XML
by Example

ISBN 0-13-960162-7

90000

9 780139 601620

**An accompanying
CD is enclosed
inside this book**

The Charles F. Goldfarb Series on Open Information Management

"Open Information Management" (OIM) means managing information so that it is open to processing by any program, not just the program that created it. That extends even to application programs not conceived of at the time the information was created.

OIM is based on the principle of data independence: data should be stored in computers in nonproprietary, genuinely standardized representations. And that applies even when the data is the content of a document. Its representation should distinguish the innate information from the proprietary codes of document processing programs and the artifacts of particular presentation styles.

Business data bases—which rigorously separate the real data from the input forms and output reports—achieved data independence decades ago. But documents, unlike business data, have historically been created in the context of a particular output presentation style. So for document data, independence was largely unachievable until recently.

That is doubly unfortunate. It is unfortunate because documents are a far more significant repository of humanity's information. And documents can contain significantly richer information structures than data bases.

It is also unfortunate because the need for OIM of documents is greater now than ever. The demands of "repurposing" require that information be deliverable in multiple formats: paperbased, on line, multimedia, hypermedia. And information must now be delivered through multiple channels: traditional bookstores and libraries, the World Wide Web, corporate intranets and extranets. In the latter modes, what starts as database data may become a document for browsing, but then may need to be reused by the reader as data.

Fortunately, in the past ten years a technology has emerged that extends to documents the database's capacity for data independence.

And it does so without the database's restrictions on structural freedom. That technology is the "Standard Generalized Markup Language" (SGML), an official International Standard (ISO 8879) that has been adopted by the world's largest producers of documents and by the World Wide Web.

With SGML, organizations in government, aerospace, airlines, automotive, electronics, computers, and publishing (to name a few) have freed their documents from hostage relationships to processing software. SGML coexists with graphics, multimedia and other data standards needed for OIM and acts as the framework that relates objects in the other formats to one another and to SGML documents.

The World Wide Web's HTML and XML are both based on SGML. HTML is a particular, though very general, application of SGML, like those for the above industries. There is a limited set of markup tags that can be used with HTML. XML, in contrast, is a simplified subset of SGML facilities that, like full SGML, can be used with any set of tags. You can literally create your own markup language with XML.

As the principal enabler for OIM of documents, the SGML family of standards necessarily plays a leading role in this series. We provide tutorials on SGML, XML, and other key standards and the techniques for applying them. Our books vary in technical intensity from programming techniques for software developers to the business justification of OIM for enterprise executives. We share the practical experience of organizations and individuals who have applied the techniques of OIM in environments ranging from immense industrial publishing projects to websites of all sizes.

Our authors are expert practitioners in their subject matter, not writers hired to cover a "hot" topic. They bring insight and understanding that can only come from real-world experience. Moreover, they practice what they preach about standardization. Their books share a common standards-based vocabulary. In this way, knowledge gained from one book in the series is directly applicable when reading another, or the standards themselves. This is just one of the ways in which we strive for the utmost technical accuracy and consistency with the OIM standards.

And we also strive for a sense of excitement and fun. After all, the challenge of OIM—preserving information from the ravages of technology while exploiting its benefits—is one of the great intellectual adventures of our age. I'm sure you'll find this series to be a knowledgable and reliable guide on that adventure.

About the Series Editor

Dr. Charles F. Goldfarb invented the SGML language in 1974 and later led the team that developed it into the International Standard on which both HTML and XML are based. He serves as editor of the Standard (ISO 8879) and as a consultant to developers of SGML and XML applications and products. He is based in Saratoga, CA.

About the Series Logo

The rebus is an ancient literary tradition, dating from 16th century Picardy, and is especially appropriate to a series involving fine distinctions between things and the words that describe them. For the logo, Andrew Goldfarb incorporated a rebus of the series name within a stylized SGML/XML comment declaration.

The Charles F. Goldfarb Series on Open Information Management

As XML is a subset of SGML, the Series List is categorized to show the degree to which a title applies to XML. "XML Titles" are those that discuss XML explicitly and may also cover full SGML. "SGML Titles" do not mention XML per se, but the principles covered may apply to XML.

XML Titles Available

Goldfarb, Pepper, and Ensign
- SGML Buyer's Guide™: Choosing the Right XML and SGML Products and Services

Megginson
- Structuring XML Documents

Leventhal, Lewis, and Fuchs
- Designing XML Internet Applications

McGrath
- XML by Example: Building E-commerce Applications

Goldfarb and Prescod
- The XML Handbook™

Jelliffe
- The SGML Cookbook

SGML Titles Available

Turner, Douglass, and Turner
- ReadMe.1st: SGML for Writers and Editors

Donovan
- Industrial-Strength SGML: An Introduction to Enterprise Publishing

Ensign
- $GML: The Billion Dollar Secret

Rubinsky and Maloney
- SGML on the Web: Small Steps Beyond HTML

McGrath
- ParseMe.1st: SGML for Software Developers

DuCharme
- SGML CD

XML by Example:

Building E-Commerce Applications

■ Sean McGrath

 Prentice Hall PTR, Upper Saddle River, NJ   07458
http://www.phptr.com

Library of Congress Cataloging-in-Publication Data

```
McGrath, Sean.
    XML by Example: Building E-Commerce applications/ Sean McGrath.
      p.    cm. -- (The Charles F. Goldfarb series on open information
  management)
    Includes index.
    ISBN 0-13-960162-7
    1. XML (Document markup language) 2. Electronic commerce. I. Title.
II. Series.
  QA76.76.H94M3883  1998
  005.7'2--dc21                                              98-7398
                                                                CIP
```

Editorial/Production Supervision: *Joanne Anzalone*
Acquisitions Editor: *Mark L. Taub*
Marketing Manager: *Dan Rush*
Manufacturing Manager: *Alexis R. Heydt*
Cover Design: *Anthony Gemmellaro*
Cover Design Direction: *Jerry Votta*
Series Design: *Gail Cocker-Bogusz*

© 1998 Prentice Hall PTR
Prentice-Hall, Inc.
A Simon & Schuster Company
Upper Saddle River, NJ 07458

Prentice Hall books are widely used by corporations and government agencies for training, marketing, and resale.

The publisher offers discounts on this book when ordered in bulk quantities. For more information, contact Corporate Sales Department, Phone: 800-382-3419; fax: 201-236-7141; email: corpsales@prenhall.com or write Corporate Sales Department, Prentice Hall PTR, One Lake Street, Upper Saddle River, NJ 07458.

Printed in the United States of America

10 9 8 7 6 5 4 3 2

ISBN 0-13-960162-7

Prentice-Hall International (UK) Limited, *London*
Prentice-Hall of Australia Pty. Limited, *Sydney*
Prentice-Hall Canada Inc., *Toronto*
Prentice-Hall Hispanoamericana, S.A., *Mexico*
Prentice-Hall of India Private Limited, *New Delhi*
Prentice-Hall of Japan, Inc., *Tokyo*
Simon & Schuster Asia Pte. Ltd., *Singapore*
Editora Prentice-Hall do Brasil, Ltda., *Rio de Janeiro*

All product names mentioned herein are the property of their respective owners.

Opinions expressed in this book are those of the Author and are not necessarily those of the Publisher or Series Editor.

The Author of this book has included a diskette or CD-ROM of related materials as a convenience to the reader. The Series Editor did not participate in the preparation, testing, or review of the materials and is not responsible for their content.

For my precious baby daughter Aoife

A remarkable instance of Nature's formidable markup language: "46, XX, 5p-"

May you always be happy

Contents

I Part One

XML Jumpstart   3

Chapter I
XML—An Executive Summary   4

I Part Two

XML by Example

Chapter 6
Using XML with Internet Explorer 4

▌ Part Three

A Close Look at XML and Related Standards   247

Chapter 11
The XML Standard   248

Part Four

E-Commerce Initiatives Based on XML

Chapter 17
OFX—Open Financial Exchange

Chapter 18
XML/EDI—XML and Electronic Data Interchange

Foreword

In a few short years, the World Wide Web has grown from a novelty to the world's library. At the heart of this universal information resource is the Hypertext Markup Language—HTML.

Now HTML has a brother, the eXtensible Markup Language—XML. And XML is in the process of turning the Web into the world's commercial and financial hub.

XML and HTML are similar because both are based on SGML, the International Standard for structured information. But while HTML lets you describe the way data should look, XML lets you say what the data *means*. And smart data is what is powering the electronic commerce revolution.

We've all seen the beginnings of commercial activity on the Web: online book stores, computer dealers, and music services. But there are things less obvious, like the XML documents that power the financial interchange between your broker's web site and your personal finance program.

Sean McGrath is aware of all of the e-commerce activity, and he brings it to you in this book, with clear examples at every step. He has personally built e-commerce applications for top financial firms like

Coopers & Lybrand, Deloitte & Touche, and Price Waterhouse, and his expertise shows on every page.

With Sean's help, you'll soon be building your own e-commerce applications with XML and profiting from this revolutionary change in the World Wide Web.

Charles F. Goldfarb
Saratoga, CA
May, 1998

Preface

"XML may just be the 'killer application' needed to open up the Worldwide Web for electronic commerce."

CommerceNet

http://www.commerce.net/news/press/ 0821.html

Quotes such as this are common on the World Wide Web at the moment. An ever increasing number of Web pages seem to feature "XML" and "electronic commerce" in the same sentence! So just what is XML? Where did it come from? Why is it being heralded as the kick start that the electronic commerce revolution has been waiting for? In this book I hope to answer these questions.

XML is the most exciting technology I have been involved in since I first tapped a computer keyboard in 1982. The excitement around XML is positively palpable. You can cut it with a knife! Nobody knows for sure where this technology is headed but the smart money (and lots of it!) points to a healthy future for XML in the increasingly Web centric world of business.

Is XML some major technical breakthrough cooked up by research scientists?

—No it is not.

Is XML something that could only have happened in recent years because of other technology constraints?

—No it is not.

XML could have happened at any time since the late 1960s when the seeds of the ideas it embodies drew their first breath. Perhaps the world was simply not ready for it? Perhaps the world then did not need what XML has to offer badly enough.

The Internet revolution and in particular, the frenzied excitement about electronic commerce on the Web has changed all that. We are in a new world order now. A world in which the World Wide Web, the Internet, intranets, and extranets will change both the technological and commercial landscape of our planet for good.

The plain fact of the matter is that electronic commerce today needs what XML has to offer. XML is not, like some hot technologies before it, a solution waiting for a problem. It is a solution to a very real existing problem—how to make the Web a better place to do business.

Evidence of XML's promise as an enabling technology for electronic commerce abound. Just look at the number of start-up companies where the words "XML" and "e-commerce" feature prominently on their home pages! Although XML certainly has killer applications far removed from commerce[1] it is surely no accident that much of the early buzz around XML features phrases such as "business transactions", "open financial exchange", "open trading protocol", and so on.

In this book, I will flesh out what XML is all about and illustrate how it can be applied to electronic commerce. I will show how enterprising companies, both large and small, can wield XML for commercial benefit today.

I hope it illustrates why XML is good for business and triggers ideas for applying it in your own endeavors, as I've done for my company After all, it is people like you and I who will make e-commerce happen by building real solutions to real commercial problems with the power that XML provides.

---

1. You can find out about them in my book "XML Killer Applications" also in this series.

I've hope this book will help you get started with XML, building e-commerce applications.

Sean McGrath
Enniscrone
County Sligo
Ireland

About this book

This book is structured into four major parts

Part I—Jumpstart

This intention of this part of the book is to provide a rapid overview of XML, illustrate how it is currently being put to use in the real world, survey the benefits to be gained, and provide just enough of the details to get you up and running with XML.

Chapter 1 is an executive summary of XML laid out like an internet FAQ (Frequently Asked Questions). Even if you know nothing about XML, reading this one chapter will give you a broad grasp of the technology and its business applications.

Chapter 2 is a collection of eight independent and varied examples of where organizations and individuals are putting XML to practical commercial use today.

Chapter 3 reflects on the uses of XML illustrated in chapter 2 and categorizes the various commercial benefits that result from using XML based technologies.

Chapter 4 is a pragmatic look at the areas where XML can be gain-fully deployed in achieving competitive advantage. This chapter introduces a theme which pervades the rest of the book. Namely, an e-business selling computer equipment via a Web site. The various ways in which an e-business, *any* e-business, can deploy XML to their advantage are illustrated.

Chapter 5 rounds out part 1 with a dip into the important details of the XML standard. The coverage is intentionally at a high level introducing just enough of the details to get started designing XML e-commerce applications.

Part II—XML By example

In this part of the book we take real world examples of XML technologies and build e-commerce applications with them.

Chapter 6 presents the XML technologies built into Microsoft Internet Explorer version 4 and show how it can be used today to leverage the benefits of XML. We illustrate how the data binding features of Dynamic HTML can be used with XML and also show how XML's sister standard for stylesheets—XSL—can be used to convert XML into HTML for deployment on today's Web browsers.

Chapter 7 provides a compelling example of what can happen when you have the freedom to create your own markup language—a freedom that XML provides. In this chapter we develop an application for transparently publishing a Microsoft Access database on a Web site.

In *chapter 8* we look at how XML can be used to describe and capture the details of interactive Web services in a way that allows them to be batch automated. This application is a good example of how a small amount of XML can pack quite a punch!

In *chapter 9* we implement push publishing using the XML based Active Channels technology of Internet Explorer 4.

Chapter 10 rounds out this part of the book with practical examples of building XML utility applications in the Perl, Python and Java programming languages.

Part III—A closer look at XML and related standards

In this part of the book we dig into the details of the core standards and proposed standards. We also take a look at how SGML (from which XML was born) can usefully be used in tandem with XML.

Chapter 11 presents many of the details of the XML standard. This chapter is a reference resource rather than a casual read. Use it to dip into for the details as you need them. Some further details are also provided in Appendix A.

In *chapter 12* we take a look at XLL, the proposal for a standard way of layering powerful hypertext functionality onto XML documents.

In *chapter 13* we take a look at XSL, the proposal for a standard way of specifying formatting for XML documents. We illustrate many of the ideas using Microsoft's XSL technology preview application MSXSL.

In *chapter 14* we take a look at Unicode—the character encoding standard on which XML and HTML 4.0 are based.

Chapter 15 presents the Document Object Model (DOM) proposed standard. The DOM provides a language and application independent interface to both HTML and XML documents.

Chapter 16 finishes this part of the book with a raid on the richly stocked larder of technologies developed over the years around the SGML standard. It provides an overview of the differences between SGML and XML and how you can gainfully use both.

Part IV—E-Commerce Initiatives based on XML

Even though XML is still hot out of the oven, a variety of far-reaching initiatives are under way to make XML the platform of choice for electronic commerce.

Chapter 17 presents the Open Financial Exchange initiative that promises to make XML a vital part of the e-commerce revolution.

Chapter 18 presents current thinking on how XML can help jump-start the e-Commerce revolution by embracing and perhaps replacing the pre-Web e-commerce standards such as ANSI X.12 and EDI-FACT.

Chapter 19 presents the Open Trading Protocol, a comprehensive e-commerce proposal for capturing and interchanging trading data with XML.

Acknowledgments

Many, many people contributed to this book in many different ways. For contributions to content, my knowledge, my sanity or all of these I would like to thank Dr. Charles F. Goldfarb, James Clark, Jon Bosak, Tim Bray, Michael Sperberg-Mc Queen, David Megginson, David Durand, Dr. David Abrahamson, Michael Kilcawley, Dr. John Spinosa, Eve Maler, Henry Thompson, Chris Maden, Norman Walsh, Paul Prescod, Rick Jelliffe, Len Bullard, Adam Denning, Andrew Layman, Chris Lovett, Jeremie Miller, Joakin Östman, Caren De Witt, Charles Axel Allen, Irene Vatton, Kirsten Castagnoli, Laurie Doherty, Peter Murray-Rust and Traci Massaro. To all those whose names I have failed to mention, apologies and thank you.

For sterling work picking the worst of the fluff off the drafts my thanks go to Noel Duffy. Thanks also to Noel for grappling with some of the conundrums that inevitably arise when you attempt to install a crazy mix of Web browsers, Web Servers, programming languages, applets and databases onto a single machine.

For the use of his house as a writers retreat, my thanks to Neville Bagnall. To JC the dog, heartfelt thanks for your constant absence while this book was being written. Both the postman and I are very grateful.

To all at Prentice Hall: Mark Taub, Joanne Anzalone, Patti Guerrieri, Christa Carroll, my thanks for all your help, encouragement and hard work.

Finally, I wish to thank my wife Johanna who is, as I write this, still speaking to me! Given what she has had to put up with since this project began, I can only thank her profusely. Truly a woman amongst women. Johanna, I promise I will not write another book! Well, not this month anyway:-).

A Note about URI and URL

In this book you will come across numerous examples of the term "URI" (Universal Resource Indicator) as well as the more familiar "URL" (Universal Resource Locator). The term URI and its precise usage is a work in progress by Tim Berners Lee—the inventor of the Web. The term URI is a more general term for resources on the Web of which URLs are one particular type. The term URI is used exclusively in XML and related standards. Earlier technologies continue to use the term URL; hence the mix of terms in the book.

Disclaimer

The example web site used throughout this book is http://www.acmepc.com. At the time of writing this book no such web site is registered on the Internet. This is a purely fictional web site created for the explicit and sole purpose of teaching XML concepts.
Prentice Hall PTR

Part One

XML
Jumpstart

XML—An Executive Summary

∎ XML explained

∎ Advantages of XML

∎ Relating XML to HTML

∎ Relating XML to SGML

∎ Existing users and uses of XML

This chapter takes a look at the world of XML from a height of approximately 30,000 feet! It is intended to serve two purposes. Firstly, it gives readers with only 20 minutes to spare right now, a single chunk of reading to familiarize themselves with XML. Secondly, it sets the scene for the more comprehensive treatment presented in the rest of the book.

Having read this chapter, you will know enough about XML to discuss it in general terms with your boss or with your colleagues. This chapter will give you some idea of the broad areas of application of XML and, I hope, trigger some thoughts about how you can apply this exciting technology in your own projects.

I hope that it will also whet your appetite to dig into the rest of the book in order to flesh out your understanding of XML. Even if you are rushing off after this chapter, intending to return later on, please take the time to peruse Chapter 2, which provides practical illustrations of some areas where XML is being successfully deployed today.

This chapter is set out as a dialog of questions and answers, not unlike an Internet FAQ (Frequently Asked Questions) list. For best results, please read the questions and answers in the order they are presented. Ready to get started?

1.1 | Can you explain XML in less than half a page?

No! Too many good ideas and too many *killer applications* of XML exist for half a page to do it justice. But if you can only read half a page right now, try this for size . . .

XML is a computer language for describing information. So too is HTML. XML improves on the HTML approach and makes the Web a better place in which to do business, to learn, and to have fun.

HTML is a great technology, and it has changed the world. However, a great deal of useful information is *lost* when data is converted into HTML—information that, if preserved, can be used to build a whole new world of computer applications on the Web.

Compare this little document:

```
<!-- HTML Snippet -->
<h1>Invoice</h1>
<p>From: Joe Bloggs
<p>To : A. Another
<p>Date : 1 Feb 1999
<p>Amount : $100.00
<p>Tax : 21 %
<p>Total Due : $121.00
```

To this little document:

```
<!-- XML Snippet -->
<Invoice>
<From>Joe Bloggs</From>
<to>A. Another</To>
```

```
<Date year = '1999' month = '2' day = '1'/>
<Amount currency = 'Dollars'>100.00</Amount>
<TaxRate>21</TaxRate>
<TotalDue currency = 'Dollars'>121.00</TotalDue>
</Invoice>
```

Now put yourself in a computer's shoes. Which little document is easier to process? Which one captures the most useful information? Which has the most potential uses?

The distinction illustrated in these two snippets is the very essence of XML. XML is all about *preserving* useful information—information that computers can use to be more intelligent about what they do with our data.

You might be thinking, "Why not just add tags for **<Invoice>**, **<TaxRate>**, etc. to HTML?" This step could certainly be taken, but where does this process end? *No* set of tags, no matter how large, will ever come close to providing all the tags we might conceivably want. There must be a better way!

Well, a better way does exist, and it is called XML. XML is not a "go-faster HTML." It is a fundamentally different technology that liberates information from the shackles of a fixed-tag set. For example, if you are describing an invoice, why not call it an **<Invoice>** rather than a level 1 heading?

In my country (Ireland), the phrase "call a spade a spade" means "Speak plainly. Tell it like it is." This phrase captures the core idea of XML rather well. It could be a mantra for XML—"call a spade a **<spade>**"!

1.2 | Where did XML get its name?

XML is an acronym. It stands for e**X**tensible **M**arkup **L**anguage. Like all the best acronyms, it is a TLA—**T**hree-**L**etter **A**cronym.

1.3 | What does it do?

XML is not a software program and thus does not *do* anything unaided. The same can be said of HTML. XML provides a standard approach for describing, capturing, processing, and publishing information. It is a language that has significant benefits over HTML, as you shall see.

1.4 | Sounds complicated

Far from it! Indeed, the opposite is the case. XML is a set of ideas—all of them quite simple ideas. However, it will take a while to present all these ideas thoroughly enough to do them justice yet simply enough to be easily digested. Trust me on this one! By the time you have reached the end of this chapter, you will know what XML does and how it does it.

1.5 | Can you explain the term "markup language"?

I can use the book you are now reading to illustrate the concept of a markup language. This book, like many books before it, began life as a collection of electronic files. These files were created in a word processor. As the content was created, the word processor stored extra information, over and above the words you are now reading. This extra information consisted of instructions to control the layout and appearance of the words themselves. Such information is collectively known as *markup*.

The term *markup* dates back to the days before electronic documents, when publishing professionals used to take basic text from authors on paper and write markup instructions to tell the typesetter how to make the document look good on the final printed page—e.g., "insert a paragraph break here, make this word bold, double space this text," etc.

The digital world we live in is positively awash with different markup languages. Firstly, you have the proprietary markup languages used by word processors, desktop publishing packages, etc. Then you have open nonproprietary markup languages such as TeX, Troff, and, of course—the most famous nonproprietary markup language of them all—HTML (**HyperText Markup Language**).

1.6 | So XML is just another markup language?

No. XML is a markup language with a very important twist. Most markup languages, HTML included, are *fixed* markup languages. That is to say, they provide a certain feature set in their markup, and that set is fixed in the design of the language. HTML, for example, has a fixed set of *tags* with which you craft your documents—**<H1>**, **<P>**, **<TABLE>,** etc. XML, on the other hand, does not define *any* particular set of tags. Rather, it provides a standardized framework with which to define your own, or to use those defined by others that best fit your needs.

1.7 | What does XML look like?

It looks an awful lot like HTML! (This is not a coincidence, as you will see later on.) XML documents—just like HTML documents—

consist of a mixture of data and markup. The syntax for the markup is very reminiscent of HTML. Here is an example:

```
<Spice>
<Name>Sichuan Peppercorns</Name>
<CountryOfOrigin Country = "China"/>
<Description>Pungent, distinctive. Excellent with
slow cooked, earthy dishes.
</Description>
<Example>Sichuan Braised Chicken</Example>
</Spice>
```

With XML, you have the freedom to use pretty much any names you like to tag up your data. You can literally roll your own tags, just as I have done here!

1.8 | So XML is extensible because I can use it to make up my own tags?

Exactly. Unlike most other markup languages, XML is a flexible framework in which to create your *own* customized markup languages. All XML-based languages will share the same look and feel. They will all share a common basic syntax. Beyond that, the sky is the limit in terms of the diverse markup languages that can be built on the foundation that XML provides.

Naturally, not everyone who uses XML will feel a compelling urge to create his or her own markup language. The majority of people will simply use the XML-based markup languages created by others that best fit their purpose. Already, a number of industry standard XML-based languages exist in fields such as Push Technologies (CDF—Channel Definition Format), Electronic Commerce (OTP—Open Trading Protocol) and mathematics (MML—Mathematical Markup Language).

Any language based on XML consists of a set of *element types* that have been given certain names and certain meanings. Examples we have encountered so far in this chapter include Invoice, TaxRate and Spice element types. The presence of elements of various types in documents is indicated by *tags* that serve to indicate where the element starts and ends. For example the Spice element in the previous document starts with a start-tag "<Spice>" and ends with an end-tag "</Spice>".

A set of element types serves to define *types* of documents and are referred to as *Document Type Definitions,* or *DTDs* for short. Thus you will read and hear references to the CDF DTD, the OTP DTD, the MML DTD and so on.

1.9 | But why would people bother to invent their own XML-based markup language (DTD)?

The main advantage of being able to define your own markup language is that it gives you the freedom to capture and publish useful information about what your data is and how it is structured, instead of having to shoe-horn it into someone else's often ill-fitting format. This advantage is best illustrated by example. Consider a company running an e-Business selling PCs on the Internet.[1] Here is the sort of information the company needs to publish:

```
Maker : Acme PC Inc
Model : Blaster 555
Storage:
    RAM: 72 MB
    Hard Disk : 2 GB
```

---

1. A scenario I use extensively in this book

In order to publish this information using HTML, they need to create a document looking something like this:

```
<!-- snippet of HTML -->
<h1>Personal Computers For Sale</h1>
<h2>Maker : Acme PC Inc</h2>
<h3>Model : Blaster 555</h3>
<table border = 1>
 <tr>
   <td>Storage:</td>
 </tr>
 <tr>
   <td>RAM</td><td>72 MB</td>
 </tr>
 <tr>
   <td>Hard Disk</td><td>2 GB</td>
 </tr>
</table>
```

Opened in an HTML browser, this information looks like Figure 1–1. The original data has been transformed into HTML for publishing purposes. In the course of that transformation, useful information

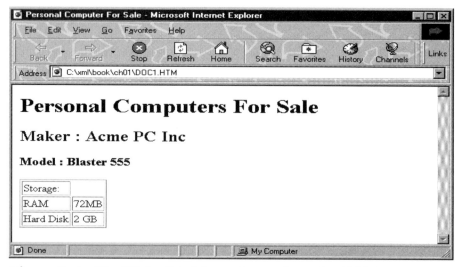

Figure 1–1   The PC for Sale information as shown in a Web browser

about what the information *really is* has been lost. The HTML version of the data knows nothing about PCs or hard disk sizes. All it knows about are heading levels, tables, italic text, etc. As a consequence, when this document is let loose on the World Wide Web, search engines and users alike see only a collection of levels, tables, italic text, etc., as in Figure 1–2.

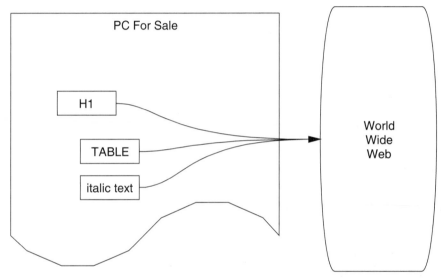

Figure 1-2   HTML document linked to the World Wide Web

Ignoring the details (and perhaps suspending disbelief!) for a moment, let your mind chew over the possibilities arising if the company could publish this on the Web instead:

```
<!-- Snippet of an XML document -->
<PcForSale>
 <Maker>Acme PC Inc</Maker>
 <Model>Blaster 555</Model>
 <Storage>
  <Ram Units = "MB">72</Ram>
  <HardDisk Units = "GB">2</HardDisk>
 </Storage>
</PcForSale>
```

I think you will agree that this representation opens up some pretty interesting possibilities. This document can have a much richer interface to the Web, an interface that presents all sorts of possibilities about how it might be put to use, as in Figure 1–3.

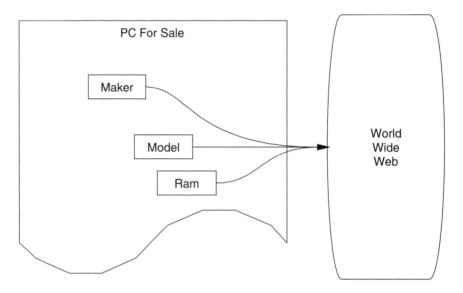

Figure 1–3   XML document linked to the World Wide Web

By keeping information about what the pieces of data *really* are—i.e., a hard disk capacity, a PC model name, etc.—you can contemplate:

- Letting the browser do the work to format the data on the user's screen. Perhaps allowing users to choose between a variety of "looks" or presentation formats for the same data.

- Letting the user's browser perform calculations on the data, and manipulate and display the results in a variety of ways.

■ Allowing intelligent searching of the information, e.g., "find all PCs for sale on the Web with disk drive capacity greater than 2 GB."

■ Intelligently checking that all the pieces of information required for a proper entry on the PC selling Web page are actually there, e.g., "all PCs must have a RAM size element and can optionally have a hard disk size element."

■ Performing complex queries on the data either for your own management purposes or as a service to customers, e.g., "how many laptop PCs with built-in CD-ROM drives were sold last month in Arkansas?"

■ Building rich links between different types of information—for example, linking a sales invoice (itself perhaps an XML document!) with the particular makes/ models of PCs it references.

■ Standardizing a set of XML element types for an entire industry, such as PC vendors. Users and vendors alike would benefit from the standardization. Software "robots" could trawl the Web to find the perfect PC for you, based on criteria you specify. Vendors would be able to easily contrast their offerings with those of the competition via "tick sheets" and so forth.

■ Avoiding the need to "dumb down" data into HTML prior to publishing. This activity often involves complex software and is frequently error prone. With XML, the data can be stored and published in the *same* format. You don't need either batch or on-the-fly translation into HTML (although XML allows you to continue doing that if you so wish).

1.10 | Is some philosophical stuff going on here that I need to know?

Yes. The core philosophy of XML has come about as a result of a long and thoughtful analysis of what is really meant by the term "document" in the digital world. By and large, documents consist of three distinct components, namely:

- Data content—the words themselves
- Structure—the document type and the organization of its elements, i.e., memo, contract, cooking recipe. Also, what kind of elements it can contain and in what order they can occur.
- Presentation—the way the information is presented to the reader, on a piece of paper, a browser screen or via voice synthesis. Also, which fonts or voice inflections are used for each element type and so on.

The central idea of XML is that *significant* benefits accrue to the document owner if these three aspects of a document are kept separate and made explicit in a computer system. Now compare and contrast the treatment of these three strands of a document in traditional word processors to their treatment in XML (see Figure 1-4).

A word processor—especially a WYSIWYG word processor—entwines content and presentation in a very tight embrace. Using such tools, we create documents with a specific output device in mind—typically paper of a particular width and height. As we create the content, we are ever watchful of the appearance of the result; we inextricably bind that content to a particular presentation. Indeed, being able to do so is the very essence of the WYSIWYG (What You See Is What You Get) philosophy. As for structure—capturing what the information really is—the concept is hardly present

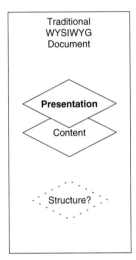
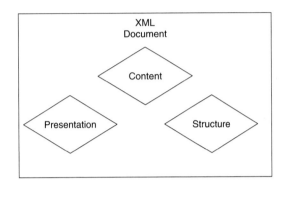

Figure 1–4 Content, structure, and presentation in traditional and XML documents

at all. The only structural information stored relates to the creation of the final paper output—details about page margins, font sizes, and so on.

This approach is in stark contrast to that espoused by the XML approach. The inherent structure of documents such as procedure manuals, invoices, and tax returns is considered just as important as the content itself. Presentation information is also, naturally, important but is kept well separated from the content. In XML, you create document content by concentrating on what the information really is and how it is structured (see Figure 1–5). We defer issues to do with presentation, leaving them to be dealt with at the point where someone needs to *look* at the document. I will come back to presentation in "But how do I make XML look nice in a browser?" later on in this chapter. For now, suffice it to say that an XML document can be made to look arbitrarily beautiful without intertwining the formatting information with the core content of the document.

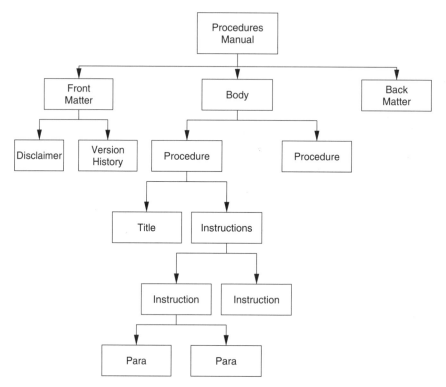

Figure 1–5   Representing the logical structure of a document

1.11 | Ah! So that is what they mean by "structured documents"!

In a word, yes.

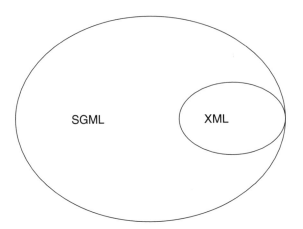

Figure 1–6 The relationship of XML to SGML

1.12 | Did someone just sit down and, you know, "invent" XML?

XML was certainly invented but not out of thin air[1]. Since 1986, an international standard has existed for doing what XML does. In fact, that standard does a lot more than XML does, in many respects. Its name is SGML—Standard Generalized Markup Language—ISO 8879.

SGML is a very powerful, very general standard, but with that power comes increased complexity. XML is a subset of SGML intended to make SGML "light" enough for use on the Web. XML is a *proper subset* of SGML. That is to say, all XML documents are valid SGML documents. However, not all SGML documents are valid XML documents (see Figure 1–6).

SGML has been used very successfully over the years in industries such as technical publishing, pharmaceuticals, aerospace and so on. Some major SGML initiatives are listed in Table 1.1.

---

1. Someone did sit down and invent the original form of SGML—Charles F. Goldfarb, the editor of this series.

Table 1.1   Some SGML Initiatives

Name	Industry
ATA	Aviation (Air Transport Authority)
DocBook	Technical manuals
Text Encoding Initiative (TEI)	Encoding of literature
J2008	Automotive maintenance
Edgar	Financial reports for public companies
HTML	Hypertext Markup Language
Pinnacles (PCIS)	Semiconductor data

1.13 | Is something wrong with SGML?

No. The complexity of implementation that is a by-product of SGML's power has had the effect of limiting its user base to big companies that need all that power. Organizations with tens of thousands of pages of information are typical SGML users. Having said that, the ideas that SGML embodies are just too good and useful to be restricted to such a niche. Hence XML—a simplified SGML that retains most of the inherent power of SGML in a simple, tidy, easy-to-use, easy-to-implement form.

1.14 | Can you draw me a picture of how all these languages are related?

Sure! In Figure 1–7, rectangle boxes indicate *applications,* and ellipses indicate *framework languages* or *meta-languages,* if you like. From it, you can see that XML is a simplified version of SGML; and CML, CDF, and so on are XML applications; whilst HTML, Edgar, and Docbook, etc., are SGML applications.

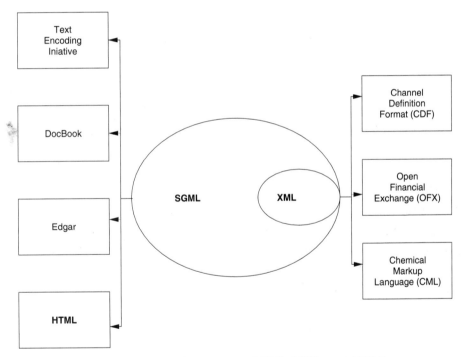

Figure 1–7   The relationships among SGML, XML, and HTML

1.15 | Can the structure of an XML document be checked somehow?

Yes. XML includes a mechanism for defining rules that control how documents are structured. In jargon, these are called *Document Type Definitions,* or DTDs for short. In a DTD, you can arrange for XML documents to be automatically checked in various ways. Here are some examples.

- A person's name consists of an optional title, a given name, and a surname.
- A TV timetable contains one or more channels. Each channel contains one or more time slots. Each time slot has a program title and an optional description.

These effects can be achieved in the Document Type Definition by listing the element types you wish to use in your document and indicating the structural order in which they can occur. A utility program called an XML Parser is then able to test whether or not the document meets the prescribed rules (see Figure 1–8).

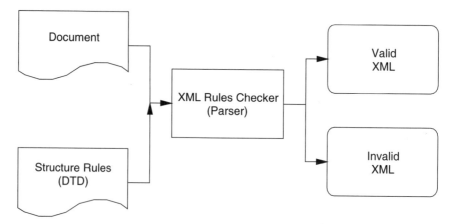

Figure 1–8   Checking the structure of an XML document with an XML Parser

1.16 | What if I do not want my structure checked?

No problem. With XML, it is perfectly okay not to rigorously check the structure of your documents against a DTD. As long as the elements *nest* properly within each other, creating a tree-like structure, the document is known as a *well formed* XML document. Well formed documents are particularly suited for Internet use because they can be processed with simple XML tools. These tools are small and light enough to be used in everything from browser applets to credit-card swipers to laboratory equipment.

1.17 | But how do I make XML look nice in a browser?

In XML, presentation and content are kept separate for reasons I discussed in "Is some philosophical stuff going on here that I need to know?" earlier in this chapter. Making XML look nice—either in a browser or on a sheet of paper—is the responsibility of an XML subsidiary standard called XSL—**X**ML **S**tyle **L**anguage.

You may be familiar with the concept of a style sheet in a word-processor, or you may have come across a style-sheet standard for HTML called Cascading Style Sheets (CSS). The core idea is to capture details about how the various elements in a document should look and then to store them in a separate document, rather than intertwine them with the content of the document. Separating the two allows the presentation to be changed by simply changing the style sheet. XSL is the proposed style-sheet language for XML. It is more powerful than CSS yet broadly compatible with it. In the same way that XML is a subset of the SGML International Standard (ISO 8879),

XSL is a simplified subset of the International Standard style language known as DSSSL (ISO/IEC 10179)—see Figure 1–9.

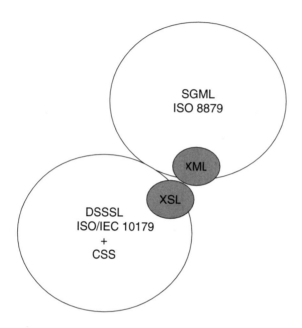

Figure 1–9   The relationship between XML, XSL, and ISO Standards

1.18 | What about hypertext?

With HTML, we are used to the idea of having hypertext-linking functionality built directly into the language. In HTML, the famous **<A>** element serves this purpose. As you know, XML does not pre-define any elements, so how do you go about specifying hypertext links? Just as in the case of presentation information, XML delegates the task of capturing hypertext information to a subsidiary standard known as XLL—e**Xtensible** **L**ink **L**anguage (see Figure 1–10).

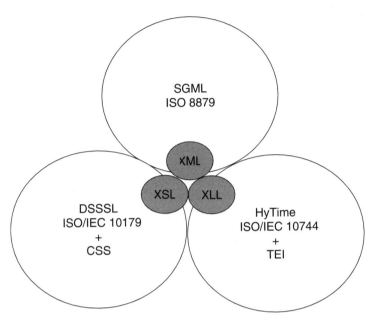

Figure 1–10   Adding XLL to the family of XML standards

The XLL standard draws heavily upon an existing standard for expressing hypertext links in SGML documents, known as HyTime (yet another ISO standard—ISO/IEC 10744). It also draws on the wealth of experience in dealing with complex hypertext linking that has built up over the years in the SGML-based Text Encoding Initiative.

1.19 | So XML is based on truly international standards?

Right down to its toes! XML is derived from SGML (ISO 8879), XSL is derived from DSSSL (ISO/IEC 10179), and XLL is derived from HyTime (ISO/IEC 10744). On top of that, the native character set of XML is Unicode (ISO/IEC 10646). Any system that declares itself to be XML-compliant must be able to handle the Unicode character set. Unicode, with its multiple byte characters, supports a wide variety of languages and alphabets. Support for Unicode is becoming increasingly common; it is directly supported in programming languages such as Java and in operating systems such as Windows NT and AIX.

1.20 | Where does all this leave HTML and the concept of a browser?

In pretty good shape, actually! XML can usefully be seen as a generalization of the information-publishing paradigm pioneered by HTML and the World Wide Web. HTML is not threatened by XML. In fact, a direct comparison of the two is meaningless. XML is a *framework* for making markup languages; HTML is an *example* of a markup language. If HTML is like a slice of bread, XML is like a bakery. If HTML is a red rose, XML is a greenhouse.

In fact, not only are HTML and XML not in competition, but HTML may well one day become an XML application!

1.21 | Why not just let people invent proprietary languages—why base them on XML?

The primary reason is to ensure that your information can leverage the existing set of open standards, tools, and expertise available for XML. For too long now, the lowest common denominator in the document world has been *plain text*. XML builds on top of plain text, allowing layers of useful information to be captured along with basic data, and it does so in a completely application-independent, vendor-independent fashion.

With the range of uses to which XML is being put and the range of XML software (much of it free!) that is available, it will become increasingly difficult for developers to cost-justify inventing yet another proprietary syntax. This difficulty is a good thing. Every proprietary syntax creates another isolated island of information and another doubling of the world's already bulging set of file conversion utilities!

1.22 | Where does XML fit in with other information technology standards?

XML is, first and foremost, a document technology. Having said that, the XML approach to information as a threesome of content, structure, and presentation cuts right across the world of Information Technology. XML can be gainfully applied to database modeling, for example. Also, nothing, in principle, can prevent XML from being used as a graphics file format! It would not be terribly space-efficient, but that is not the point. The point is that XML's modeling power has significant depth. Who knows where it will be applied outside its initial realm of documents? It may well emerge as a base interchange framework for all electronic data.

1.23 | If XML is so clever, how come the Web was not designed that way in the first place?

The Web started out with modest aims—to allow easy dissemination of information amongst a group of scientists at CERN. It has expanded somewhat since then! Given the original requirements, HTML was a very good design, easy to read and easy to write, both for humans and computers.

However, the scope of the Internet has extended at such a pace that the sheer simplicity of HTML—on one hand the Web's greatest asset—is becoming one of its greatest weaknesses. To extend the Web into areas now envisaged for it—such as electronic commerce, health-care information, on-line voting and the like—the Web needs a more extensible, robust, and formally defined standard. We owe HTML a great debt of gratitude. It has opened our eyes to a whole new vista of possibilities for Information Technology. It still has a significant role to play as a standard *display* format. However, it will become just one of a family of markup languages in everyday use on the World Wide Web—the vast majority of them based on XML.

1.24 | Okay. Sounds good, but let's cut to the chase. Who out there is using XML and for what purposes?

Here are some corporate names you may recognize:

- Microsoft
- Netscape

- Sun Microsystems
- Adobe
- IBM
- Corel
- Hewlett-Packard

Here are some XML application areas you may recognize:

- Online Banking
- Push Technology
- Web Automation
- Database Publishing
- Software Distribution

Would you care to see some proof? Proceed to Chapter 2, where I take a closer look at some of these real-world XML applications.

XML in Action

- Push technology with Microsoft Active channels
- Electronic banking
- Software distribution
- Web automation
- Database integration
- Localization
- Data representation
- Chemical Markup Language

Although the XML standard is quite new, it has a remarkably diverse set of applications already. Undoubtedly, a contributing factor to this fact is that XML's parent, SGML, has been around since 1986. Many SGML "old-timers" have been aware of the exciting potential applications of structured documents on the Web for many years now. Ideas have been cooking away in the backs of people's minds, waiting for the day when a simplified subset of SGML would make it a viable technology for the World Wide Web. The ideal subset would be simple enough to achieve broad acceptance and have a wide appeal. XML is exactly what these old-timers have been waiting for. Indeed XML's explosion onto the Internet scene has been dubbed "the revenge of the forty-somethings!"

In this chapter, I present some of the exciting areas of XML innovation on the Web today. This chapter provides overviews only—I return to those most applicable to e-commerce in greater detail later on in the book.

- Push Technology—Microsoft Active Channels
- Online Banking—Open Financial Exchange Initiative
- Software Distribution—Open Software Distribution
- Web Automation—Web Interface Definition Language
- Database Integration
- Localization—OpenTag Initiative
- Data Interchange—the Lotus Notes Flat File Initiative
- Scientific Publishing—Chemical Markup Language

2.1 | Push Technology with Microsoft Active Channels

The amount of time-critical information on the Web is growing rapidly. Daily news, stock prices, special offers, and so on are all examples of this sort of information. How can technology help to ensure that time-critical information gets to the desks (browsers) of those who need it in a timely fashion?

2.1.1 *Overview of a solution*

Methods of delivering information of any form to a consumer can be broadly categorized into two approaches—push and pull.

2.1.1.1 Pull Publishing

Purchasing a newspaper and visiting a library are examples of pull publishing methods. You, the consumer, have to make a conscious effort to search for and locate interesting information. Having found something interesting on, say Monday, you then have to come back again on Tuesday if you wish to see Tuesday's updates. You must regularly initiate the transfer of information from your end of the chain. You have to "pull" it down yourself (see Figure 2–1).

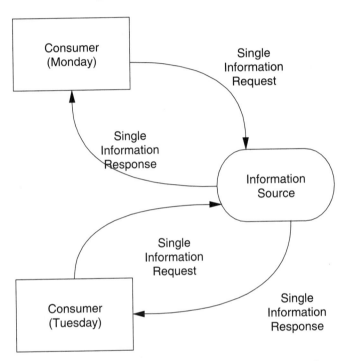

Figure 2–1   How pull publishing technology works

2.1.1.2   Push Publishing

Tuning in to a TV news station and listening to the sports results on the radio are examples of "push" publishing. In this model (pictured in Figure 2–2), the publisher is constantly broadcasting the latest information. The user simply has to "tune in" to the TV or radio station to automatically receive new information as it becomes available.

The World Wide Web is basically a pull publishing system. If the contents of your favorite Web site change for whatever reason, you remain oblivious to the change until such time as you revisit the site.

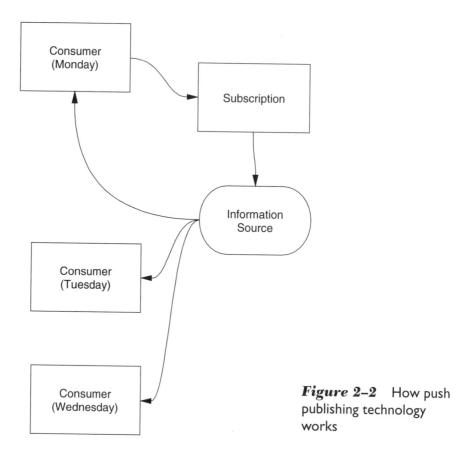

Figure 2–2   How push publishing technology works

For many possible applications of the Web—especially commercial applications that require the timely delivery of business-critical information—the push model has many advantages over pull. Users, having located interesting information of use to them in their business, are likely to prefer to have any changes to that information appear *automatically* rather than to have to revisit and redownload the information. Examples abound, ranging from stock price information, to announcements of economic statistics, to football results. In an intranet environment, push can be used to keep employees up to date on everything from quality procedures to company announcements to racquetball league tables.

Clearly, a mechanism is needed for capturing details about particular sources of information (channels). For each channel, we will need to know what Web pages constitute the content of that channel. We also need to know how to go about checking the channel for updates. Should we check the site every hour, every day, or every week? Also, storing some simple titles and abstracts for the information would be nice, so we can download a small document that acts as a table of contents, listing the information available in the channel.

2.1.2 *Enter XML*

To achieve push technology, we need an open data representation. We need to define the component parts of the representation, each of which will define one or more channels. Each channel in turn will have a title and an associated update schedule. An update schedule will have optional start and end times and a mandatory interval setting. And so on.

In the best circumstances, these documents would be plainly readable, easy to create, easy to check for completeness, and easy to process. How about something like this:

```
<CHANNEL>
    <TITLE>My truly wonderful news channel</TITLE>
    <LOGO HREF = "www.acme.com/logo.gif"/>
    <ABSTRACT>Dramatic savings on tape backup
      units</ABSTRACT>
    <SCHEDULE>
        <INTERVALTIME DAY = "1" />
    </SCHEDULE>
</CHANNEL>
```

If browsing tools could be made aware of such a standardized channel definition format, they could then use these documents to allow users to browse/subscribe to interesting channels from the comfort of their familiar Web browsing environment. These channel documents can be used as "subscription cards" by the browser to allow it to intelligently and automatically seek out and download updates to the content.

Apart from some simplification and pruning, the previous tagged snippet conforms to the XML Application Initiative known as CDF—Channel Definition Format. The process of subscribing to and subsequently receiving updates from a channel is illustrated in Figure 2–3.

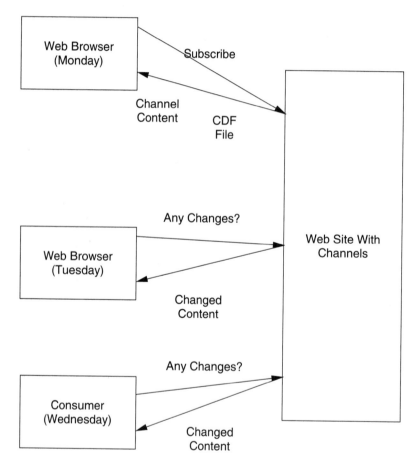

Figure 2–3   Subscribing to and receiving updates from a channel

Figure 2–4 shows a screenshot of the Web site http://www.iechannels.com. This site houses a directory of publishers providing Active Channels supporting the Channel Definition Format.

Having selected a channel for preview (in this case, the *New York Times*), you can see more detailed information about the chosen channel (see Figure 2–5).

After you select "subscribe," the top level contents of the channel are downloaded and an entry is added to the channel list on the browser, as you see in Figure 2–6.

Right-clicking on the *New York Times* Channel pops up a menu, as in Figure 2–7.

Selecting the Explore option presents a view of the channel that exposes its hierarchical structure (see Figure 2–8).

Beneath all these fancy graphics and dynamic HTML, the bedrock of this push architecture is simple XML documents conforming to

Figure 2–4 Searching for interesting channels on http://www.iechannels.com

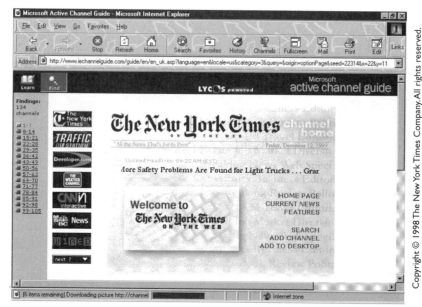

Figure 2–5   Preview page from the *New York Times* channel on http://www.iechannels.com

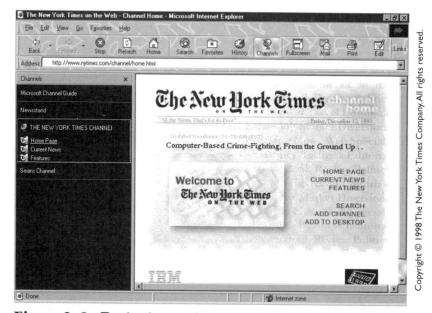

Figure 2–6   Top-level view of the *New York Times* Channel in Internet Explorer

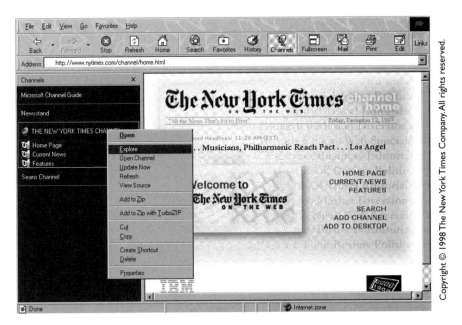

Figure 2–7   Options for manipulating the *New York Times* Channel in Internet Explorer

the Channel Definition Format (CDF) Document Type Definition. To see this, use the same menu as before and select the "view source" option, and you will open a text editor containing the raw XML used to define the *New York Times* channel. The first few lines are included here.

```
<?xml version="1.0"?>
<CHANNEL HREF = "http://www.nytimes.com/channel/
   home.html">
  <TITLE>THE NEW YORK TIMES CHANNEL</TITLE>
  <LOGO LASTMOD="1997-08-27T03:08" HREF="http://
  www.nytimes.com/channel/images/NYT16x16.gif"
  STYLE="ICON"/>
  <LOGO LASTMOD="1997-08-27T03:08" HREF="http://
  www.nytimes.com/channel/images/NYT32x80.gif"
  STYLE="IMAGE"/>
  <ABSTRACT>The New York Times Channel - All the News
  That's Fit to Print</ABSTRACT>
  <SCHEDULE>
```

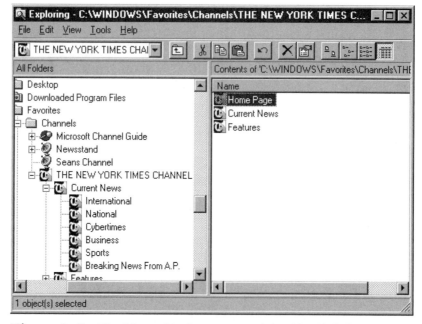

Figure 2–8   The hierarchical structure of the *New York Times* Channel

```
<INTERVALTIME DAY = "1" />
<EARLIESTTIME HOUR = "3" />
<LATESTTIME HOUR = "2" />
</SCHEDULE>
<ITEM HREF="http://www.nytimes.com/channel/screen-
saver/index.html">
<USAGE VALUE="Screensaver"/>
</ITEM>
```

Another view of this XML document is available by loading it into a CDF editing tool such as CDFGen from Microsoft (included on the CD). You can see it in Figure 2–9.

2.1.3   *Concluding thoughts*

The CDF initiative illustrates some important points about XML. The whole principle of CDF relies on the fact that the data representation is *standardized*. Publishers and tool developers would have

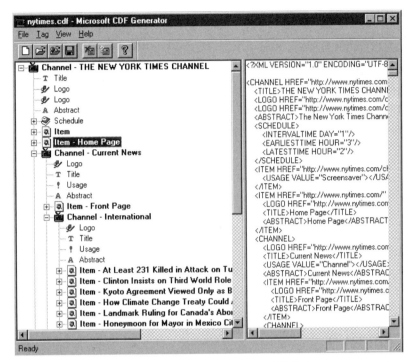

Figure 2–9   The *New York Times* Channel CDF document as viewed in the CDFGen utility

grave difficulty building a worldwide push publishing system on the Internet if such a standard did not exist. And yet, the CDF representation is *really simple.* It takes a mere moment to understand what it is saying—even if you have never seen one before.

Finally, given that the structure of CDF documents is to a large extent specified in a DTD, new CDF developers/publishers have access to an excellent piece of documentation about CDF documents in general. A quick scan through a two-page DTD can tell you as much, if not more, than hundreds of pages of hand-crafted documentation or many megabytes of sample data.

The CDF specification has been submitted to the World Wide Web Consortium for consideration as a standard. The specification was developed and proposed for standardization by Microsoft, Pointcast, and others.

2.2 | Online banking

Financial institutions are one of the world's biggest users of Information Technology. Indeed the modern commercial infrastructure is completely dependent on IT. Every teller machine transaction, every interest rate hedge, and every mortgage repayment are essentially digital data. Although the *types* of data involved in digital financial transactions are well defined and easily classified, the world is awash in proprietary, mutually incompatible formats for representing this data in digital form.

With the advent of the Web, the need for an interchange data representation for financial data becomes more important than ever before. Users want to be able to purchase goods from anywhere on the Web with funds drawn from institutions anywhere on the Web without having to concern themselves with the particular data representations for financial transactions required by each.

2.2.1 *Outline of a solution*

What is needed is a Web-friendly, internationally agreed, standard notation for expressing financial transactions. The notation should be extensible to allow new financial transaction types to be added in the future without breaking existing applications. The standard should be easy to develop software for and completely open.

2.2.2 *Enter XML*

The hierarchical structure of the information found in many financial transaction types is easily represented using the structured document philosophy of XML.

A statement request might look like this.

```
<StatementRequest>
  <BankAccount>
    <BankID>123456</BankID>
    <AccountID>9999</AccountID>
    <AccountType>CHECKING</AccountType>
  </BankAccount>
</StatementRequest>
```

The transaction from a customer to a bank, requesting the establishment of a recurring payment with 12 monthly installments, might look like this.

```
<Recurrence>
    <Number>12</Number>
    <Frequency>MONTHLY</Frequency>
</Recurrence>
<PaymentInfo>
    <FromBank>
        <BankId>555432180</BankId>
        <AccountId>763984</AccountId>
        <AccountType>CHECKING</AccountType>
    </FromBank>
    <Amount>395.00</Amount>
    <PayeeID>77810</PayeeID>
    <PayAccount>444-78-97572</PayAccount>
    <DateDue>19971115</DateDue>
    <Memo>Auto loan payment</Memo>
</PaymentInfo>
</Recurrence>
```

Apart from some simplifications and changes in element type names, both of these examples conform to the Open Financial Exchange (OFX) specification. This is an XML[1] application developed jointly by Microsoft, Intuit, and Checkfree.

---

1. The OFX initiative predates XML and at the time of writing is still based on SGML rather than XML. A variety of both SGML and XML resources are linked to *from* the OFX home page (http://www.onestandard.com).

The latter transaction could be conducted using an OFX-compliant application such as Microsoft Money, as shown in Figure 2–10.

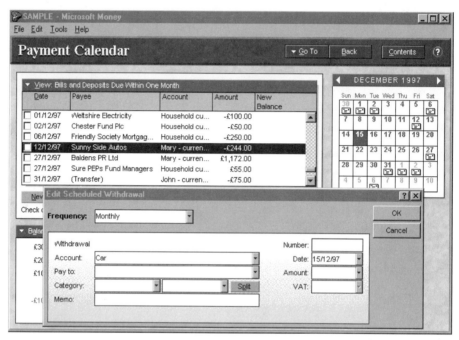

Figure 2–10   Entering a recurring transaction in Microsoft Money

This application will create an OFX document at the point where it goes online to the financial institution. At the far side of the link, the financial institution will field the OFX data and perhaps transform it into the notation required for its internal software. This process is illustrated in Figure 2–11.

2.2.3   *Concluding thoughts*

The OFX initiative is a good example of how members of a highly competitive industry can use XML to the benefit of all. As consumers of financial services, we get a better choice and better access to services because of OFX.

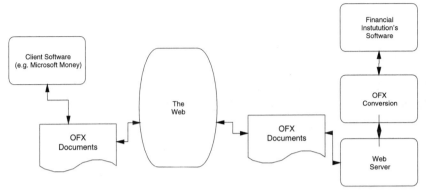

Figure 2–11 OFX interchange between a customer and a financial institution over the Web

For their part, the financial institutions know that in this new frontier of electronic commerce, chaos is in nobody's interest. The entire industry thrives on confidence. Electronic commerce standards such as OFX and OTP contribute to that confidence.

2.3 | Software distribution

As more and more digital data of all forms finds its primary distribution medium on the Internet, the likely outcome is that it will become the standard way of installing application software onto users' PCs. Even if bandwidth issues make initial distribution via the Internet prohibitively expensive, a clearly attractive alternative is to have some way of doing an initial software distribution on CD but deliver updates, bug fixes, etc., via the Web.

The crux of the problem is that we need a way to describe what the component parts of a software distribution *really are* and how they interrelate. How great the tools for installing applications from the Web would be if they were intelligent enough to only download the components you need—ignoring the ones you already have. On Windows platforms in particular, a large number of component files (dlls, ocxs, etc.) can be shared across all applications built with a particular tool. Much download time could be saved if an intelligent software downloading agent could say to itself, "This application needs vbrun300.dll, size 398,416 bytes, but the user already has that installed. No need to download it."

2.3.1 *Outline of a solution*

A data representation is needed to capture information such as:

- What the software is
- Summary details of what the software does
- Version information
- Platform requirements (i.e., Windows, UNIX, Macintosh, etc.)
- Component parts

2.3.2 *Enter XML*

We need to create a data representation with certain predefined components. Each document will capture all that is required to specify a complete software package. Each package will typically contain one or more subpackages. A snippet of a data representation describing a software package is shown here.

```
<Package Name = "Currency Calculator" Version = "1.0">
<Title>Currency Calculator Package</Title>
<Abstract>This calculator allows conversions of
   amounts of money between currencies</Abstract>
<Component Name = "com.digitome.calculator" Version =
   "1.0">
</Package>
```

Apart from some simplification and pruning, the previous snippet is a valid example of a document conforming to an XML application known as OSD—Open Software Distribution. OSD is an initiative by Microsoft, Marimba, and others to standardize a data representation for software distribution via the Internet.

As far as a computer is concerned, digital data is digital data. No significant difference exists between a software package consisting of multiple component files and a push channel consisting of multiple Web pages. Thus the fact that some overlap occurs between OSD and CDF is not surprising.

Indeed, CDF includes support for OSD by standardizing so-called Software Distribution Channels. Out of the box, Internet Explorer Version 4 comes with just such a channel preconfigured to allow downloads of updated versions of itself. It sits under the Favorites menu, in the Software Updates submenu. The top-level HTML page in this channel is shown in Figure 2–12.

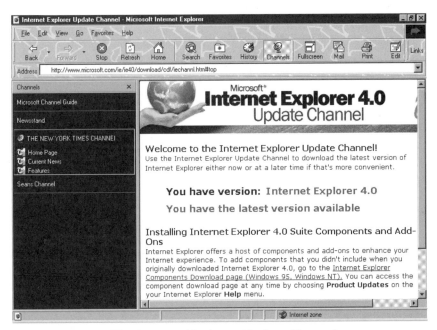

Figure 2–12 The Internet Explorer Update Channel

A snippet of the actual CDF document used for the Internet Explorer Software Update Channel is shown here.

```
<CHANNEL HREF="http://www.microsoft.com/ie/ie40/down-
load/cdf/iechannl.htm">
<TITLE>Microsoft Internet Explorer</TITLE>
  <ABSTRACT>
    The Internet Explorer Software Update Channel is
    designed to notify you when a new version of IE is
    available.
  </ABSTRACT>
  <USAGE VALUE="SoftwareUpdate"/>

<SCHEDULE>
        <INTERVALTIME DAY="14" />
      <LATESTTIME DAY="2"/>
</SCHEDULE>

<SOFTPKG  HREF="http://www.microsoft.com/ie/ie40/
  download/cdf/iechannl.htm"
        NAME="{89820200-ECBD-11cf-8B85-00AA005B4383}"
        VERSION="4,72,2106,8"
        STYLE="ActiveSetup">
<IMPLEMENTATION>
    <LANGUAGE VALUE="en"/>
    <PROCESSOR VALUE="x86"/>
    <OS VALUE="winnt"/>
</IMPLEMENTATION>
```

2.3.3 *Concluding thoughts*

The OSD initiative is a good example of how even small XML documents can carry a tremendous amount of useful information. An OSD document of 1 KB or so, incorporated into an OSD-aware installation package, could avoid many megabytes of unnecessary download. Also, given that all XML documents are in plain text, OSD documents provide technicians with a rich, succinct description of how a software distribution is constructed and how the parts interrelate.

2.4 | Web Automation

The act of browsing a Web site is, naturally enough, considered an interactive activity. A user sits at a terminal and interactively enters URLs, clicks a mouse to follow links, keys data into forms, and so on.

As the technology has matured and the sheer volume of material/applications on the Web has increased, so too has interest in developing methods of *automating* Web interaction. Perhaps the best known applications of a noninteractive Web application are search engine spiders. Also known as Web Robots, these applications spend their time trawling the Internet for content by pretending to be interactive Web browsers. Their mission: to seek out and index new content to add to their centralized search engine databases.

Batch automating the process of visiting Web sites and traversing links is relatively straightforward. However, complexities quickly arise if user interaction via HTML forms, for example, is required.

Consider a stock quotation Web site where the user enters a ticker symbol, a chart type, and clicks **OK** in order to receive a graph of the stock's price (see Figure 2–13).

Obviously, business applications such as this can benefit from automation. Once automatic download of stock prices/graphs is achieved, any number of interesting possibilities present themselves:

- Stock portfolio applications can schedule downloads of the latest information and update stock portfolios accordingly.
- Buy and sell signals can be programmed into stock-watching applications.
- Stock watchers can send e-mails to investors once certain trigger conditions are met.

The automation of access to this sort of site and the construction of business applications on top of them are nothing new. Many developers have developed *robots* or *Web Agents* in Java, Perl, Visual Basic,

More Info: News , SEC Filings , Profile , Research , Msgs					
Last Trade 4:36PM · **102 $^{1}/_{8}$**	Change +2 $^{1}/_{8}$ (+2.13%)		Prev Cls 100	Volume 6,816,700	Div Date Dec 10
Day's Range 97 - 102 $^{15}/_{16}$	Bid N/A	Ask N/A	Open 99 $^{1}/_{4}$	Avg Vol 4,259,590	Ex-Div Nov 6
52-week Range 63 $^{9}/_{16}$ - 113 $^{1}/_{2}$	Earn/Shr 5.97	P/E 16.75	Mkt Cap 99.283B	Div/Shr 0.80	Yield 0.80

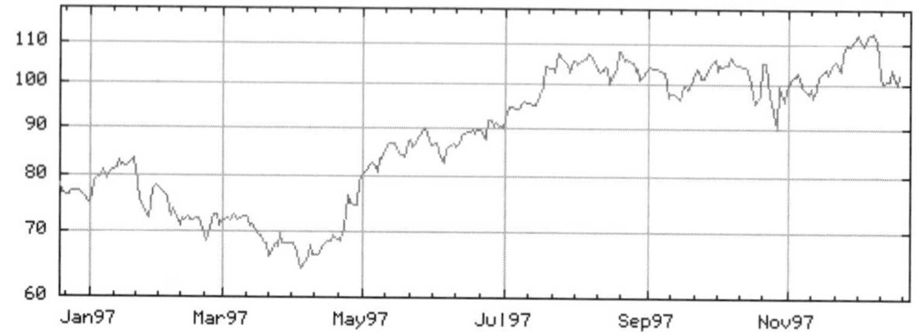

Figure 2–13   A typical stock quotation from http://quote.yahoo.com

Python, etc., to do this sort of thing. The trouble is that hand crafting these things is both error prone and time consuming. Moreover, they are very easily broken. Typically, if a service provider changes a site layout or adds a new field to a form or changes a URL, these robots can come crashing down. Changing them takes valuable time.

2.4.1 *Outline of a solution*

Only a limited number of user interaction types are in common usage. Could someone *generalize* the interaction types and create a little language in which to express interactive sessions? Such a language would have numerous advantages.

- Increasing the speed with which robot applications can be developed.

- Removing the need to hard-code Java, Perl, and VB code to achieve the automation.
- Simplifying the process of modifying the robot to cope with change.

2.4.2 *Enter XML*

A little language is needed to capture the details of the Web service to be automated, perhaps something like this:

```
<Service Name="Stock Quote"
URL="http://quote.yahoo.com/">
```

Within the service, we need a data entry form of some description. For each field in this form, we will need to provide a piece of data of our own. We will call that process *binding*. Perhaps the code will be something like this:

```
<Binding Name="QuoteInputForm">
 <Variable Name="stock" TYPE="String"/>
</Binding>
```

Once such a Web automation description document is in place, it can be automatically converted into the HTTP protocol commands that Web servers expect to get from HTML forms.

Once the stock quote comes back from the service, we have an HTML page. Somewhere on that HTML page are the pieces of information we need. Browsers can expose this information to applications in the form of a "Document Object Model." For example, "doc.img[0]" might mean "the first image in the full list of images for this page."

Supposing the graph is the first image on the page, we might capture this as.

```
<Variable Name="Image" Type="String[]" Refer-
ence="doc.img[0]"
```

Apart from some simplifications and pruning, this snippet of XML conforms to the WIDL proposed standard for Web automation.

WIDL—**W**eb **I**nterface **D**efinition **L**anguage—is an XML application developed by WebMethods, Inc. to support the rapid development of Web Automation applications. It is included on the CD with this book. WIDL uses XML to capture the important details of a Web conversation in a form that allows such conversations to be automated.

The WebMethods software (and indeed any software that understands the WIDL format) can take this information and auto-generate the Java, JavaScript, Visual Basic, etc. required to build a stand-alone Robot application.

As a simple example of how WIDL can be used to describe the contents of an HTML document, Figure 2–14 shows a screenshot of the small HTML document created in Chapter 1, loaded into the Web Automation Toolkit.

The various locations within this structure are identified via the Document Object Model descriptions pictured in Figure 2–15.

The WIDL representation of the information objects available in this simple HTML document looks like this:

```
<SERVICE NAME="watt_Doc1Doc"
 METHOD="GET"
 URL="file:C:\xml\book\ch01\Doc1.htm"
 OUTPUT="watt_Doc1DocOutput" />


<!-- ----------------------------------------- -->


<BINDING NAME="watt_Doc1DocOutput" TYPE="OUTPUT">
 <VARIABLE NAME="title" TYPE="String" REFER-
   ENCE="doc.title[0].text" USAGE="DEFAULT" />
 <VARIABLE NAME="doctext" TYPE="String" REFERENCE="doc.text"
   USAGE="DEFAULT" />
 <VARIABLE NAME="headings" TYPE="String[]" REFERENCE ="doc.head-
   ing[].text" USAGE="DEFAULT" />
 <VARIABLE NAME="table0" TYPE="String[][]" REFER-
   ENCE="doc.table[0].tr[].th|td[].text" USAGE="DEFAULT" />
</BINDING>
```

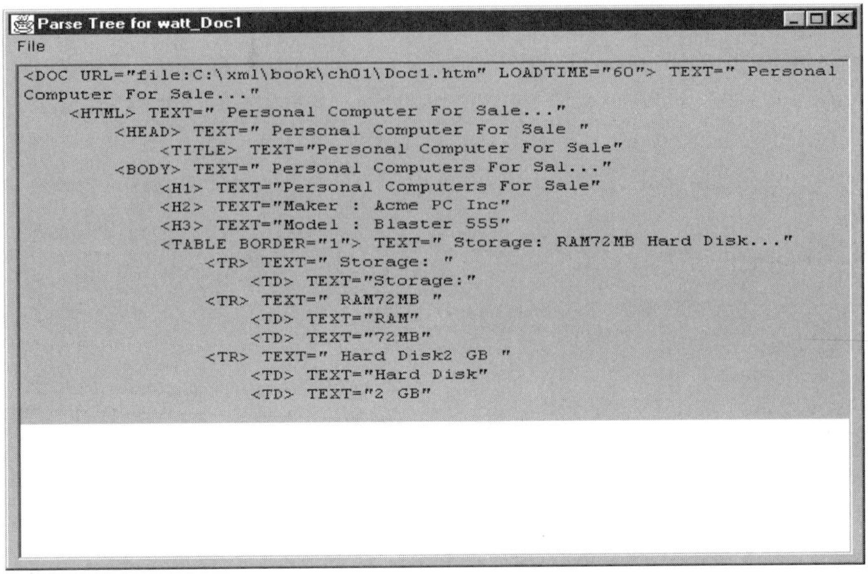

```
Parse Tree for watt_Doc1                                          _ □ ×
File
<DOC URL="file:C:\xml\book\ch01\Doc1.htm" LOADTIME="60"> TEXT=" Personal
Computer For Sale..."
    <HTML> TEXT=" Personal Computer For Sale..."
        <HEAD> TEXT=" Personal Computer For Sale "
            <TITLE> TEXT="Personal Computer For Sale"
        <BODY> TEXT=" Personal Computers For Sal..."
            <H1> TEXT="Personal Computers For Sale"
            <H2> TEXT="Maker : Acme PC Inc"
            <H3> TEXT="Model : Blaster 555"
            <TABLE BORDER="1"> TEXT=" Storage: RAM72MB Hard Disk..."
                <TR> TEXT=" Storage: "
                    <TD> TEXT="Storage:"
                <TR> TEXT=" RAM72MB "
                    <TD> TEXT="RAM"
                    <TD> TEXT="72MB"
                <TR> TEXT=" Hard Disk2 GB "
                    <TD> TEXT="Hard Disk"
                    <TD> TEXT="2 GB"
```

Figure 2–14   Tree structure of the HTML document

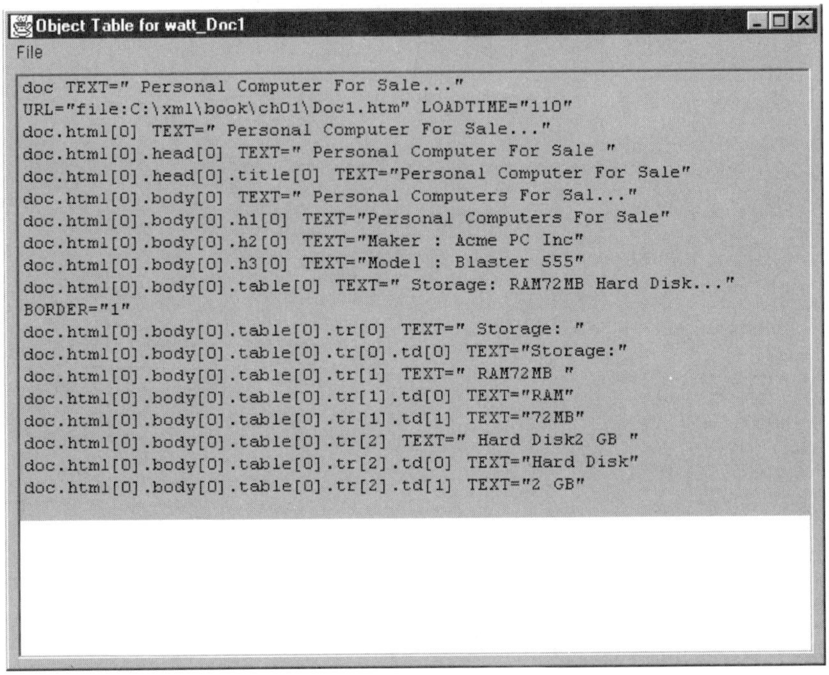

```
Object Table for watt_Doc1                                        _ □ ×
File
doc TEXT=" Personal Computer For Sale..."
URL="file:C:\xml\book\ch01\Doc1.htm" LOADTIME="110"
doc.html[0] TEXT=" Personal Computer For Sale..."
doc.html[0].head[0] TEXT=" Personal Computer For Sale "
doc.html[0].head[0].title[0] TEXT="Personal Computer For Sale"
doc.html[0].body[0] TEXT=" Personal Computers For Sal..."
doc.html[0].body[0].h1[0] TEXT="Personal Computers For Sale"
doc.html[0].body[0].h2[0] TEXT="Maker : Acme PC Inc"
doc.html[0].body[0].h3[0] TEXT="Model : Blaster 555"
doc.html[0].body[0].table[0] TEXT=" Storage: RAM72MB Hard Disk..."
BORDER="1"
doc.html[0].body[0].table[0].tr[0] TEXT=" Storage: "
doc.html[0].body[0].table[0].tr[0].td[0] TEXT="Storage:"
doc.html[0].body[0].table[0].tr[1] TEXT=" RAM72MB "
doc.html[0].body[0].table[0].tr[1].td[0] TEXT="RAM"
doc.html[0].body[0].table[0].tr[1].td[1] TEXT="72MB"
doc.html[0].body[0].table[0].tr[2] TEXT=" Hard Disk2 GB "
doc.html[0].body[0].table[0].tr[2].td[0] TEXT="Hard Disk"
doc.html[0].body[0].table[0].tr[2].td[1] TEXT="2 GB"
```

Figure 2–15   List of locations within the tree structure

This WIDL representation of the contents of HTML documents can be programmatically converted for use in any required scripting language. The following is a snippet of WIDL-driven Java that prints out all the images in an HTML document:

```
Document doc = c.loadDocument(args[0]);
String[] images =
  doc.getPropertyArray("img[].src");
for (int i = 0; i < images.length; i++)
      {
          if (images[i] != null)
              System.out.println(i+") "+images[i]);
      }
```

2.4.3 *Concluding thoughts*

WIDL is illustrative of an entire family of automation applications that can be envisioned for XML. Anywhere where a Web conversation occurs with a predefined structure is a candidate WIDL application. The WIDL description of the conversation is language-independent, allowing the automatic generation of source code to conduct the conversation in a variety of languages.

The WIDL language has been submitted to the World Wide Web Consortium for consideration as a standard language for Web Automation.

2.5 | Database Integration

A lot of information in the world is stored in databases—terabytes worth of personnel files, health records, football results, stock prices, etc. Much of this information can be put to use on the Web. The problem is how to get it there. A once-off conversion to a Web page is not an option because these databases need to be constantly updated and often change rapidly. What is needed is a mechanism allowing such database data to be accessed/modified via a Web interface, yet remain in its original database format.

2.5.1 *Outline of a solution*

One of the great attractions of the Web is that users do not need to know or care how Web pages are created by Web servers. A Web browser simply issues a request and awaits a response. In many cases the Web pages are static—sitting on the server waiting to be requested, as illustrated in Figure 2–16.

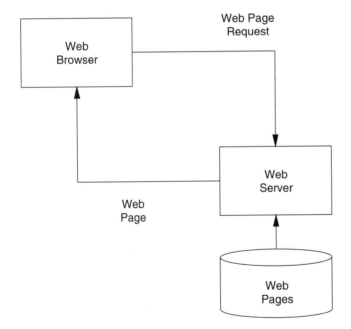

Figure 2–16   Static Web pages served up on a Web Site

However, you can introduce a level of indirection here completely transparent to the Web browser (see Figure 2–17).

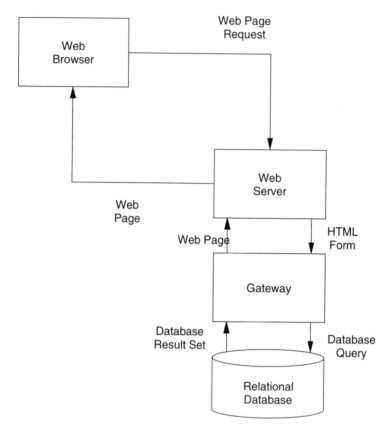

Figure 2–17   Dynamically created Web pages served up on a Web Site

What is needed is some way to capture database-related information such as tables, fields, values, and so on in a form that can be
translated to HTML "on the fly" so that the whole thing is transparent to the applications that can deal only with straight HTML, i.e.,
the Web browser.

2.5.2   *Enter XML*

Suppose that we have a database called Personnel with a table called
Names. It might be defined as follows:

```
Database Personnel
  Table Names
    Field Surname,text,40
    Field Given,text,40
    Field DateOfBirth,date
```

Taking this table definition and generating a Web page form that can act as a data entry screen for that information is a straightforward process, as you can see in Figure 2-18.

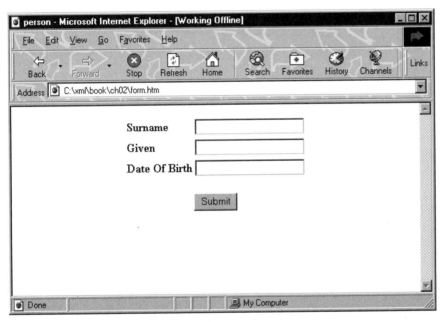

Figure 2–18   Data entry screen for a database as an HTML form

Once the form has been filled in, the next simple matter is to create a new record in the Names database using the field values supplied by the user who filled in the form and pressed the submit button. The sequence of operations is illustrated in Figure 2–19.

1. Use the database scheme to construct an HTML data entry form

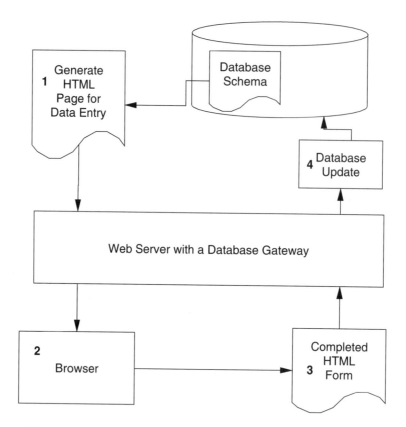

Figure 2–19　Sequence of operations required to interface a database to the Web

2. The browser displays the form and the user fills in the fields

3. The user presses the submit button, and the complete form is sent back to the web server

4. The database gateway component of the Web server plucks out the fields and creates a record for submission to the database

To provide maximum flexibility, we control operations via *template* documents, which can contain a mixture of straight HTML and our new little language for expressing database functions. To describe the interaction above, we could use something like the following:

```
<!-- The HTML Form for data entry -->
<DATABASEINSERT DATABASE="Personel" TABLE="Names">
<!-- From here is the page to send back after an
    update-->
<HTML>
<HEAD>
<TITLE>My Input Template</TITLE>
</HEAD>
<BODY>
<p>Database record entered successfully.
```

Naturally, we can go a lot further than that. We could, for example, embed a database query right in the middle of an HTML page:

```
<H1>Here is a list of all the Marys on the payroll</H1>
<QUERY DATABASE="Personnel" TABLE="Names">
    SELECT * from database
    WHERE Given like "Mary"
     ORDER By Given
</QUERY>
```

Apart from simplification, pruning, and element type names, the examples in this section are illustrations of how CFML—Cold Fusion Markup Language—works. Cold Fusion is from Allaire Corp. An evaluation edition of the software is provided on the CD with this book. The CFML markup language is XML-like but unlikely to become fully XML compliant owing to the needs of the 4GL programming language it includes. However, the language has been designed to be extensible using XML. Developers can develop their own element types as add-ons to the core CFML language. Moreover, given that CFML is a powerful technology for accessing *structured* information it can just as easily be applied to accessing XML. Using CFML, it will be possible to query, update and generate reports on XML data using the same techniques applicable to relational databases.

2.5.3 *Concluding thoughts*

Although you can argue that XML can do everything a traditional database can do, the need to build bridges to existing database technology—especially relational database technology—is very real. The way the Web works lends itself to seamless integration of the two via on-the-fly conversions, as the example illustrates.

Historically, these conversions have been into HTML, but as native XML browsing tools become mainstream the need to perform a down translation to HTML can be removed, as illustrated in Figure 2–20.

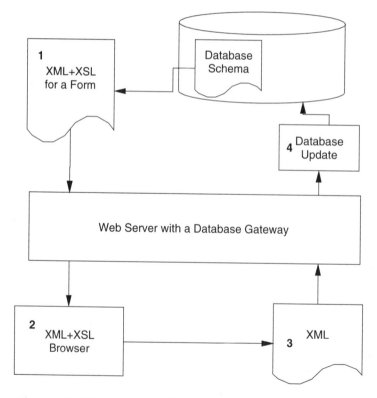

Figure 2-20   Native XML+XSL used to perform a database update

The advantages of *not* down translating to HTML can be significant, especially in the case where database results are being sent back to the Web browser for display. Even in the simple example used here, we can see some possibilities. For example, the most recent query has *wired* the ordering of the query results to be in given name order. If the data arrives at the browser in straight XML like this:

```
<Names>
  <Surname>Bloggs</Surname>
  <Given>Joe</Given>
  </DateOfBirth>1/1/2097</DateOfBirth>
  <!-- more names here -->
</Names>
```

Then the browser user would be able to search, sort, and otherwise process the data in any number of ways *locally*.

2.6 | Localization

The Web has accelerated the rate at which the Earth is shrinking. The speed with which digital information can now be published to a worldwide audience makes it increasingly important to have localized versions of software/documentation available very quickly after the launch of, say, the English language version.

The localization process is slowed down and thus made more expensive by the diversity of data representations in which translatable material can exist. Dozens of popular DTP/WP packages, programming languages, graphic file formats, resource file formats, and so on are available. Many of these formats are mutually incompatible. With every new data representation or variation on an existing representation, the poor translators run into more problems.

2.6.1 *Outline of a solution*

Many of the problems with language translation stem from the fact that traditional document formats blend formatting and content so closely together. More often than not, the only way to get at the text is to use exactly the same editing tool that was used to create it in the first place. This restriction is far from ideal from a translation point of view.

If a data representation could be agreed on that would *temporarily* separate content from formatting but maintain the link between the two, life would be a lot easier for the translators. They could translate the content part of a document without having to use the software package used to create it. Software could then *merge* the original formatting back in with the content to recreate the original document. Furthermore, if the data representation for the content part could be standardized, a variety of tools from different vendors could all operate on the same data. The process is illustrated in Figure 2–21.

For example, assuming the original document contains the following fragment of RTF (**R**ich **T**ext **F**ormat):

```
{\plain\cf2\b Hello World }
```

We could use the pretranslation filter to generate a document for translation like this:

```
<1>Hello World<2>
```

Note the two placeholder codes, **<1>** and **<2>**. The pretranslation filter would also generate a document to store the formatting information ready for merging after the translation.

```
<1> {\plain\cf2\b
<2> }
```

The translation then takes place, taking care not to disturb the place holders.

```
<1>Bonjour le Mond<2>
```

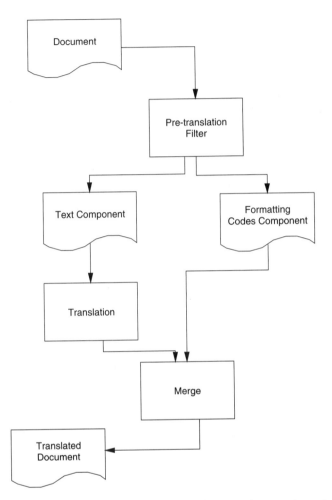

Figure 2-21   The workflow of a translation via an intermediate data representation format

Finally, the posttranslation filter, reconstitutes the document by merging the translated content with the formatting codes.

```
{\plain\cf2\b Bonjour le Mond }
```

2.6.2   *The XML advantage*

Using XML for the intermediate document notation for this application makes a lot of sense, for the following reasons.

- XML's parent, SGML, has been used in the past to provide a common denominator for word processing data representations, and a lot of knowledge has been built up about how to go about it, what element types are required, etc.
- XML is language friendly "out of the box" with its native support for Unicode.
- XML's ability to validate documents can be used to ensure that translated documents do not break their original structure.
- The significant scope for automation in XML processing fits well with the growing availability of automatic and semiautomatic translation systems.

The following XML snippet is taken from a document that conforms to the OpenTag format. OpenTag is an initiative of ILE, and full details are available from their Web site at http://www.ile.com.

```
<FILE lc="EN-US"
tool="Borneo 1.00-017"
datatype="RTF" original="//brazil/recife/devile/
  data/help.rtf">
<P id="1">This is a text in <G type="bold">bold
  </G> and <G id="1">all caps red</G></P>
<P id="2">Second paragraph with graphic
  <X id="1"/>.</P> </FILE>
```

2.6.3   *Concluding thoughts*

A lot of effort has gone into ensuring that XML is as multilingual as possible. The use of Unicode as the character encoding is the most visible evidence of that effort. XML users can not only use all of Unicode's capabilities in the content of their documents—but they can use it in the markup as well. In other words, XML's ability to use arbitrary names for elements extends to full Unicode, accented characters, etc., and can will be commonly used in XML element type names.

2.7 | Intermediate data representations

Intermediate data representations are a vital technique for facilitating the interchange of data from one platform/software package to another. The more powerful a particular computing tool is, the more likely it is to benefit from having an intermediate representation *tuned* to its own particular feature set. This need for specific functionality in an intermediate representation often leads to the development of yet another syntax for essentially the same sort of information. RTF, MIF, DCF, CSV, SYLK, DIF, etc., are all examples of interchange data representations.

With each new data representation comes the need for software developers to understand it in detail and then develop processing software to work with the new representation. The low-level aspects of processing a representation—analyzing the syntax and checking the structure—are typically highly specific to that representation. Each one seems to have its own set of "magic" characters, for example. In RTF, characters such as "{" and "}" are special. In Maker Interchange Format, "<" and "\" are special, and so on. The overall task generally consists of three phases illustrated in Figure 2–22.

Developing software to implement the basic syntax and structure parsing of these representations is a lot of tedious and tricky work. Can this be avoided? Specifically, can a basic syntax be agreed upon so that developers could rely on using an off-the-shelf component to do the time-consuming and error-prone parts, leaving them free to concentrate on the specifics of the data interchange task at hand?

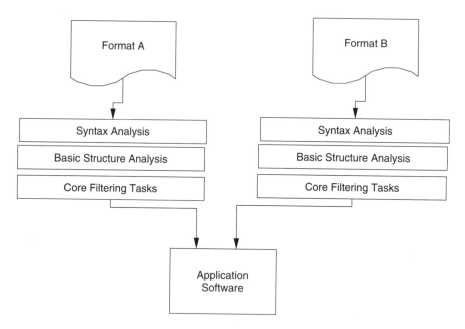

Figure 2–22   Three stages of processing an intermediate data representation

2.7.1   *Outline of a solution*

We need to move the base notation for such interchange representations up a level so that the functionality to do with syntax analysis, basic error checking, etc., can become an off-the-shelf module to be reused over and over again.

2.7.2   *The XML advantage*

One way to allow reuse of the low-level details of parsing an interchange representation is to base them all on the same notation—XML. That way, a generic piece of code for parsing XML can be used over and over again to deal with such low-level details, as Figure 2–23 shows.

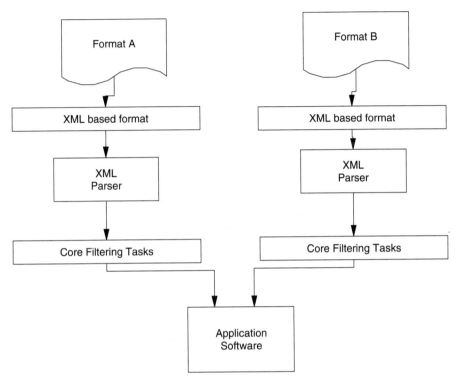

Figure 2–23 Processing intermediate data representations based on XML

Lotus Notes is a good example of a powerful computing platform that benefits from an intermediate data representation specific to it. In Notes, some concepts, such as composite text fields, doclinks, multi-valued fields, and so on, need to be comprehensively catered for in an intermediate representation if it is going to be worth using.

An XML application—Notes Flat File—has been developed to provide such an intermediate data representation for importing data into Lotus Notes.

A segment of an NFF file is shown here.

```
<NFFBOOK>
 <STYLES>
  <PARAS>
   <PARA AFTER="1.5" NAME="Style1" ALIGN="CENTRE"
  LM="2880">
  </PARAS>
```

```
</STYLES>
<NOTE FORM = "Main Form">
 <ANCHOR NAME = "anchor1">
 <FIELDS>
  <FIELD NAME = "Age" TYPE = "Number">
 </FIELDS>
 <COMP NAME = "Body">
  <P STYLE = "Style1">
  <TEXT>Hello World</TEXT>
  </P>
  <P STYLE = "Style1">
  <TEXT>I am a </TEXT>
  <DOCLINK ANCHOR = "anchor1">
  <TEXT>link.</TEXT>
 </COMP>
<NOTE>
<NFFBOOK>
```

A standard Notes Import Filter has been developed that understands this XML application. It supports all the features of the Notes platform in terms of fields, rich text formatting, doclinks, and so on. A screen shot of a Lotus Notes Application created with the Notes Flat File import filter is shown in Figure 2–24.

Notes Flat File is an initiative of Digitome Electronic Publishing, at http://www.digitome.com.

2.7.3 *Concluding thoughts*

Just as authors using WYSIWYG tools can spend too much time formatting the content they create, software developers can spend too much time struggling to implement low-level parsing routines to get access to yet another badly defined interchange representation. Using XML for this task means that from the word go, the software developer has a wealth of experience and tools to bring to bear on the task of processing the data. Moreover, since many XML parsers are being written with speed as a primary concern, fewer and fewer good reasons will exist for developing custom data representations. Just use XML!

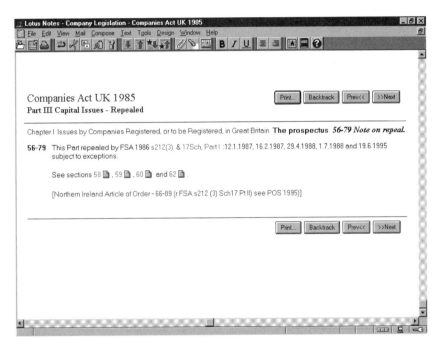

Figure 2–24   A sample NFF document as it appears after import into Lotus Notes

2.8 | Scientific Publishing—Chemical Markup Language

Publishing scientific documents has always proven a testing task, owing to the complexity and variety of the formatting required. The mathematician and computer scientist Donald E. Knuth invented the TeX typesetting system in order to improve the typesetting quality of his own, often highly mathematical books.

TeX has been, and continues to be, very popular, particularly in the scientific community. However, TeX is very format oriented, building up publications in terms of fixed page sizes consisting of nested rectangular areas. Once coded in TeX, the underlying structure and content of the information is clouded behind complex typesetting markup.

Reusing text in TeX notation is thus made rather difficult. Moreover, for things like mathematical equations, chemical compounds, etc., a lot of opportunities to interact with the data are lost. For example, if a chemical compound could be published on the Web with the information that it *is* a chemical compound made explicit, browser applets could render the compound in different ways on the screen, perhaps creating three dimensional models, calculating the results of applying various formulae, and so on.

How can the inherent information content of, say, chemical compounds be retained in order to be put to better use in Web browsers and elsewhere?

2.8.1 *Outline of a solution*

We need a little language that allows us to build models of molecules in terms of atoms, bonds, etc. We could conceivably have something like this:

```
<Molecule>
  <Atoms>
    <Locations>
       <X Coords>1.0 1.1 3.2 4.6
       <Y Coords>2.3 2.4 5.5 7.3
    </Locations>
    <Elements>
       C H H H H C C
    </Elements>
</Molecule>
```

2.8.2 *Enter XML*

This is exactly the sort of thing that Chemical Markup Language (CML) is designed for. CML is an XML application developed by Peter Murray-Rust. Using CML and its associated browser applet, Jumbo, you can bring data such as this to life. Figure 2–25 shows a CML document in the Jumbo browser applet within Internet Explorer 4.0.

Figure 2–25 A tree view of a CML document using the Jumbo applet in Internet Explorer 4.0

Part of the molecule data in tree view mode is shown in Figure 2–26.

The numerical data within these elements can be used to produce renderings such as in Figure 2–27.

An example rendering of the CML document for Adenosin is shown in Figure 2–28.

2.8.3 *Concluding thoughts*

Scientific data is particularly well suited to the XML approach. It is often rigorously structured and lends itself to processing, both on the client and server sides of a Web-based publishing system. The scien-

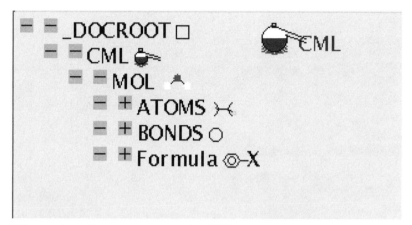

Figure 2–26   A tree view of a CML compound in Jumbo

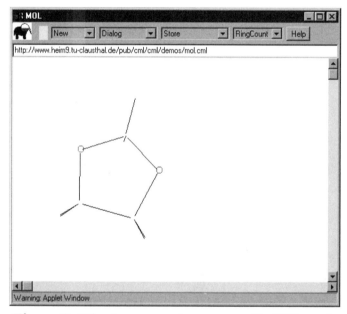

Figure 2–27   A compound represented in CML rendered using the Jumbo applet in Internet Explorer 4.0

tific community has over the years developed an array of data formats and notations ranging from chromosome classifications to hydrocarbons. As in other fields of endeavor, we are bound to see an upsurge in

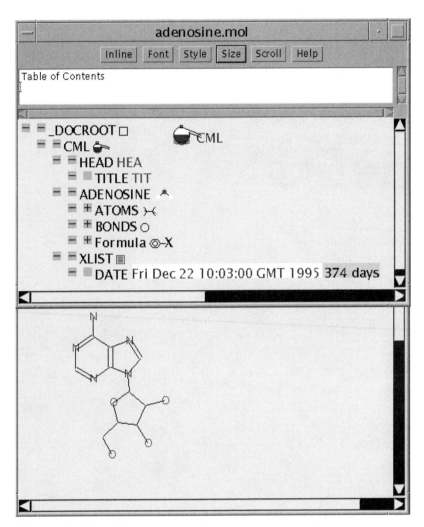

Figure 2-28 The compound Adenosin rendered in Jumbo

the use of XML as replacements for these notations and also as a hub notation for scientific data interchange.

The Commercial Benefits of XML

- Letting the browser do the work
- Authors should generate content, not formatting
- I'll show you mine if you show me yours
- Documentation—what documentation?
- Work smarter, not harder

Chapter

3

Before you delve further into the realms of XML, pause for breath and let us attempt to classify the various benefits that XML brings to the world in general and the Web in particular.

Letting the browser do the work

With HTML, most of the decisions about how information will look are made at the point when the content is created. To a very large extent, the presentation information is *wired* or *hard coded* into the HTML. All the browser can do is render it to the best of its ability, using its best guess as to what the author intended. Style sheets are a recent addition to HTML and are a step in the right direction. Allowing arbitrary element type names is a logical pro-

75

gression for the style sheet approach, a progression that nicely dove-tails with XML and XSL.

With XML, browsers can do much of the work of processing, render-ing documents. This capability has a number of far-reaching benefits.

- The content can be manipulated and rearranged. Calculations can be performed to generate extra content on the fly and so on. This work can all be done at the client end with the aid of scripting languages such as Java, JavaScript, and the like.

- The same content can be made to look completely different for different users or different uses. For example, the printed version produced by printing the data from within the browser could use a completely different layout from the one used for on-screen presentation. Popups could become footnotes, page numbers and running headers could be added, a serif font such as Times could be used, and so on.

- The content can be intelligently searched within the browser, based on what it contains, e.g., "find the first PC with a RAM capacity in excess of 32 MB."

3.1.1 *Author once, format many times*

Traditional documents are difficult to reuse. This fact of life is simple. If you doubt it, just ask people who have pulled their hair out trying to take a document created for paper and reformat it, ready for deployment on the Web, for example. Alternatively, ask people who have tried to move a document from software package X to software package Y. Ask them what happened to all their lovely formatting, their table layouts, and their floating graphics. If all else fails, and you still doubt that documents are difficult to reuse, consider this: often, *rekeying* document information is more cost effective than using a software-based conversion!

With every passing year, this problem gets worse for two reasons. Firstly, the sheer volume of document production is increasing year after year. Secondly, we demand much more from our documents these days than we used to. Paper output is no longer enough! We want online help files, Web pages, multilingual versions, speech synthesized versions, Braille versions, and so on.

Why are traditional documents hard to reuse? The reason can be found in the tight coupling between presentation and content found in most document-authoring technologies. As Brian Kernighan of AT&T Bell Labs once said, "The trouble with WYSIWYG is that what you see is *all* you get." When content and format are closely intertwined, extricating the former in anything other than plain text format is extremely difficult.

3.2 | Authors should generate content, not formatting

Authors using WYSIWYG tools can spend an inordinate amount of time formatting rather than creating content. Yet for the most part, the formatting follows well defined rules such as these:

- "Set the first paragraph after a level heading flush left. Subsequent paragraphs, left indent half an inch."
- "Warning paragraphs should be set in Helvetica, bold, 18 point."

Simply put, if the author concentrated on creating the content and telling the computer what the component parts represent—"this is a level heading," "this is a warning paragraph," etc.—then *software* could attend to the formatting.

Not only can high-quality formatting be added automatically, but also different types of formatting can be applied to the same content in order to achieve different results. Paper today, online help tomorrow, Braille the day after. This reuse concept is illustrated in Figure 3–1.

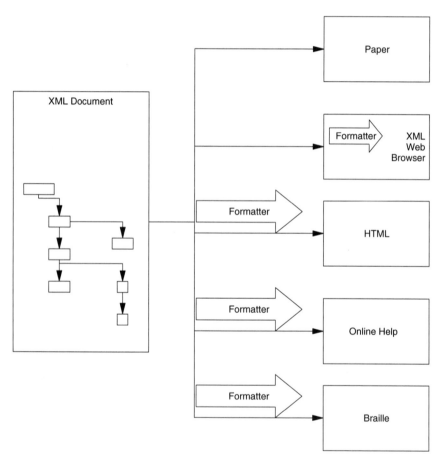

Figure 3–1   Using a single XML document to create multiple formatted outputs

With XML, your content is freed from the shackles of any one particular formatting system. Over its lifetime, an XML document can metamorphose into many different shapes and sizes. All the while, though, the structure and the content are retained independently, thus allowing the document to be reformatted over and over again to the myriad of formats around today—and the myriad of formats yet to be invented.

Note that in Figure 3-1, the formatter for the XML browser is shown as an integral part of the browser. This is to indicate that the process of applying formatting can be achieved "on the fly" just before the content is displayed.

3.2.1 *Live long, and prosper*

XML is an open standard. Nobody can monopolize it. No single person or commercial entity has control over its destiny. Nothing about it is hidden. Documents in XML belong to their *owner.* They do not belong to any software package, any computer configuration, or any operating system.

XML documents will be intelligible and useful long after many of today's proprietary, binary word processing formats have descended into hieroglyphic obsolescence. Consider this: a paper document, with a small amount of tender love and care, will still be legible in 20, 50, maybe 100 years from now. What are the odds on today's proprietary binary, word processor formats being legible in 10 years, let alone one hundred? Operating systems and software packages may come and go, but XML is for keeps.

3.2.2 *Author once, reuse many times*

In the section titled "Authors should generate content, not formatting" I talk about reuse in the context of using the same content to produce differently formatted outputs. An important second aspect exists to reuse: reusing the same content in many different documents—for example, having a single copy of some disclaimer text and reusing it in many publications, or having a document that consists entirely of component parts *harvested* from other documents (see Figure 3–2).

With XML, such reuse is not only technically feasible but considered good design. XML allows the creation of customized documents that would hitherto have proven prohibitively expensive. The ironic commercial reality is that in most instances the market is willing to pay a premium for such customization. The commercial implications of this fact are left as an exercise to you.

3.2.3 *Where did I put that memo?*

When creating documents, we typically have a very clear idea what they are, what components they contain, and how the components are structured. In our heads we differentiate among client telephone numbers, copyright notices, disclaimers, and so on. Unfortunately, this information is not stored with the document's content in the computer.

Instead, we store formatting information such as "right align, double space, bold," and so on. Such formatting information is of little use when in six months time, we wish to locate telephone numbers, copyright notices, or disclaimers. If only we had told the software what was *in* the documents . . .

With XML, telling the computer what is in a document is par for the course. You just *name* the component parts based on what they *are*. For a copyright segment, perhaps something like this:

```
<Copyright>
<Para>This document is copyright...</Para>
</Copyright>
```

For a disclaimer segment, perhaps something like this:

```
<Disclaimer>
<Para>This information is provided...</Para>
</Disclaimer>
```

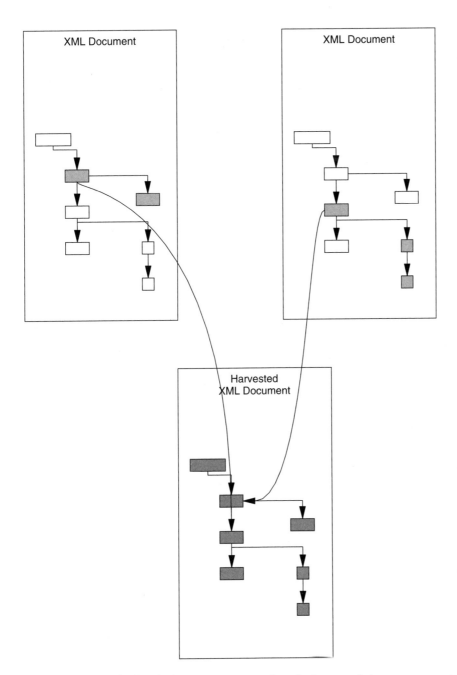

Figure 3–2   An XML document created entirely out of the component
parts of other documents

For a client telephone number, perhaps something like this:

```
<Client>
 <ContactInfo>
  <Telephone number = "555-1234"/>
  <!-- More contact info here -->
 <ContactInfo>
</Client>
```

As you can see, XML documents are self-describing. When documents contain such rich structural information about themselves, you can contemplate formulating quite complex queries and get very precise answers. Searches for information that would once have been prohibitively labor intensive can be automated with XML.

3.2.4 *All present and accounted for*

Not only does XML allow you to use arbitrary sets of element types to capture and describe your data, but it also allows you to detect automatically whether or not your documents have all the right pieces in all the right places. This facility occurs in an optional component of an XML document known as the Document Type Definition or DTD for short (see Figure 3–3). For example, in the Open Financial Exchange application of XML, an element type describes the structure of a credit card payment. This structure—or blueprint, if you like—for a credit card payment can be used to automatically check the structure of credit card payments.

3.2.5 *I'll show you mine if you show me yours*

Many organizations—even those that compete fiercely in the commercial world—can benefit from the ability to seamlessly exchange information. A setup in everyone's interest is if health care profession-

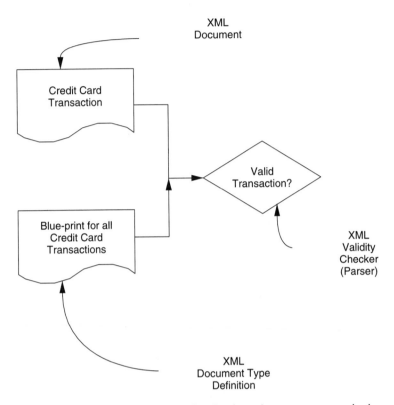

Figure 3–3   XML can check whether documents match the structures defined in their DTDs

als can interchange data. A setup in everyone's interest is if purchase orders can be exported from one accounting system in a form acceptable to another accounting system, and so on.

In industries where such standards do not exist, the characteristic pattern of information interchange in Figure 3–4 emerges.

All players with proprietary notations potentially need two-way notation converters for every third party with which they do business. Even in a field of four players, as illustrated in Figure 3–4, you can see that the number of converters can quickly get out of hand!

By using an *industry-standard interchange notation* (often called a *hub notation*), the number of converters required can be tamed as shown in Figure 3–5.

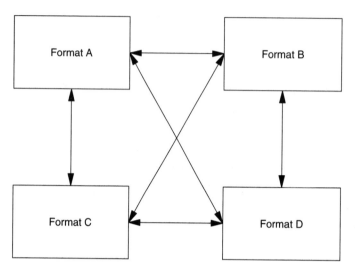

Figure 3–4 The number of notation converters required between communicating parties

Obviously, XML is not the only choice for such an interchange notation. A notation could be invented out of thin air by the cooperating parties. However, using XML as a base makes a lot of sense. It has been standardized. It is well known. And software—much of it free software—exists to process XML.

3.2.6 *Documentation—what documentation?*

XML documents can be very self-describing. Years after their creators have moved on and the question "what is this document all about?" fails to elicit a response from your co-workers, XML documents can answer such questions themselves. Even the little XML snippets in Chapter 1 describe themselves. Long after I have gone, "Sichuan Peppercorns" will obviously be a spice and "Blaster 555" will obviously be a brand of PC.

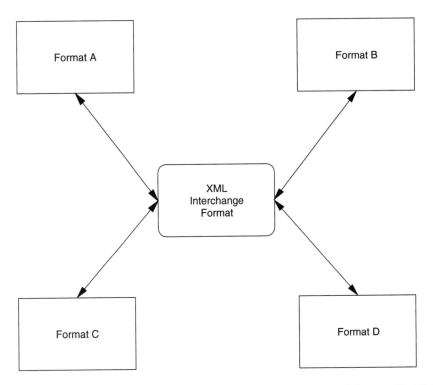

Figure 3–5   Taming the number of converters using XML as a "hub" format

3.2.7 *Work smarter, not harder*

A number of the benefits of XML outlined in this section contain the word "automatic." Automation is such a major benefit of XML that it is worthy of its own section, even though it is an intrinsic part of most of the others.

Managing large documentation sets used to be the realm of a handful of specialists. Today, especially with the growth in Web-based technologies, document management is as pervasive and complex a task as database management, if not more so.

Documents have a deserved reputation for being a labor-intensive form of information. We are used to the idea that computer programs can batch modify databases, but batch modifying documents takes human effort. With XML, the levels of automation achievable with documents are on par with those achievable with databases. Indeed with XML, documents become less like, well, documents and more like, um, databases!

3.3 | To summarize

We will wrap up this chapter with a summary of the main points raised.

- XML will be an intrinsic part of the Web and built directly into the next generation of Web browsers.
- XML is a completely open standard that safeguards your ownership of your own data.
- XML processing software and XML expertise will be ubiquitous and thus relatively cheap compared to proprietary software and format-specific expertise.
- Over its lifetime, an XML document can be used and reused in many different ways and in many different formats—including those yet to be invented.
- Authoring tools based on XML will allow authors to concentrate on authoring rather than formatting and thus to be more productive.
- XML documents *describe themselves,* making searching, indexing, and locating your information easier long after

you have forgotten what exactly you created and where
you put it!

- XML allows a high degree of automation to be achieved
  in areas that were previously highly labor intensive.

- XML documents are essentially *databases* of information.
  They can be processed, harvested, reported on, and
  queried just like traditional databases (only better).

Gaining Competitive Advantage with XML

- Setting up shop
- Creating a product catalog
- Publishing the catalog
- Keeping customers informed
- Enhancing the experience
- Money matters

4

Previous chapters have illustrated some of the areas where XML is being used to great effect by some of the biggest players on the Internet. Some of these applications actually came into being and were deployed *prior* to XML 1.0 being finalized by the experts involved in drafting it! Such was the compelling need for a way of achieving what XML achieves. In software development centers all over the world, from California to Cairo to Dublin to Bombay, new and innovative XML applications are being hatched in ever increasing numbers.

The day will come when no part of the Web will remain untouched by XML. This chapter illustrates some areas where XML either has already popped up or is going to pop up really soon now. To ground the discussion in a plausible reality, I use the concept of an Internet-based business (e-Business) selling Personal Computers. Assume that the little business operates from the URL **http://www.acmepc.com**.

4.1 | Setting up shop

The virtual shop, like any shop, will have a stock of goods to sell. In the case of acmepc.com, the stock is hidden away, perhaps in a warehouse or perhaps ordered from suppliers purely on an as-needed basis. The customer's sole point of contact with the stock is the electronic catalog on the Web site. It is vital to the viability of the business that this catalog is accurate, attractive, distinctive, and helpful. In this business, a good Web site is not simply a "nice-to-have" item. It *is* the business. A top-level view of how the business will operate is shown in Figure 4–1.

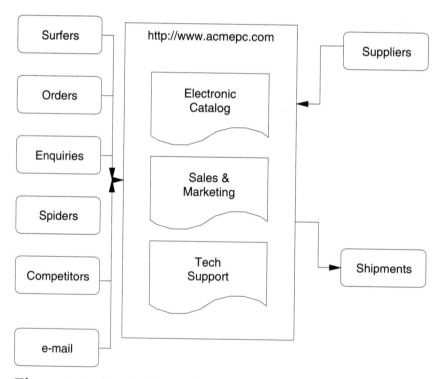

Figure 4–1   Top-level view of the e-business

4.2 | Creating the product catalog

Catalogs are by their very nature highly structured objects and lend themselves readily to an XML treatment. Catalogs can be large with a high density of information that benefits from the availability of a variety of access methods. In the acmepc.com catalog, I can envision having:

- Table of Contents
- Index
- Catalog Sorted by Price
- Catalog Sorted by Brand Name
- Catalog Sorted by CPU Speed
- Full text search
- Query by Example
- "Pick a PC" Wizard

and so on.

Having the catalog in XML makes it feasible to *generate* all of these from a single-source XML document. As long, that is, as the information required for sorting, keyword indexing, etc., is made explicit in the markup.

Start by free-wheeling your way towards a mini-catalog in XML. Do not concern yourself with syntax that is new to you at this stage!

```
<acmepc>
<item type = "PC">
 <make>
  <brand>Acme Delux</brand>
  <supplier id = "Acme"/>
 </make>
 <specification>
  <cpu type = "986" speed = "500"/>
  <harddisk type = "IDE" size = "10" units = "GB"/>
 </specification>
 <price n = "2000" units = "USD"/>
 <blurb>
```

```
  <p>A versatile PC for home or business use. Featur-
  ing as standard:</p>
  <ul>
   <li><index term = "Multimedia"/>Sound card</li>
   <li>90-day money back guarantee</li>
   <li>Mouse mat</li>
  </ul>
 </blurb>
 <internal>
  <instock num = "44"/>
  <supportcalls num = "6"/>
  <perunitcost n = "1800" units = "USD"/>
 </internal>
</item>
</acmepc>
```

Some things to note about this snippet of XML:

- Indentation has been added here to make the hierarchical structure of the document more obvious.
- The content includes certain information not for publication—the internal element. Keeping everything together this way makes for easier management of the catalog. This data will be removed from the copy of the catalog that is actually seen on the Web site.
- Some presentation-oriented markup has been mixed in with the more content-oriented markup. Specifically, the blurb element is intended to map pretty much directly onto a section/paragraph/list type display.

4.3 | Publishing the catalog

So far, so good. You have identified the important information that needs to be stored in the catalog and created a sample entry. How do you go from that to an electronic catalog on a Web site?

You can go a number of ways:

- Process the XML into HTML on the server
- Process the XML into HTML on the client
- Display the XML directly

4.3.1 *Process the XML into HTML on the server side*

This is perhaps the most straightforward way to publish the catalog. You can use XML processing tools to process the XML into a collection of interlinked HTML pages (see Figure 4–2).

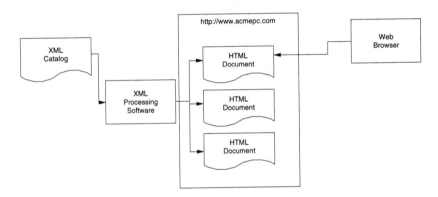

Figure 4–2   Converting XML to HTML on the server

This approach has the advantage of great simplicity. You, the owners of acmepc.com, have all the advantages of XML, yet the "public face" of acmepc.com does not contain any evidence of XML at all. All the user sees is a large set of very consistent HTML pages containing product information, a variety of "drill down" tables of contents, indices, and so on.

I want to point out that although XML is relatively new, numerous large organizations have been using SGML to auto-generate their HTML for years now. However, some of these companies are reticent about broadcasting to the world the information about *how* they do it, for competitive advantage reasons. You could take that view for acmepc.com. You can easily see that the high level of automation achievable with this approach would allow acmepc.com to roll out an updated product catalog of perhaps thousands of interlinked HTML pages in a matter of minutes. Furthermore, since it is all *generated,* it is possible to make wholesale changes to both content and "look and feel" of the catalog by simply modifying the XML conversion software and regenerating the HTML.

Note that the conversion into HTML can be scheduled, ad hoc, or on the fly. On-the-fly conversions have the benefit of ensuring that the HTML the user sees is always the most recent information available. However, it also puts a load on the server and can slow down the rate at which HTML pages are presented to the user.

4.3.2 *Process the XML into HTML on the client side*

Using this approach, you move the conversion from XML into HTML over onto the client—typically a Web browser (see Figure 4–3).

Perhaps the most straightforward way of achieving the conversion is to use an XML-aware applet, programmed in a language such as Java or JavaScript. The applet can process the XML and *bind* the required parts of the XML document onto particular HTML elements for display.

For example, the Microsoft Internet Explorer Version 4.0 browser ships with XML utilities as both Java applets and ActiveX controls. These programming tools present a wealth of options for processing and displaying the catalog at the client side. Some features you might consider for acmepc.com include:

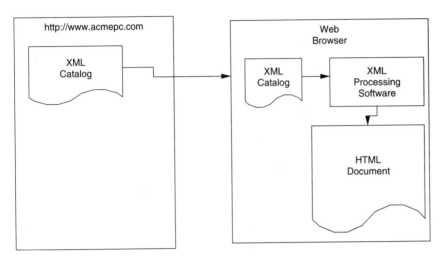

Figure 4–3 Converting XML to HTML on the client

- Generating HTML tables, sorted as requested by the user (price, speed, etc.), complete with hypertext links to pages of the full catalog.

- A "select a PC wizard" applet to walk the user through the options of picking the best PC to fit his or her needs.

- Adding value to the print-outs from the catalog by generating print-oriented HTML specially for that purpose. You might, for example, use serif fonts, which look better on paper than the sans-serif fonts most often used for online viewing.

- Personalizing the Web pages, including the customers' account details in the title and so on.

- Allowing the user to store parts of the catalog in, say, comma-delimited ASCII for direct import into a spreadsheet or a database.

- Creating a Query By Example Applet that allow the users to fill in fields of information to narrow the catalog down to those entries that meet their criteria.

4.3.3 *Display the XML directly*

Browsers are emerging that support the display of XML documents *directly,* thus sidestepping the requirement to down translate the XML to HTML. The XML is translated into a pleasant display format by applying formatting rules from a style sheet. This style sheet language is known as XSL, a companion standard to XML (see Figure 4–4).

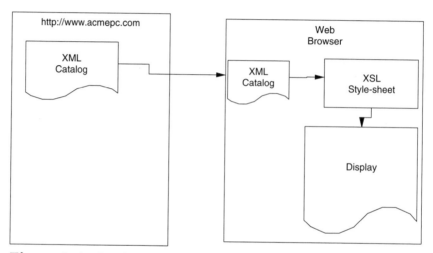

Figure 4–4   Rendering XML in an XML-aware Web browser

This approach is certainly the one with the most scope for innovative use. Users could store the catalog offline and use any XML aware tool to process it any way they want. As XML support in desktop applications expands, so too do the processing options. Users will be able to link into the catalog from word processors, spreadsheets, and so on. They will be able to extract full details of the machines they buy for direct import into the fixed assets component of their accounting system. They will be able to put the catalog on their own Intranet and blend it into their own full-text search indices. They will be able to create direct comparisons between the offerings in the acmepc catalog with other catalogs, in order to search for the best deals and so on.

4.4 | Keeping the catalog accurate

The catalog might have many thousands of entries. How can you be sure that entries are not missing vital pieces of information? A reasonable rule would be that all items in the acmepc.com catalog must have a unit price and a brand name. Another reasonable rule would be to make disk capacity for PCs an optional item, given that diskless workstations might be in the catalog and so on.

XML allows such rules to be captured and enforced using a Document Type Definition. A sample rule from a DTD for the acmepc catalog is shown below:

```
<!ELEMENT specification (cpu,harddisk?)>
```

This says "there is an element known as *specification*. It consists of a mandatory *cpu* element, optionally followed by a *harddisk* element."

The process of checking an XML document against the rules expressed in a DTD is known as *validating* the XML document. A utility program called a *validating XML parser* performs this task. You can choose to leverage the power of validation in the acmepc.com application in a variety of ways:

- Validation at the client side
- Validation at the server side

4.4.1 *Validation at the client side*

Client side validation is illustrated in Figure 4–5.

This approach has a number of advantages and a number of disadvantages. On one hand, there is comfort in knowing that the XML is being checked for validity every time someone tries to access it. Knowing that all the XML components that must be there *are* actually there is a great help when it comes to, for example, picking out

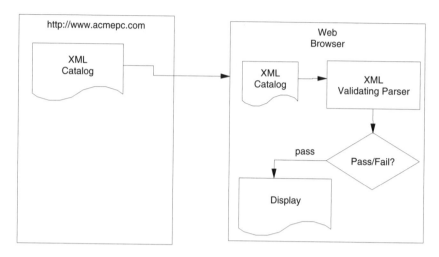

Figure 4–5　Validating an XML document on the client

price elements for display in Dynamic HTML, or generating a sorted list based on CPU speed.

4.4.2　*Validation at the server side*

On the other hand, validating takes time and might be an annoyance in some situations. Also, a validating XML parser that encounters a validation error may *stop* the processing of the document dead in its tracks. In some situations, this sort of error is best checked for on the server. Server-side validation is illustrated in Figure 4–6.

In Figure 4–6, the XML validation happens prior to the XML finding its way to the client. In this situation, the client can sensibly not validate the XML because validation is being done on its behalf prior to transmission. This design is obviously at its most powerful if the validation is happening on the fly on the server.

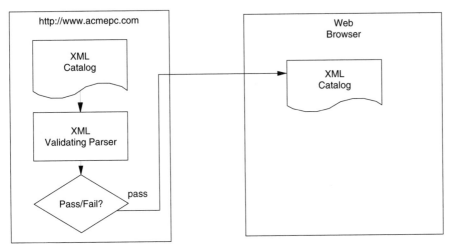

Figure 4–6   Validating an XML document on the server

4.5 | Keeping it pretty

The look of a Web site is often as important as the message it contains when it comes to attracting new customers to an e-business. As I mentioned earlier in the section "Display the XML directly," making XML look good is the responsibility of a sister standard called XSL. An XSL style sheet is typically quite a short document, but its impact on the display of an XML document can be profound. Using XSL, you can.

- Rigorously apply a style to ensure a standard, quality look
- Re-arrange document components prior to display
- Delete document components prior to display
- Add new components to the document prior to display
- Apply complex typesetting

■ Use a built-in scripting language (ECMAScript—the standardized version of JavaScript) to create complex effects

In the same way that the previous DTD snippet expresses a "rule" concerning how the XML document is structured, XSL expresses rules for how XML should be displayed. In the acmepc.com application, you could have the following XSL snippet (don't worry about the details for now).

```
<!-- A acmepc.com catalog Stylesheet (Snippet) ->

<rule>
 <!-- trigger this rule for item elements -->
 <target-element type = "item">
<!-- create a table -->
  <TABLE>
   <!-- wade through the descendants of the item -->
   <select from = "descendants"/>
    <!-- locating the brand elements -->
    <target-element type = "brand"/>
   </select>
  </TABLE>
  <!-- create another table -->
  <TABLE>
   <!-- wade through the descendants of the item -->
   <select from = "descendants"/>
    <!-- select those with a type attribute == "IDE" -
->
    <attribute name = "type" value = "IDE"/>
    <!-- restrict to just harddisk elements -->
            <target-element type = "harddisk"/>
   </select>
  </TABLE>
 </rule>
```

For now, suffice it to say that this snippet will create two tables: one containing all the brand names from the catalog, and one containing information on all the IDE hard disks in the catalog. XSL will have the same effect on the quality of Web pages that Postscript has had on the quality of desktop paper publishing. A Postscript file is actually a computer program written in the Postscript programming language that is executed within the printer. The program itself is independent of any particular printer, and thus different printers will render the same Postscript file with different qualities. So too with XSL. XSL style sheets are, in effect, programs that get executed inside the browser. They may one day be executed inside printers.

The XSL approach also makes much better use of the resources available between the client and the server in a Web-based application. With the client side handling the formatting via XSL, the server is free to dish out content without spending CPU cycles generating formatting in the form of HTML, for example. Likewise, document creators are free to avoid presentation-oriented markup in their documents, safe in the knowledge that formatting can be dealt with at the point the document is viewed by applying an XSL style sheet.

The XSL standard will also have an effect on what actually gets put into Web documents. You will have no need to put in content that can be automatically generated, such as tables, running headers, fancy list item adornments, and so on. A lot of the presentation-oriented markup familiar from HTML such as alignment, color, and font selection will not be necessary.

Of course, once the formatting of content is outside the document proper, other interesting possibilities present themselves. Firstly, by simply changing a single, small, style sheet file, you can instantaneously change the look and feel of the entire acmepc.com web site. You could present users with a selection of style sheets from which to choose when they visit the site. You could use a user identification mechanism such as cookies to use style sheets personalized to particular customers. The entire look and feel of the site can be soft-coded in style sheets rather than hard-coded in the documents themselves.

4.6 | Helping surfers to help themselves

Liberal use of hypertext will help make the acmepc.com catalog a more useful resource for browsers and is thus clearly good for business. The HTML notion of a hypertext link is extremely simple. Essentially all you can say is: link this piece of text (anchor 1) to this document or location within a document (anchor 2).

With something as volatile as a product catalog having more intelligent anchor addressing would be useful. Take an example. Supposing the marketing department decides to have a special offer always present somewhere in the catalog. They wish to be able to move it around from time to time, perhaps on an hourly basis. They want a link on the acmepc.com Web site, saying something like:

For today's special offer **click here.**

Using HTML, you would have to keep track of where in the catalog this link should point and change it whenever the special offer changed. In XML, addressing is much more powerful. Linking and addressing in XML are the responsibility of a sister standard known as XLL—XML Link Language. Do not worry about the details for the moment. Suffice it to say that using XLL, you can say this:

```
root()descendant(1,blurb)string(1,"Special Offer")
```

This says, starting at the top of the document, select the first **blurb** element that contains the string "Special Offer." This is effectively a *search* and is an example of the powerful forms of anchor addressing possible using XLL.

As well as flexibility in locating things, XLL provides flexibility in how they are displayed. For example, you could indicate traversal to the above anchor address by clicking on a piece of text. However, you could also arrange for the traversal to occur automatically when the containing page loads and the target resource (in this case, the **blurb** element) could be embedded right into the text of the acmepc.com home page!

Once in place, this powerful anchor address is self-maintaining. Every visit to the acmepc.com page is *guaranteed* to automatically retrieve the most up-to-date special offer from the catalog. The marketing department can move it around the catalog all they like!

4.7 | Keeping customers informed

Obviously, acmepc.com is heavily reliant on getting the message about its products out into the Web browsers of customers and potential customers alike. Using the XML-based CDF (Channel Definition Format) standard presented in Chapter 2, acmepc.com could establish a *push channel* on their Web site. Subscribers could be informed of additions to the product range, special offers, and so on.

The content of the channel will most likely be a blend of sales/marketing commentary and content auto-generated from the catalog—things like the most popular PC, the best cost per megabyte system, and so on (see Figure 4–7).

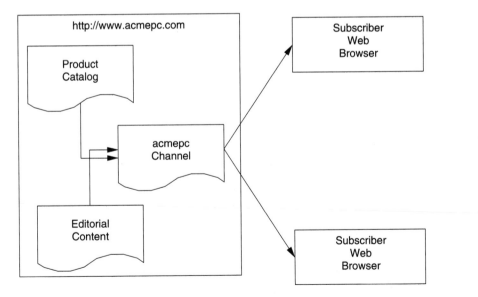

Figure 4–7   Establishing a push channel at acmepc.com

The fact that CDF documents are XML documents presents some interesting possibilities. After all, processing CDF documents can be achieved with precisely the same tools used for manipulating the electronic catalog. You can, for example, contemplate personalizing the acmepc.com channel for each customer, as follows.

Imagine a scenario in which customers are asked to specify what price range is of most interest to them. Naturally you would capture this as an XML document:

```
<customer id = "1234567890">
 <Name>Joe Bloggs</Name>
 <price lower = "2000" upper = "4000"/>
</customer>
```

When a customer connects to the site, you can determine who they are—perhaps using the cookie mechanism. From there, you can find out whether they have specified a price range and, if so, the acmepc channel can contain information specific to this customer. Perhaps something like this:

Hi Joe,

This month we have 5 new machines within your specified price range . . .

The process of generating a personalized channel for the acmepc.com application is illustrated in Figure 4–8.}

4.8 | Enhancing the experience

Surfers from all over the world will visit acmepc.com. What if their local currency is, say, Irish Punts, but the catalog quotes Dollars? You could add a currency calculator applet to the catalog. When the user clicks on the calculator, it could pick up the dollar price from the catalog. The user could enter the exchange rate for their local currency.

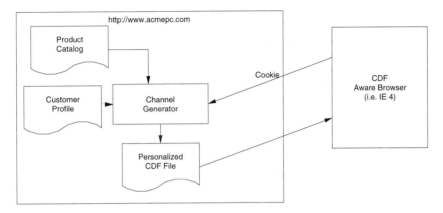

Figure 4–8   Establishing a personalized push channel at acmepc.com

You could go further and get the applet to connect to a financial Web site and find the up-to-the-minute rate automatically!

XML excels at providing opportunities for innovation such as this. In the highly competitive market that acmepc.com trades in, every little bit of market differentiation helps. The currency calculator is only one of a myriad of possibilities that the XML + Scripting Language cocktail presents to Web architects. As Jon Bosak of Sun Microsystems (chairman of the W3C's XML working group) put it, "XML gives Java something to do!"

4.9 | Money matters

At acmepc.com, you obviously have a need for bank accounts, mechanisms for taking credit card orders, mechanisms for checking account balances, and so on. You might also contemplate establishing credit facilities for trade customers and wish to allow them to query their own accounts and settle their bills with you electronically.

This domain is the forte of the Open Financial Exchange and Open Trading Protocol applications of XML. I discussed OFX briefly in Chapter 2. At acmepc.com, you will need to establish a relation-ship with a financial institution to handle the authorization of, for example, credit card purchases. You may collect this data (name, card number, expiration date) using a normal HTML form, but you can choose to store it in XML, using element type names and structures conforming to the OFX specification. In so doing, you are in a posi-tion to present the financial institution with data in an industry-stan-dard notation (see Figure 4–9). (You may be able to haggle for a better rate of commission as a result.)

Also, since you have the transactions stored in XML, you can add them to your "data warehouse"—a central repository of data about your business, all in XML. You can use all the XML tools you are using for the catalog and so on to process the data warehouse and learn more about your customers and their buying patterns.

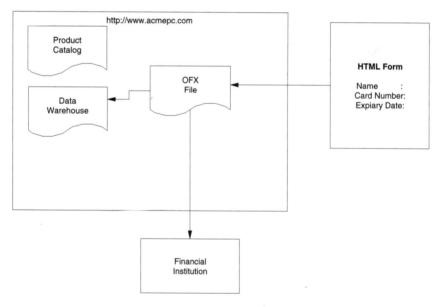

Figure 4–9   Routing credit card authorizations at acmepc.com

I return to the data warehouse idea in the section "Keeping ahead of the customer" later in this chapter.

4.10 | Integrating existing systems

As the saying goes, if it ain't broke, don't fix it. The world is full of databases—especially relational databases—that work perfectly well without having to become part of the XML revolution. The Cold Fusion Markup Language briefly outlined in Chapter 2 is an example of a technology for bridging the gap between these systems and the Web. At acmepc.com, you could well have standard relational database systems for handling customer accounts and so on (see Figure 4–10). If you wish to allow customers to access their account balances via a secure part of your Web site, you can most quickly achieve this facility with the help of something like CFML.

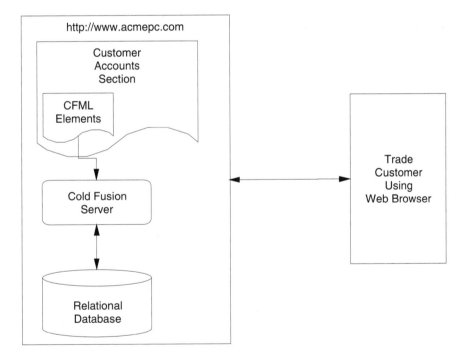

Figure 4–10 Integrating a relational database with the acmepc.com Web site

4.11 | Saving on browse time

The management at acmepc.com will need to keep track of what is going on in their business in order to stay competitive. They will need to hunt down the best prices for component parts, track what their competitors are doing, stay abreast with new technologies, etc. Obviously, an increasingly large amount of this information is to be gleaned from the Web. Furthermore, as XML usage gathers momentum, an increasing amount of it is available in XML format.

Repetitively revisiting sites to fill in forms and retrieve information is both labor intensive and error prone. In Chapter 2, I discussed an XML application known as Web Interface Definition Language (WIDL), which promises to simplify the process of "batch automating" Web interactions and downloads.

At acmepc.com, WIDL could be used to automate scheduled visits to interactive Web sites to hunt down the best prices for components, gather intelligence about what the competition is doing, and so on. If that information is available for download in XML format, so much the better! At acmepc.com, a powerful tool chest of XML processing tools is at hand to help in the analysis of this information, in order to make it work harder for the enterprise.

4.12 | Keeping ahead of the customer

The next time you are in your local store on a Friday evening, see if the diapers are stocked beside the beer. Believe it or not, a large supermarket chain has identified a correlation between beer sales and diaper sales on Friday evenings. The reasons behind the correlation can be speculated upon at great length, but how did the organization determine that this was true?

They operate a "data warehouse"—an ultra-large repository of all the data available to the enterprise that is gathered from disparate sources, cleaned up, and loaded into a database for the specific purpose of searching for trends and correlations that would otherwise go unnoticed.

At acmepc.com, a data warehouse could be established to search for trends in customers' buying patterns. What day of the week produces the most credit card orders and why? Does a correlation exist between customer age and the rate at which consumables such as ink cartridges are purchased? And so on.

The results of such trend spotting can be fed back into the acmepc channel publishing system to ensure that channel subscribers get the most appropriate material presented to them.

XML, with its focus on capturing what information *really is* and the homogeneity between disparate data sets that it produces, is a compelling base notation for a data warehouse.

4.13 | Working the market

One of the signs of a mature market is the emergence of standards amongst competing entities aimed at improving the commercial well-being of the entire industry. Standard sizes for spanners, washing machines, and TV tubes all help these industries to help themselves. The existence of a standard increases the overall size of the market and benefits consumer and producer alike.

As e-commerce matures, more XML-based standards will emerge to complement the financial-transaction-standard OFX and the trading standard OTP. For example, the big players in the PC direct-sales industry might agree on an XML-based data notation for describing PCs in their electronic catalogs.

At acmepc.com, the emergence of such a standard would be good for business. Indeed, supporting such a standard might even be vital to *stay* in business. Web agents for PC buyers could be developed, either by PC vendors or third parties, to perform intelligent, Web-wide searches for products meeting the customers' needs. You could see the emergence of a PC Buyers Search Engine capable of answering the question "Tabulate all the PCs for sale on the Web that are based on the 986 processor with 50 GB of hard disk space, selling for less than 10,000 US Dollars." At acmepc.com, you would ignore such search engine technology at your own peril.

4.14 | Preparing for change

XML is an open standard. XML lends itself to the automation of document-processing tasks. Taken together, these twin strands of open systems and automation permeate the entire XML concept. At acmepc.com, the management and staff appreciate that they may have to move very quickly to modify their business practices to meet new challenges. They need to know that they can move voluminous quantities of information from HTML 3.2 to HTML 4.0. They know that they may need to edit thousands of documents in a single day in order to conform to new regulations. They know that the Web in five years' time will not be like the Web today. Who knows what new publishing paradigms or commercial paradigms will emerge? By capturing the information their business needs in an open notation supporting a high degree of automation, they know that they can move and move *quickly.* They will need to in order to survive.

Thank goodness for XML . . .

Just Enough Details

- Two views of XML documents

- Two classes of XML processor

- Tags

- Attributes

- Entities

- DTDs

- Validating XML documents

n this chapter, you take a look under the hood at the nuts and bolts of XML documents. The coverage is intentionally both brief and simplified, intended to present just enough detailed information to get you started on the road to creating your own XML applications. I mull over the finer points in Part 3 of the book.

In earlier chapters, you see snippets of XML but never a fully blown XML document. In this chapter, you create one based on the acmepc.com catalog idea sketched in the Chapter 4. To get there, you need to wade through some terminology, battle with some syntax details, and learn to wield some XML software.

Note that covering the various forms of markup that make up XML documents presents a slight chicken-and-egg situation. To fully understand the things that can occur in a document, you must know about the things that can occur in a DTD. To fully understand the things that can occur in a DTD, you need to know about the things that can occur in a document. As a result, a certain amount of forward referencing is unavoidable. I have kept it to a minimum, and all forward references are to places later on in this chapter. You might find it useful to read this chapter twice—a quick first pass to scout out the territory and then a closer second pass.

5.1 | The big picture

A minimalist example of an XML-based system involves at least three distinct items as illustrated in Figure 5–1.

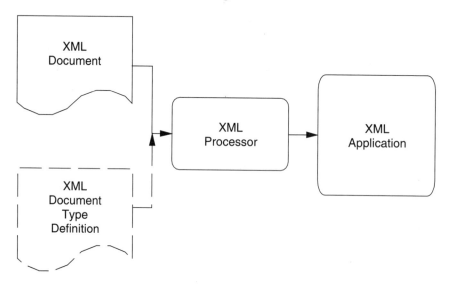

Figure 5–1   A minimalist XML-based system

Firstly, you have the XML document itself. It will consist of a mixture of XML character strings known collectively as *markup*, along with the actual information content of the document, known as *character data*.

Examples of markup include start-tags, end-tags, comments, and so on. Examples of character data include: the price of a PC in the acmepc.com catalog, the text of Joyce's *Ulysses,* the lead story in the *Financial Times,* and so on.

An XML document can optionally be associated with a set of rules that specify what order and occurrence of markup and character data is permitted. Examples of such rules would be:

- All items in the catalog must have a unit price.
- A Shakespearean play consists of one or more acts.

and so on.

These rules are housed in a *Document Type Definition,* or DTD for short. The fact that the DTD component is optional is denoted by the dashed lines in the diagram.

A program known as an *XML Processor,* also commonly referred to as an *XML Parser,* is responsible for combing the XML document— with or without the presence of a DTD—in order to split it up into "chunks" of markup and chunks of character data. The XML Processor/Parser feeds this information through to an *XML application.*

Examples of XML Processors (all available on the accompanying CD) include those listed in Table 5.1.

Table 5.1   Some XML Processors

Name	*Origin*
msxml	Developed by Microsoft Corporation. Versions available in both Java and ActiveX component forms.
Ælfred	A Java-based XML Processor developed by David Megginson of Microstar Corporation.
nsgmls	This C++ based program by James Clark is a full SGML parser. Given that all XML documents are conformant SGML documents, it can be used as an XML Processor.
XP	A Java-based XML Processor developed by James Clark.

Examples of XML Application implementations discussed in earlier chapters include the Active Channel components of Internet Explorer 4.0, the Jumbo browser for Chemical Markup Language, the Lotus Notes Import Filter, and so on.

5.2 | Two views of an XML document

The overall structure of any given XML document can be looked at in two very distinct ways. Firstly, it has a *logical* structure. Viewed from this angle, an XML document is a hierarchy of information. The character data of the document hangs in individual chunks out of a tree-like structure created by the markup. A branch of this logical tree structure from the acmepc.com application is shown in Figure 5–2.

At the very top of the tree is the so-called *root* element (in this case, **acmepc**), from which all the further logical structure springs.

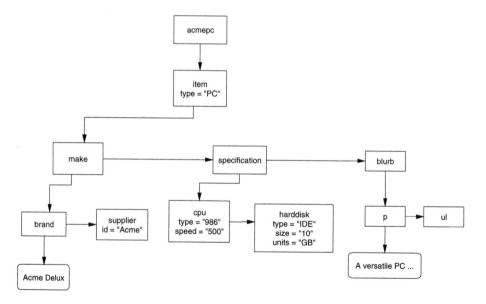

Figure 5–2   The logical structure of the acmepc catalog XML document

Side by side with the logical structure, XML documents have a *physical* structure. A single logical XML document can be made up of a number of distinct physical files known in XML as *entities*. The full document is rooted in the entity known as the *document entity*. As with the logical structure, the physical structure of an XML document is hierarchical in nature. That is to say, an entity can contain references to other entities, which themselves can contain references to other entities, etc. In Figure 5–3, the full XML document is split across five separate entities—typically files on some storage medium or other.

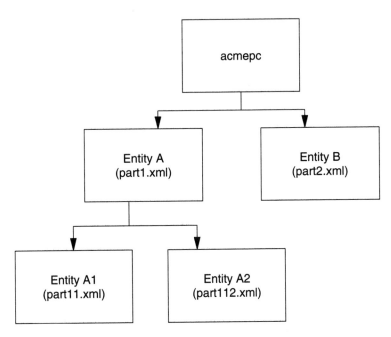

Figure 5–3 Physical view of an XML document

5.3 | Two classes of XML documents

In order for a document to conform to the XML standard, it must be *well formed*. Essentially, a well-formed XML document is one from which an XML Processor can successfully build a tree structure such as illustrated in Figure 5–2. An XML Processor can do this much *without* a DTD and without a large amount of processing effort. Well-formed XML documents can be further classified as *valid* if they meet the constraints spelled out in an associated DTD. The term *type valid* is also used to mean the same thing. If an XML document is valid, it is also well formed. The set of all valid XML documents is thus a subset of the set of all well-formed XML documents (see Figure 5–4).

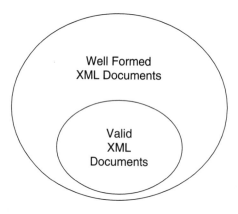

Figure 5–4   "Valid" XML as a subset of "Well–Formed" XML

5.4 | Two classes of XML processors

An XML processor capable of checking for validity is known as a *validating* XML processor. The msxml processor from Microsoft is an example of a validating XML processor.

An XML processor that ignores any validity constraints spelled out in DTDs is known as a *nonvalidating* XML processor. Ælfred is an example of this class of XML processor. Any processor capable of checking for validity is capable of checking for well-formedness (see Figure 5-5).

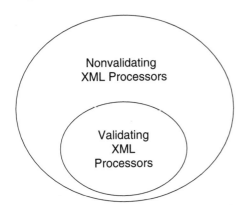

Figure 5–5   Validating XML Processors as a subset of non-validating XML Processors

The term *XML parser* is more commonly used than the phrase *XML processor*, and I use it from here on out.

5.5 | Introducing msxml

In order to illustrate the nuts and bolts of XML, this chapter uses the MSXML XML parser from Microsoft. This parser is included on the CD and is also available on the Internet at http://www.microsoft.com/XML.

The parser is available both as an ActiveX component and as a Java application. In this book, I use version 1.8 of the Java-based parser. Like all Java programs, msxml runs within a Java Virtual Machine (JVM). These are prebuilt into most modern Web browsers. At different points in this chapter, you use the JVM of Internet Explorer 4.0

and the command-line-activated JVM supplied with Internet Explorer known as *jview*.

5.6 | A minimalist XML document

Let me get the ball rolling with a very small XML document:

```
C>type foo.xml

<greeting>Hello World</greeting>
```

This one-line-long XML document has three component parts:

- a start-tag (<greeting>)
- an end-tag (</greeting>)
- character data ("Hello World")

This document can be parsed with msxml on the command line as follows:

```
C>jview msxml foo.xml
```

By default, the msxml XML parser does not produce any output apart from error messages. The -d1 option is used to get the parser to emit a simple representation of the tree structure it has built from the XML document:

```
C>jview msxml -d1 foo.xml

DOCUMENT
|---ELEMENT greeting
|    +---PCDATA "Hello World"
+---WHITESPACE 0xa
```

Note the hierarchical structure captured by this simple textual representation. The "Hello World" text has been encapsulated beneath a "greeting" element. At the same level as this element is some white space in the form of the end-of-line code added to the file by my text editor. The parser reports this as a line feed character, denoted by 0xa. This is the base sixteen representation for character 10—line feed—in Unicode (and ASCII). A graphical representation of this little document is shown in Figure 5–6.

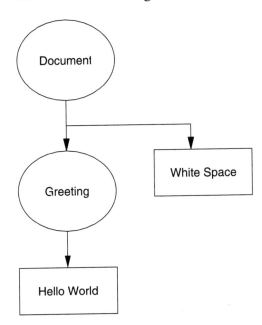

Figure 5–6 Graphical representation of a simple XML document

Before moving on, see what happens when you purposely introduce an error into this XML document:

```
C>type foo.xml
<greeting>Hello World</item>
```

This is not well-formed XML because the start-tag, <greeting>, does not have a matching end-tag.

```
C>jview foo.xml

Close tag item does not match start tag greeting
Location: file:/C:/xml/book/ch05/foo.xml(1,24)
Context: <greeting>
```

This tells us the nature of the error and points to a location within foo.xml where the error was encountered, namely, character 24 on line 1. At the point where the error occurred, the parser was in the process of capturing a "greeting" element, which is reported as the *context* in which the error occurred.

In order to illustrate a simple parse of a simple XML document, I have used local files in these early examples. However, remember that this technology has its roots firmly in the Web! We can just as easily parse an XML document from the far side of the globe. Something like this:

```
C>jview msxml http://www.digitome.com/foo.xml
```

This command will cause msxml to connect to the World Wide Web and attempt to find the document foo.xml on the Digitome Web site. No such document exists, so we get an error message:

```
C>Error opening input stream for "http://www.digit-
ome.com/foo.xml":
java.io.FileNotFoundException: http://www.digit-
  ome.com/foo.xml
Location: Parsing(0,0)
Context: <>
```

Web sites springing up all over the world contain collections of XML documents. To parse any one of them with msxml, all you need is the URL and a Web connection.

5.7 | Creating XML documents

Now it is time to get stuck in some details about creating real XML documents. Seven forms of markup can occur in XML documents:

1. start- and end-tags
2. attribute assignments
3. entity references
4. comments
5. processing instructions

6. CDATA sections
7. document type declarations

5.7.1 *1. Start- and end-tags*

Elements are the primary building blocks of the hierarchical structures XML allows us to represent. The presence of elements in an XML document is denoted by *tags* of various forms. The majority of elements are intended to contain something—perhaps character data, perhaps other elements, or perhaps a mixture of the two. These elements have start- and end-points denoted by start- and end-tags, respectively (see Table 5-2).

Table 5.2   Start- and End-Tag Examples

Tag	*Meaning*
`<greeting>`	Start a greeting element.
`</introduction>`	End an introduction element.
`<Joe Bloggs>`	Bad start-tag. No spaces allowed in the element type name.
`<42>`	Bad start-tag. Element type names cannot begin with a number.
`</ product>`	Bad end-tag. No space allowed between the slash and the element type name.

Elements can be nested to an arbitrary depth to describe very rich information structures. Here is an XML document with some nesting elements:

```
C>type names.xml
<TypesOfCar>
```

```
<Saloon>
<Normal>
<automatic>
<car>
Model A
</car>
</automatic>
<manual>
<car>
Model B
</car>
</manual>
</Normal>
<FourWheelDrive>
<automatic>
<car>
Model B
</car>
</automatic>
</FourWheelDrive>
</Saloon>
</TypesOfCar>
```

The hierarchical structure this represents can be clearly seen by using other command-line options to the msxml parser. The -d option tells the parser to recreate the XML document it has parsed as the output from the parse. The -p option modifies this command to tell the parser to "pretty-print" the XML to show off its hierarchical structure:

```
C>jview msxml -d -p names.xml

<TypesOfCar>
        <Saloon>
                <Normal>
                        <automatic>
                                <car> Model A </car>
                        </automatic>
                        <manual>
                                <car> Model B </car>
                        </manual>
                </Normal>
                <FourWheelDrive>
                        <automatic>
```

```
                         <car> Model B </car>
                    </automatic>
               </FourWheelDrive>
          </Saloon>
     </TypesOfCar>
```

For a more graphical view of the same document, you can use the XMLViewer applet supplied with msxml. You will find it in the viewer subdirectory of wherever you install msxml. Load the document XMLViewer.htm into your browser. This page auto-loads the XMLViewer applet and creates a separate viewer window. The above XML document is shown in Figure 5–7 viewed in source form in the XML Viewer applet window:

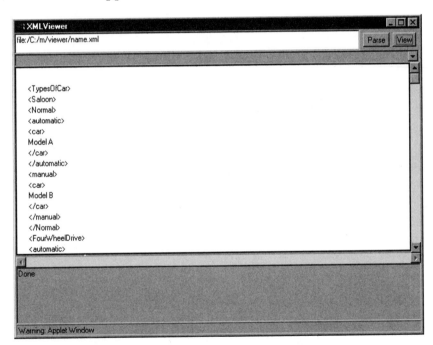

Figure 5-7 The XML document viewed in source form in the Microsoft XMLViewer applet

Clicking the Parse button initiates parsing of the XML and yields the tree view of the same document (see Figure 5–8).

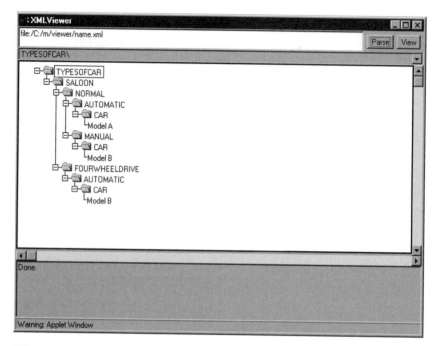

Figure 5–8   XML document viewed in hierarchical form in the Microsoft XMLViewer applet

The concept of *content* within an element does not sit comfortably with all possible elements that can be imagined. For example, in HTML the **br** (line break) element cannot sensibly have any content. In SGML/XML parlance, it is an *empty* element. As a result

feels a lot more sensible than

</br>

Although omitting end-tags like this is permitted in SGML, end-tags are mandatory in XML. In order to preserve the "feel" of an omitted end-tag, in XML, an empty element can also look like this:

Note the backslash tacked on before the closing ">". Here is an example of an empty element occurring within another element:

```
C>type empty.xml
<Document>
Some content
<IAmEmpty/>
Some more content</Document>
```

Viewed in Microsoft's XMLViewer applet, the empty element is denoted by a circle (see Figure 5–9).

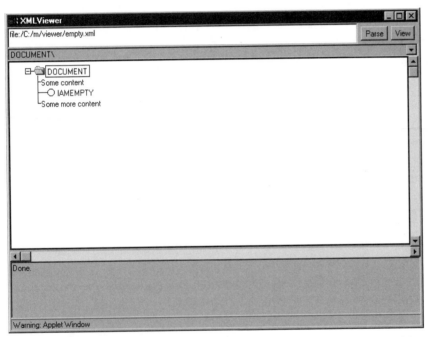

Figure 5–9   An empty element viewed in hierarchical form in the Microsoft XMLViewer applet

5.7.2   *2. Attribute assignments*

Attributes are pieces of information, typically small, that are associated with XML elements. In HTML, examples include the align attribute of the **p** element, the border attribute of the **table** element, and so on.

Attributes come in a variety of shapes and sizes that are controlled in the DTD, as you see later on. However, in an XML document, they all take the same simple form. Attribute assignments always appear within the start-tag of an element in this format:

```
[name of attribute] "=" [value of attribute]
```

Some examples appear in Table 5-3.

Table 5.3   Examples of Attribute Assignments

Attribute Example	*Interpretation*
`<apple variety = "Granny Smith">`	The variety attribute of the apple element has the value "Granny Smith"
`<apple variety = 'Granny Smith'>`	Single quotes can also be used. The variety attribute of the apple element has the value "Granny Smith"
`<table border=2>`	Not well formed XML. All attribute values must be quoted.

`<animal`
`legs = "4"`
`blood= "cold">`
	The legs attribute of the animal element has the value "4". The blood attribute of the animal element has the value "cold." Any white space (e.g. new lines) within start-tags are ignored by the parser.

The Microsoft XMLViewer applet shows attributes when the cursor hovers over an element, as you see in Figure 5–10.

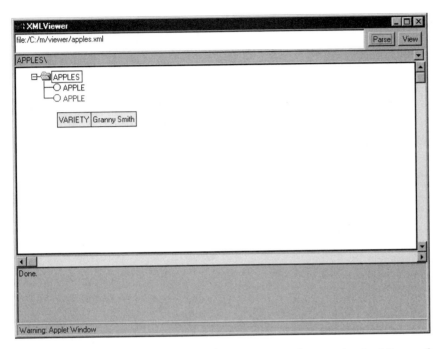

Figure 5–10   Display of the attributes of an element in the Microsoft XMLViewer applet

5.7.3 *3. Entity references*

Entities, as you will remember from earlier on in this chapter, are the physical building blocks of XML documents. An entity is a unit of text—perhaps as simple as a single character, perhaps as complex as an entire document. Entities are included in XML documents by means of an *entity reference*. Armed with an entity reference, an XML parser can hunt down the entity referenced and slot in its contents in place of the reference.

A simple and common usage of an entity reference is to slide characters into an XML document that cannot be entered directly without confusing the XML parser. The classic example of this is the "<" character, which causes the parser to try and interpret what follows as markup. Supposing you wish to have the following content in an XML document:

```
C>type ent.xml
<Document>
if a<b and b<c then a<c
</Document>
```

As it stands, this is not well-formed XML because an XML parser will complain when it sees the second "b" character (see Figure 5–11). Why? Because at that point, it is expecting an equals sign to start the value for the "and" attribute of the b element!

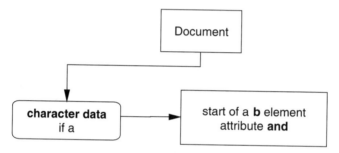

Figure 5–11   The parser's view of the text "if a<b and"

```
C>jview msxml ent.xml

Expected = instead of NAME 'b'
Location: file:/C:/m/viewer/ent.xml(2,12)
Context: <Document><b>
```

XML comes "out of the box" with a number of predefined entities to circumvent this sort of thing. In an XML document, an entity reference always takes the same form—prepend an "&" and append a ";" to the name of the entity. The built-in entity for "<" in XML is the same as it is in HTML, namely "lt".

```
C>type ent.xml

<Document>
if a&lt;b and b&lt;c then a&lt;c
</Document>
```

```
C>jview msxml -d1 ent.xml

DOCUMENT
|---ELEMENT Document
|    |---PCDATA " if a"
|    |---ENTITYREF lt "<"
|    |---PCDATA "b and b"
|    |---ENTITYREF lt "<"
|    |---PCDATA "c then a"
|    |---ENTITYREF lt "<"
|    +---PCDATA "c. "
+---WHITESPACE 0xa
```

Note that the parser has successfully detected three entity references (displayed in the output above as ENTITYREF lines) for the entity "lt". This entity is built into the parser, and thus the parser knows that the "content" of the entity (commonly referred to as the replacement text) is "< ". Viewed in the Microsoft XMLViewer applet, it looks like Figure 5–12.

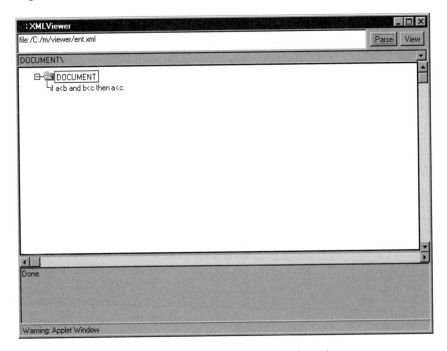

Figure 5–12   Expansion of entity references for <

The five built-in entities in XML appear in Table 5.4.

Table 5.4   The Entities Built into XML

Entity Reference	*Interpretation*
&lt;	<
&gt;	>
&amp;	&
&apos;	'
&quot;	"

Entities can also be used for bigger things. Entity references can be used to include entire files of XML text within the text of other files or act as handy shorthand for often used text snippets. You can arrange, for example, for this XML snippet

```
<Book>
&chapter1;
&chapter2;
&chapter3;
</Book>
```

to cause three chapters of a book stored in separate entities to be gathered into a single Book element.

To illustrate another usage, you can arrange for the string "spbm" to be available as a handy shorthand for "Stately, plump Buck Mulligan" so that

```
<ulysses>
&spbm; climbed...
```

is expanded by the XML parser into

```
Stately, plump Buck Mulligan climbed...
```

In order to do so, we need to feed the parser names and values for these entities. This is done in the DTD, and you will see how in "Creating DTDs" later on in this chapter.

5.7.4   *4. Comments*

XML comments take exactly the same form as HTML comments:

```
<!-- this is a comment -->
```

Note that for compatibility with SGML, the string "--" cannot occur with a comment:

```
<!-- this is not -- well formed XML-->
```

5.7.5   *5. CDATA sections*

Sometimes a document must contain large numbers of characters that are considered special by an XML parser, characters such as "<" and "&" principle amongst them. XML allows a block of text to be insulated from attention of the parser using a CDATA section, as illustrated:

```
C>type cdata.xml
<Document>
<![CDATA[
if a<b and b<c then a<c.
]]>
</Document>
```

Under normal circumstances, the "<" in the above document would attract the attention of the parser, as you have seen. By prefixing the string "<!CDATA[" and appending the string "]]>" you insulate the entire section, which magically becomes plain old character data as far as the parser is concerned.

```
C>jview msxml -d1 cdata.xml

DOCUMENT
```

```
|---ELEMENT Document
|    |---WHITESPACE 0xa
|    |---CDATA [CDATA[ "
if a<b and b<c then c<d.
"
|    +---WHITESPACE 0xa
+---WHITESPACE 0xa 0xa
```

Note that the parser has detected the presence of a CDATA section and waved the entire string "if a<b and b<c then a<c" through to the application unquestioned. In the Microsoft XML Viewer applet, CDATA marked sections are displayed as gray text, as shown in Figure 5–13.

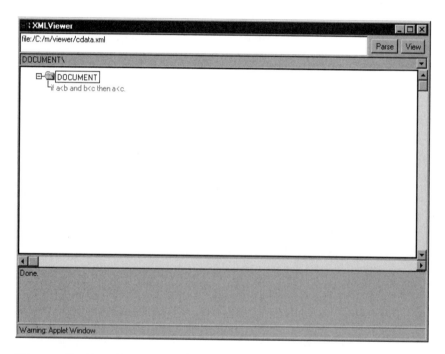

Figure 5–13   CDATA marked section displayed in the Microsoft XML Viewer applet

The term "CDATA" and the slightly surprising syntax of CDATA sections are a result of the fact that such sections in SGML come in a variety of shapes and sizes. Although XML documents only ever use the CDATA variety, maintaining the SGML syntax ensures SGML compatibility.

5.7.6   *6. Processing instructions*

In SGML, a mechanism known as a *processing instruction* can be used to store application-specific information in an SGML document. The idea is to provide an "escape hatch" to allow an SGML document to "talk" specifically to a particular application, yet clearly delineate where such application-specific conversations are taking place. A common example in SGML would be to use a processing instruction to force a particular typesetting device to output a page break at a particular place:

```
<?rtf \page>
```

An RTF generator engine processing a document containing this processing instruction would spot that the processing instruction is aimed at it, by matching against the "rtf" string in the processing instruction. This is known as the processing instruction *target*. Such processing instructions pass straight through an SGML parser because they are for the consumption of some application or other, in this case the RTF generator engine.

In XML, the notion of a processing instruction has been carried over from SGML but with a slightly modified syntax from SGML's default syntax to make it easier for XML parser writers to spot where they end:

```
<?rtf \page?>
```

XML itself makes use of a processing instruction in what is known as the *XML declaration*. This is a processing instruction that the standard suggests should head up all XML documents (I start doing so as of now!). In its simplest form, it looks like this:

```
<?xml version = "1.0"?>
```

So, to be fully in line with what the XML standard recommends, we hereby modify our minimalist XML document.

```
C>type foo.xml
<?xml version = "1.0"?>
<greeting>Hello World</greeting>


C>jview -d1 foo.xml
DOCUMENT
|---XMLDECL
|   +---CDATA " version = "1.0""
|---WHITESPACE 0xa
|---ELEMENT greeting
|   +---PCDATA "Hello World"
+---WHITESPACE 0xa
```

Note how the parser has interpreted the processing instruction as the XML Declaration (denoted by the XMLDECL entry above).

5.7.7 7. Document Type Declaration

Finally in this whirlwind roundup of XML markup, you arrive at the *Document Type Declaration*. As you know, XML documents can have DTDs. In the event that a DTD is to be associated with an XML document, the association is achieved using what is termed the Document Type Declaration. A simple form is shown here:

```
<!DOCTYPE foo SYSTEM "foo.dtd">
```

This says, "The DTD for this document is available in the file foo.dtd." These document type declarations come in various shapes and sizes that I return to in Appendix A. A common one used for HTML documents is shown here:

```
<!DOCTYPE HTML PUBLIC "-//W3C//DTD HTML 3.2//EN">
```

5.7.8 *Pulling it all together*

I have covered all the details needed to make a real, perfectly well formed XML document for the acmepc catalog application. Note that I have included—but commented out—the Document Type Declaration for now. You will reinstate it once you have pored over the details of what goes into a DTD in the next part of this chapter.

```
C>type acmepc.xml
<?xml version="1.0"?>
<!--
Commented out for the moment
<!DOCTYPE acmepc SYSTEM "acmepc.dtd">
-->
<acmepc>
<item type = "PC" code = "ACME1">
 <make>
  <brand>Acme Deluxe</brand>
          <supplier id = "Acme"/>
 </make>
 <specification>
  <cpu type = "986" speed = "500"/>
  <harddisk type = "IDE" size = "10" units = "GB"/>
 </specification>
 <price n = "2000" units = "USD"/>
 <blurb>
  <p>A versatile PC for home &amp; business use. Fea-
  turing as standard:</p>
  <ul>
   <li><index term = "Multimedia"/>Sound card</li>
   <li>90 day money back guarantee</li>
   <li>Mouse mat</li>
  </ul>
 </blurb>
 <internal>
  <instock num = "44"/>
  <supportcalls num = "6"/>
  <perunitcost n = "1800" units = "USD"/>
 </internal>
</item>
</acmepc>
```

The catalog is now well-formed XML and can be parsed into a tree structure as shown in Figure 5–14.

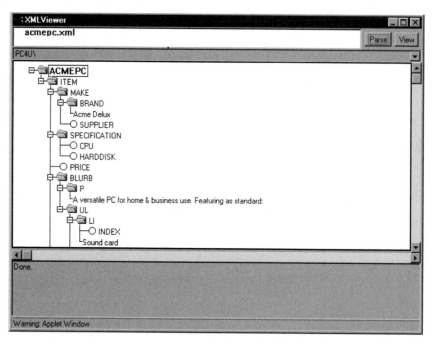

Figure 5–14   The acmepc catalog displayed in the Microsoft XML Viewer applet

Note the "&" sign that has resulted from the use of the "&" built-in entity to include an ampersand character into the document.

5.8 | Creating XML DTDs

You are now in a position to move on to the subject of DTDs. Take a spin through the required details first and then put the theory into practice by building the DTD for the acmepc catalog application. You then round out this chapter by using the msxml parser to validate the acmepc catalog document.

5.8.1 *Element Type Declarations*

In order to be able to validate an XML document, a validating XML parser needs to know three principle things about each element.

- What the element type is named
- What elements of that type can contain (known as its *content model*)
- What attributes an element of that type has associated with it.

I deal with the first two items here and defer the third to the treatment of attributes later in the next section. Both the element type name and its content model are declared together in what is known as an *element type declaration*. Table 5.5 contains some examples and their interpretation.

Table 5.5   Element Type Declarations and Their Interpretation

Declaration	*Interpretation*
<!ELEMENT contact (name,address,telephone)>	An element of type **contact** must contain three subelements, namely, **name**, **address**, and **telephone** in exactly that order. **Example:** <contact> <name>Joe Bloggs</name> <address> Tumbolia </address> <telephone> 555-1245 </telephone> </contact>

Table 5.5   Element Type Declarations and Their
             Interpretation*(continued)*

Declaration	Interpretation
<!ELEMENT contact (name,address?,telephone)>	An element of type **contact** can contain three subelements. Firstly, it must have a **name** element. This is optionally followed by an **address** element. Lastly, you have a **telephone** element. **Example**: <contact> <name>Joe Bloggs</name> <telephone> 555-1245 </telephone> </contact>
<!ELEMENT fruit (apple|orange)>	An element of type **fruit** contains either a single **apple** element or a single **orange** element.
<!ELEMENT fruit (apple|orange)+>	An element of type **fruit** contains one or more subelements that are either **apple** elements or **orange** elements. **Example**: <fruit> <apple>...</apple> <apple>...</apple> <orange>...</orange> </fruit> **Example**: <fruit> <orange>...</orange> </fruit>

Table 5.5 Element Type Declarations and Their
Interpretation*(continued)*

Declaration	*Interpretation*
<!ELEMENT fruit (apple|orange)*>	An element of type **fruit** contains zero or more subelements that are either **apple** elements or **orange** elements. **Example:** <fruit> <apple>...</apple> <orange>...</orange> </fruit> **Example:** <fruit> </fruit>
<!ELEMENT InStock EMPTY>	An element of type **InStock** does not contain anything. **Example:** <InStock/>
<!ELEMENT para (#PCDATA|list)*>	An element of type **para** contains a mixture of character data and **list** elements in any order. **Example:** <para> Here is my list: <list>...</list> </para> **Example:** <para>Stately, plump, Buck Mulligan...</para> **Example:** <para> <list>... </para>

Table 5.5   Element Type Declarations and Their
Interpretation *(continued)*

Declaration	Interpretation
<!element InStock EMPTY>	This is an error. The keyword "ELE-MENT" must always be in uppercase. This applies to all XML keywords.

An important distinction exists between elements that can contain character data (i.e., those with #PCDATA starting their content model) and those that cannot. The former are said to have *mixed content,* and the latter, *element content.* For now, just bear in mind that this distinction is important and that it affects the way the XML parser treats newlines.

5.8.2 *Attribute List Declarations*

Just like the element types they are attached to, attributes need to be declared in the DTD in order for a validating XML parser to check that they have been used properly in an XML document. An attribute list declaration has four aspects:

- The element type to which it belongs

- What the attribute is named

- What type of data the attribute value can contain (the attribute's *type*)

- How assignments to the attribute are treated by the parser, e.g., what to do if a value is not supplied and so on (the attribute's *default value*)

Establishing the attribute's name and associating it with a particular element type always takes the same form, as you see in Table 5.6 (the ellipsis denotes details to be filled in later on).

Table 5.6 Declaring an Attribute's Name and Associating It with an Element Type

Partial Attribute List Declaration	Interpretation
<!ATTLIST product name ... >	An element of type **product** has an attribute known as **name**... Sample usage: <product name = "...">
<!ATTLIST product name ... color ... >	An element of type **product** has two attributes known as **name** and **color**... Sample usage: <product name = "..." color = "...">
<!Attlist product name ... >	Error. The keyword "ATTLIST" must always be in uppercase.

5.8.2.1 Attribute Types

In total, nine types of attributes exist. I will limit the discussion to the three most popular ones for now. Firstly, you have the plain old string value attribute known as a CDATA attribute. This is declared using the **CDATA** keyword. Secondly, a list of permissible values for an attribute can be supplied using an *enumerated type* attribute. Thirdly, you can arrange for all attribute values for a particular attribute to have unique values. Declarations for these three attribute types are illustrated in Table 5-7, along with interpretation and some examples.

Table 5.7   Partial Attribute List Declarations and Their Interpretations

---

Partial Attribute List Declaration	*Interpretation*
<!ATTLIST product name CDATA ... >	An element of type **product** has an attribute known as **name**, whose value can be any string of characters except for three that have special meaning to the parser: "<", ">", and "&". Sample usage: <product name = "Acme Deluxe"> Sample usage: <product name = ""> Sample usage: <product name = 'Say "Hello World" today'> Sample usage: <product name = "Profit&Loss">
<!ATTLIST product name CDATA ... color (red|green) ... >	An element of type **product** has two attributes known as **name** and **color**. The **name** attribute value can have any string of characters, save the special ones:"<",">", and "&". The **color** attribute value must be either the string "red" or the string "green." Sample usage: <product name = "Acme" color = "red">
<!ATTLIST product code ID ... >	An element declared of type **product** has an attribute known as **code**. The values of the **code** attribute must be unique among attributes of the ID type across the entire XML document: Sample usage: <product code = "B42">

5.8.2.2   Attribute Defaults

The four flavors of attribute default are as follows:

- A value must be supplied (Required attribute)
- A value may be supplied but need not be (Implied attribute)
- The value is fixed in the DTD (Fixed attribute)
- In the absence of a value, use the one given in the DTD

These various attribute defaults are illustrated in Table 5.8.

Table 5.8   Attribute Defaults

Partial Attribute List Declaration	*Interpretation*
<!ATTLIST product name CDATA #REQUIRED>	An element of type **product** has an attribute known as **name**, whose value can be any string of characters except for three that have special meaning to the parser: "<", ">", and "&". A value for this attribute must be supplied when it is used in an XML document. Sample usage: <product name = "Acme Deluxe">
<!ATTLIST product name CDATA "Acme" >	An element of type **product** has an attribute known as **name**. The **name** attribute value can have any string of characters save for the special ones:"<",">", and "&". In the absence of a value for the attribute in the document, use the default value "Acme." Sample usage: <product name = "Turbo"> Sample usage: <product>

Table 5.8   Attribute Defaults*(continued)*

Partial Attribute List Declaration	*Interpretation*
<!ATTLIST product color (red|green) "red" >	An element of type **product** has an attribute named **color**. The **color** attribute must be either the string "red" or the string "green." In the absence of a value for the attribute in the document, use the default value "red." Sample usage: <product color = "red"> Sample usage: <product>
<!ATTLIST product color (red|green) #REQUIRED >	An element of type **product** has an attribute named **color**. The **color** attribute must be either the string "red" or the string "green." A value must be supplied whenever the element is used in a document. Sample usage: <product color = "red">
<!ATTLIST product color (red|green) #IMPLIED >	An element of type **product** has an attribute named **color**. The **color** attribute must be either the string "red" or the string "green." If a value is not supplied, leave it up to the XML application to decide what to do. Sample usage: <product color = "red"> Sample usage: <product>

Table 5.8   Attribute Defaults *(continued)*

Partial Attribute List Declaration	*Interpretation*
<!ATTLIST product name CDATA #FIXED "Acme" >	An element of type **product** has an attribute known as **name**. The value of this attribute is fixed to the value "Acme." Any other value is an error. Sample usage: \<product\> Sample usage: \<product name = "Acme"\>

5.9 | Entity declarations

Entities take a variety of forms and can be classified in various ways. I present examples of the simplest forms in Table 5.9.

Table 5.9   Examples of Entity Declarations

Entity Declaration	*Interpretation*
<!ENTITY spbm "Stately, plump, Buck Mulligan">	There is an entity known as **spbm**. When referenced in an XML document, the parser will insert the replacement text "Stately, plump, Buck Mulligan." Example: \<ulysses\> &spbm; stepped...

Table 5.9   Examples of Entity Declarations*(continued)*

Entity Declaration	Interpretation
<!ENTITY chapter1 SYSTEM "http://www.digitome.com/ chap1.xml">	There is an entity known as **chapter1**. When referenced in an XML document, the parser will insert the contents of the file at http://www.digitome.com/chap1.xml **Example**: <ulysses> &chapter1;

5.10 | Putting it all together

You can now construct the DTD for the acmepc catalog application. The first few declarations are liberally sprinkled with comments to illustrate what is going on. Interpreting the others would be a useful exercise to check your understanding of XML DTDs.

```
C>type acmepc.dtd

<!-- Document Type Definition for the acmepc
     catalog application -->

<!-- An acmepc document contains one or
     more items -->
<!ELEMENT acmepc (item)+>

<!-- an item contains these five subelements
     in this sequence -->
<!ELEMENT item (make, specification, price, blurb,
  internal)>

<!-- Every item is either a PC or a PRINTER.
This is indicated by its type attribute.
If a value is not supplied for this attribute,
it defaults to PC -->
<!ATTLIST item type (PC|PRINTER) "PC">
```

```
<!-- Every item also has a code attribute.
     No two items can share the same code. -->
<!ATTLIST item code ID #REQUIRED>

<!-- A specification element consists of
     a cpu element optionally followed by
     a harddisk element -->
<!ELEMENT specification (cpu,harddisk?)>

<!-- A blurb element consists of one or
     more p or ul elements -->
<!ELEMENT blurb (p|ul)+>

<!-- A p element contains a mixture of
     character data and index elements.
     Zero or more can occur -->
<!ELEMENT p (#PCDATA|index)*>

<!-- An index element is empty. It does
     not have any content -->
<!ELEMENT index EMPTY>

<!-- Ab index element has a term attribute.
     A value for this must always be supplied -->
<!ATTLIST index term CDATA #REQUIRED>

<!ELEMENT supplier EMPTY>
<!ATTLIST supplier id CDATA #REQUIRED>
<!ELEMENT make (brand,supplier)>
<!ELEMENT li (#PCDATA|index)*>
<!ELEMENT brand (#PCDATA)>
<!ELEMENT cpu EMPTY>
<!ATTLIST cpu
        type CDATA #REQUIRED
        speed CDATA #REQUIRED>
<!ELEMENT harddisk EMPTY>
<!ATTLIST harddisk
        type (IDE|EIDE|SCSI) "IDE"
        size CDATA #REQUIRED
        units (GB|TB) "GB">


<!ELEMENT price EMPTY>
<!ATTLIST price
```

```
           n CDATA #REQUIRED
           units CDATA #REQUIRED>

    <!ELEMENT ul (li)+>

    <!ELEMENT internal (instock,supportcalls,perunit-
       cost)>
    <!ELEMENT instock EMPTY>
    <!ATTLIST instock num CDATA #REQUIRED>
    <!ELEMENT supportcalls EMPTY>
    <!ATTLIST supportcalls num CDATA #REQUIRED>

    <!ELEMENT perunitcost EMPTY>
    <!ATTLIST perunitcost
           n CDATA #REQUIRED
           units CDATA #REQUIRED>
```

5.11 | Validating an XML document against its DTD

You are now in a position to un-comment the Document Type Declaration in the acmepc catalog file. You can change this:

```
<!--
Commented out for the moment
<!DOCTYPE acmepc SYSTEM "acmepc.dtd">
-->
```

to this:

```
<!DOCTYPE acmepc SYSTEM "acmepc.dtd">
```

You can now proceed to parse this document with msxml. Remember that in the absence of any command parameters, msxml simply checks the document and only emits errors. See what happens:

```
C>jview msxml acmepc.xml
```

Great! No errors. To see all the good work msxml is doing behind the scenes, purposely introduce an error. Remember that in the DTD, you specified that all **item** elements *must* have a **code** attribute. Try changing this line:

```
<item type = "PC" code = "ACME1">
```

to this

```
<item type = "PC">
```

Now re-parse with msxml:

```
C>jview msxml acmepc.xml
Attribute 'code' is required.
Location: file:/C:/xml/book/ch05/acmepc.xml(5,-1)
Context: <acmepc><item>
```

Note how msxml has rigorously applied the rules and is refusing to move forward with parsing this document until the missing code attribute is supplied. You might think that this refusal is no big deal because the omission would be easy to spot by visual inspection. This is certainly true in this case, but imagine a catalog with ten thousand entries! The beauty of DTDs is that they allow the automation of this sort of check so that you never need to worry about it. As you will readily appreciate, DTD-based checking scales up rather better than the visual inspection method.

Enough of the tedious details for now! You have covered enough theory to move on to practice. In the next part of the book, you get to put all this theory to good use by building practical applications with it. I return to round out the details in Part III.

Part Two

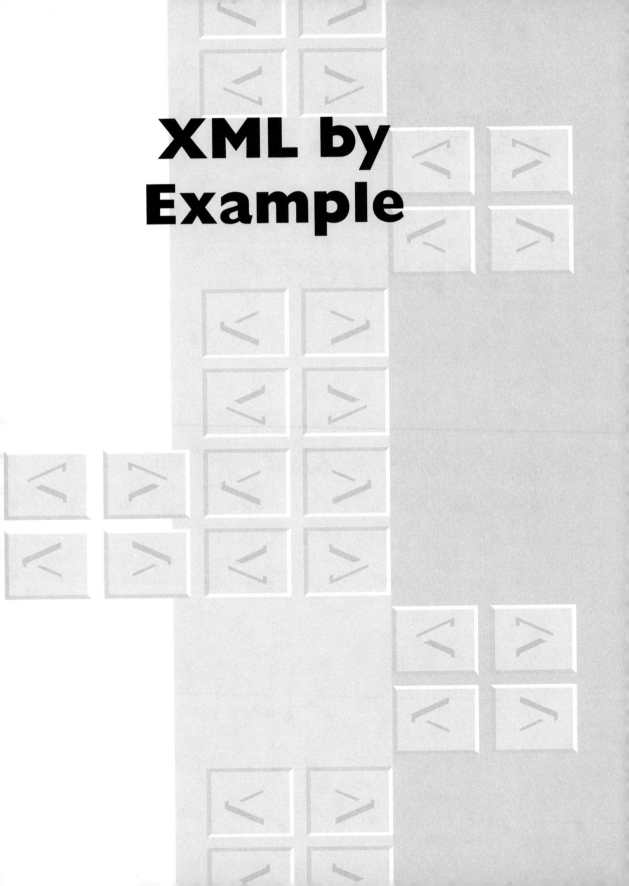

Using XML with Internet Explorer 4

- Displaying XML in an HTML browser
- Using nested HTML tables
- Performing calculations
- Navigating XML
- Converting XML to HTML with XSL

In the early days of the Web, pages of information were essentially static objects. A page of information, once displayed, was fixed until the Web browser reloaded the document from the Web server. This behavior is becoming increasingly uncommon. Simple scripting languages such as JavaScript have flourished, and Java and ActiveX controls provide essentially unlimited programming power for tasks that require it. HTML itself has been overhauled several times and has emerged as a dynamic environment in which to create user interfaces, manipulate and process data, and talk to server-based applications. This flexibility and programmability presents some interesting possibilities to utilize the rich structure of XML documents from the familiar world of HTML and today's Web browsers.

You read in Chapter 5 how the XMLViewer applet that ships with Microsoft Internet Explorer 4 could be used to create a hierarchical view of an XML document. In this chapter, I examine two more powerful techniques for seamlessly integrating HTML and XML.

- Displaying XML in an HTML browser with Microsoft's Data Source Object technology (DSO)
- Converting XML to HTML via the XSL Stylesheet Language

6.1 | Displaying XML in an HTML browser

Microsoft Internet Explorer contains built-in support for XML in the form of an XML parser technology known as msxml. The parser is built into the browser in both ActiveX and Java applet forms. It can also be used from the command line as you saw in earlier chapters.

Microsoft has an overall strategy for making structured information available to HTML browsers in the form of *Data Source Objects*. The original intent of Data Source Objects was to allow easy integration of relational database data and the Web. Microsoft has added support for XML into this technology via the XMLDSO applet—a Java applet that *exposes* XML data sources in much the same way as relational databases.

An illustration of how XMLDSO can be used to map XML to HTML is illustrated in Figure 6–1, using the acmepc.com PC catalog as an example.

In the diagram, the XMLDSO applet is shown acting as the "glue" that binds the name element of the source XML document to the first cell of the HTML table row. Similarly, the capacity element of the source XML document is bound to the second cell of the HTML table row and so on.

The XML source document I use is a very simple variant of the www.acmepc.com PC catalog.

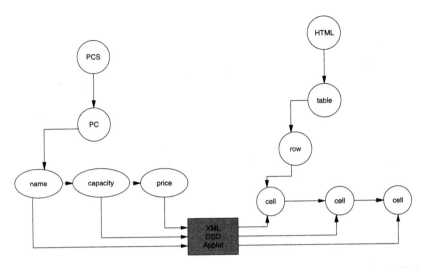

Figure 6–1   Using XMLDSO to connect XML elements with HTML elements

```
C>type cat.xml

<?xml version = "1.0"?>
<PCS>
 <PC>
    <NAME>Acme Blaster</NAME>
    <CAPACITY>100</CAPACITY>
    <PRICE>2000</PRICE>
 </PC>
 <PC>
    <NAME>Speedy PC</NAME>
    <CAPACITY>200</CAPACITY>
    <PRICE>4000</PRICE>
 </PC>
 <PC>
    <NAME>Gonzo PC</NAME>
    <CAPACITY>300</CAPACITY>
    <PRICE>5000</PRICE>
 </PC>
</PCS>
```

6.1.1 *Example 1—Displaying XML data as a basic HTML table*

Getting XML elements into HTML elements with XMLDSO consists of the following stages:

1. Create an HTML page and include an applet element to load the XMLDSO applet that specifies the name of the XML document to load.
2. Create HTML elements that are *data aware* (such as table cells). Use the datafld attribute to specify the names of the XML elements they should contain.

In this example, I create a three-column HTML table to hold the name, capacity, and price data from the XML source document cat.xml. The applet element in the HTML document looks like this:

```
<applet code=com.ms.xml.dso.XMLDSO.class
 width=100%
 height=25
 id=xmldso
>
<PARAM NAME="url" VALUE="cat.xml">
</applet>
```

Notice that the applet has been allocated some screen space, namely an area the width of the browser window and twenty-five pixels high. The applet uses this area to display progress messages, XML parsing errors, and so on. Once the application is working, this screen area can be removed, thus making the applet completely invisible on the HTML page. The id attribute has been used to give a unique name to the applet. You will see why this is required in a moment. Note also how the param element is used to specify the name of the XML document to be processed.

Next I need to create an HTML table to lay out the information from the catalog. The start of the table element looks like this:

```
<table id=table border=2 width=100% datasrc=#xmldso>
```

```
<thead>
        <th>Name
        <th>Capacity
        <th>Price
</thead>
```

This is a simple HTML table start-tag with table heading information. Note the **datasrc** attribute, which is used to connect this table to the applet with the id **xmldso**. The body of the table looks like this:

```
<tr>
  <td valign=top><div datafld=NAME></td>
  <td valign=top><div datafld=CAPACITY></td>
  <td valign=top><div datafld=PRICE></td>
</tr>
</table>
```

This table row is declared to contain three table cells. The **datafld** attribute is used to specify the name of the data field each cell will contain. In the case of XML, these fields are XML elements, namely, the name, capacity, and price elements from the source XML document.

Notice that only a *single* row is declared. The XMLDSO applet works in concert with the browser to expand this table to as many rows as are required to display all the information in the XML document. If I had 1000 PCs in the catalog, I would end up with a 1000-row table.

To finish up the application, I need to wrap these new elements in the usual HTML elements. The full HTML document appears here:

```
C:>type cat1.htm

<html>
<head>
<title>Example 1</title>
<BODY>
<h1>Example 1</h1>
<P>
XML Catalog displayed in an HTML table using
IE4.0 XML Data Binding
<applet code=com.ms.xml.dso.XMLDSO.class
width=100%
height=25
id=xmldso
  >
```

```
<PARAM NAME="url" VALUE="cat.xml">
</applet>
<table id=table border=2 width=100% datasrc=#xmldso>
<thead>
  <th>Name
  <th>Capacity
  <th>Price
</thead>
<tr>
  <td valign=top><div datafld=NAME></td>
  <td valign=top><div datafld=CAPACITY></td>
  <td valign=top><div datafld=PRICE></td>
</tr>
</table>
</body>
</html>
```

Load this document into Internet Explorer 4, causes the applet to run, parse the cat.xml document and bind the XML elements to the HTML table as specified by the **datafld** attributes. The result appears in Figure 6–2.

6.1.2 *Example 2—storing XML in an HTML document*

XMLDSO is equally at home with having XML data provided to it as part of the HTML page, rather than accessing it externally as I did in the last example. This is done by embedding the source XML within the applet element. Note that in order to do this, the applet must be allowed to access the HTML page. To allow access, set the MAY-SCRIPT attribute to TRUE. The HTML document with embedded XML looks like this:

```
C>type cat2.htm

<html>
<head>
<title>Example 1</title>
<BODY>
<h1>Example 1</h1>
```

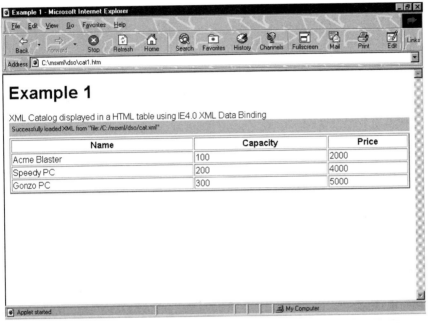

Figure 6–2 The HTML for Example I displayed in Internet Explorer 4

```
<P>
XML Catalog displayed in an HTML table using IE4.0 XML
    Data Binding
<applet code=com.ms.xml.dso.XMLDSO.class
width=100%
height=25
id=xmldso
mayscript = TRUE
>
<!-- XML stored in an HTML page as part of an applet
    element -->
<?xml version = "1.0"?>
<PCS>
 <PC>
    <NAME>Acme Blaster</NAME>
    <CAPACITY>100</CAPACITY>
    <PRICE>2000</PRICE>
 </PC>
 <PC>
    <NAME>Speedy PC</NAME>
    <CAPACITY>200</CAPACITY>
```

```
      <PRICE>4000</PRICE>
    </PC>
    <PC>
        <NAME>Gonzo PC</NAME>
        <CAPACITY>300</CAPACITY>
        <PRICE>5000</PRICE>
    </PC>
  </PCS>
</applet>
<!-- table declaration as in Example 1 -->
<table id=table border=2 width=100% datasrc=#xmldso>
<thead>
  <th>Name
  <th>Capacity
  <th>Price
</thead>
<tr>
  <td valign=top><div datafld=NAME></td>
  <td valign=top><div datafld=CAPACITY></td>
  <td valign=top><div datafld=PRICE></td>
</tr>
</table>
</body>
</html>
```

Displaying this HTML document in Internet Explorer 4 produces exactly the same output as Example 1.

6.1.3 *Example 3—Display hierarchical XML as nested HTML tables*

HTML supports nested tables, which present a natural technique for displaying nested XML data. To illustrate, I introduce another layer of hierarchy into the catalog by splitting **capacity** into two subelements for **ram** and **disk** capacities. An entry in the catalog now takes the following form:

```
<PC>
    <NAME>Acme Blaster</NAME>
    <CAPACITY>
```

```
    <RAM>10</RAM>
    <DISK>200</DISK>
  </CAPACITY>
  <PRICE>2000</PRICE>
</PC>
```

The HTML document for this example is the same as for Example 1, with the exception of the table declaration, which now looks like this:

```
<table id=table border=2 width=100% datasrc=#xmldso>
 <thead>
  <th>Name
  <th>Capacity
  <th>Price
 </thead>
 <tr>
  <td valign=top><div datafld=NAME></td>
  <td valign=top>
    <table width=100% datasrc=#xmldso
   datafld=CAPACITY
          border=2>
    <thead>
     <th>RAM
     <th>DISK
    </thead>
    <tr>
      <td><div datafld=RAM></td>
      <td><div datafld=DISK></td>
    </tr>
   </table>
  </td>
  <td valign=top><div datafld=PRICE></td>
 </tr>
</table>
```

The most important changes appear in bold. Note how the nested table is bound to the **capacity** element. This nested table has two columns, the cells of which are bound to the **ram** and **disk** subelements. The Internet Explorer 4 rendering of this HTML appears in Figure 6–3.

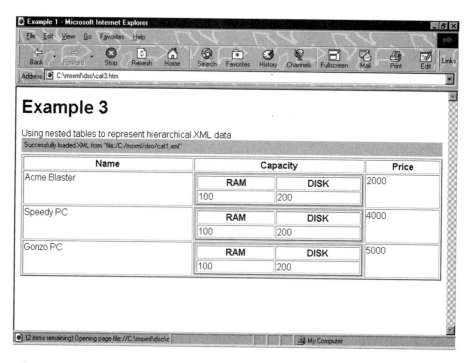

Figure 6–3 The HTML for Example 3 displayed in Internet Explorer 4

6.1.4 *Example 4—Performing calculations*

In this example, I illustrate how a scripting language such as Java-Script can access the XML document loaded by the XMLDSO applet. The XML document is exposed to JavaScript via the applet, and thus JavaScript can be used to perform calculations on the data. Here we will display the PC catalog of Example 1 in a table again, with the added twist that the user can click a button to search the table for the name and price of the most expensive (dearest) PC.

The XMLDSO applet exposes the overall structure and content of an XML document as a set of simple functions/objects that can be called from JavaScript. The **GetDocument**() fuction returns the top-level object representing the entire XML document tree. This object has a **root** property, which returns an object representing the top-level *node* in the tree. Nodes have a variety of properties, depending on their type. Nodes that represent elements have a **children** property. Nodes with data content have a **text** property and so on.

These functions/objects are used in the following JavaScript routine. The code works by accessing the array of all the PC child elements of the root node. For each PC node, the code determines the PC name and price, keeping track of the most expensive PC as it goes.

```
// Find the dearest PC
Function FindDearest()
{
    // Get the XML document root node object
    var root = xmldso.getDocument().root;

    // Get a list of all its children that are PCs
    var items = root.children.item("PC");
    var num = items.length;
    // Initalize the dearest PC name to blank
    var DearestName = "";
    // Initialize the dearest PC price to -1
    var DearestPrice = -1;
    // Traverse the list of PCs
    for (i = 0; i < num; i++) {
        // Get a list of the children of
    // this PC
        var PC = items.item(i).children;
        // Pick up the contents of the name
    // element
        var name = PC.item("NAME").text;
        // Pick up the contents of
    // the price element
        var price = PC.item("PRICE").text;
        // Convert the price string into
    // a number
        var p = parseInt(price);
        // See if this is the dearest PC we
    // have seen
        if (p > DearestPrice) {
            // Dearest PC so far - store
        // its details
            DearestName = name;
            DearestPrice = price;
```

```
            }
        }
        // Construct a string of the result
        msg = "Dearest PC is '" +
        DearestName + "' costing " +
        DearestPrice;
        // Return the string
        return msg;
    }
```

To activate this function, I add a button to the HTML page that displays the table, like this:

```
<input type=button value="Find dearest PC"
        onclick='window.alert(FindDearest())'>
```

The result of loading the catalog HTML document containing these new items and clicking the button appears in Figure 6–4.

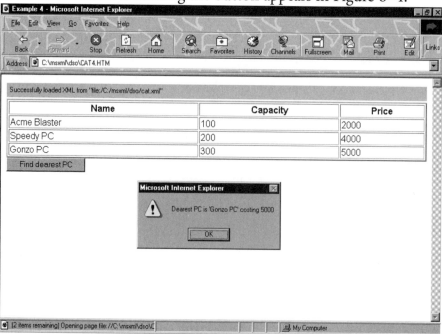

Figure 6–4   HTML from Example 4 in Internet Explorer

6.1.5 *Example 5—Navigating through the XML*

In this example, I take advantage of the database-like treatment of XML facilitated by XMLDSO. I create an XML record browser with forward and back buttons allowing the user to navigate through the XML one "record" at a time. The table template for this example consists of three rows of two cells each. It has one row each for display name, capacity, and price information:

```
<table id=table border=2 width=100%>
 <tr>
  <td><b>Name</b></td>
  <td><div datasrc=#xmldso datafld=NAME></td>
 </tr>
 <tr>
  <td><b>Capacity</b></td>
  <td><div datasrc=#xmldso datafld=CAPACITY></td>
 </tr>
 <tr>
  <td><b>Price</b></td>
  <td><div datasrc=#xmldso datafld=PRICE></td>
 </tr>
</table>
```

Note that the individual cells rather than the table specify the data source as #xmldso. This signals to the browser that it should not process the entire XML document in one go but rather process it a record at a time, keeping track of the current position.

To provide the user with the ability to move forward and back through the XML document, I provide two buttons, "Previous" and "Next" as shown here:

```
<input type=button value="Previous"
    onclick='xmldso.recordset.moveprevious();'>
<input type=button value="Next"
    onclick='xmldso.recordset.movenext();'>
```

When this new HTML document is first loaded into the browser, the first record is displayed as you see in Figure 6–5.

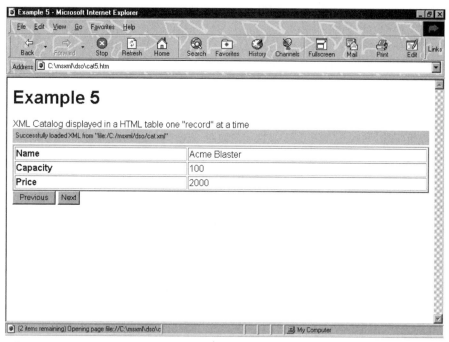

Figure 6–5   The first record in the PC catalog

Clicking Next causes the browser to activate the movenext() method and thus moves the HTML table on to the next record in the catalog, as Figure 6–6 shows.

6.2 | Converting XML to HTML with XSL

Although the XSL standard proposal is in its infancy, a number of "proof of concept" implementations are available from companies such as Microsoft and Arbortext. In this section, I use Microsoft's

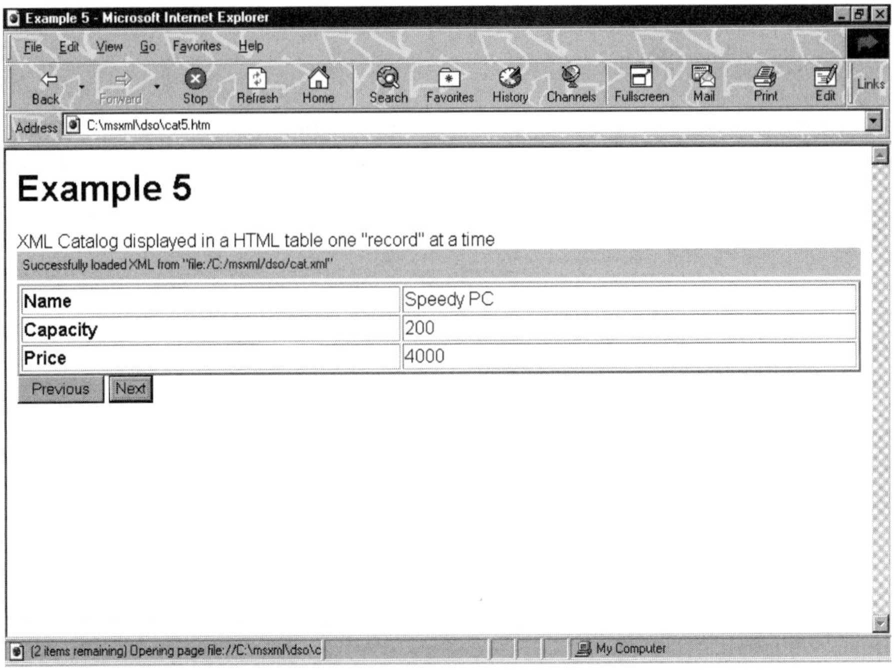

Figure 6–6   The second record in the PC catalog

partial implementation of XSL—msxsl—to convert the PC catalog XML document to various forms of HTML. You can return to look at XSL in greater detail in Part III of this book. For now, I cover just enough to illustrate how XSL can be used to achieve analogous results to those achieved with XMLDSO. The overall process is illustrated in Figure 6–7.

An XSL stylesheet consists of a set of rules that tell an XSL processor such as msxsl how to convert an XML document into some other notation. In its full generality, XSL can be used to produce stylesheets that are independent of any one output notation. In other words, a single XSL style sheet can be used to target multiple output notations, such as HTML, TeX, RTF, and so on.

In recognition of the fact that HTML output is a major use of XSL, a number of HTML-specific features have been built directly into the XSL language. I use these HTML features in Example 6.

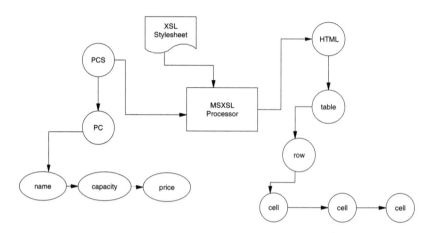

Figure 6–7   Generating HTML from XML with MSXL

An XSL stylesheet is based on the idea of *rules* that trigger when the specified elements are encountered in an XML document. Within a rule, you can specify what you would like to generate in the HTML output. This can range from nothing at all (i.e., deletion) to results generated from running JavaScript applications.

6.2.1 *Example 6—A minimalist XSL style sheet*

XSL style sheets are themselves XML documents. An XSL processor will parse and load the XSL style sheet in exactly the same way it parses and loads any XML document. Here is a minimalist XSL stylesheet for generating HTML from the PC catalog:

```
C>type cat.xsl

<xsl>
 <rule>
  <root/>
  <HTML>
   <HEAD>
    <TITLE>Example 6</TITLE>
   </HEAD>
```

```
    <BODY>
     <children/>
    </BODY>
   </HTML>
  </rule>
 </xsl>
```

This style sheet consists of a single rule. The rule is triggered by the root node in the XML tree (denoted by the XSL element **<root/>**). The tags in uppercase are HTML tags that will appear in the output document.

The XSL element **<children/>** is used to specify that the XSL processor should proceed to walk the children of this node, triggering any rules for them as required.

The msxsl processor from Microsoft can be used to process the PC catalog document with this style sheet as follows:

```
C>msxsl -i cat.xml -s cat.xsl -o cat.htm
```

Three command parameters are specified:

- **-i:** The input XML document
- **-s:** The style sheet to use
- **-o:** The output HTML document

The resultant HTML document cat.htm appears here:

```
C>type cat.htm

<HTML>
<HEAD>
<TITLE>Example 6</TITLE>
</HEAD>
<BODY>
Acme Blaster1002000Speedy PC2004000Gonzo PC3005000
</BODY>
</HTML>
```

Note how all the text of the XML document has found its way into the output document. The reason is that in the absence of any instructions to the contrary in the rules file, all text nodes in the XML document are passed through to the output.

6.2.2 *Example 7—Creating an HTML table with XSL*

In this example, I extend the style sheet to add more formatting in the HTML. Specifically, I add rules to allow the XML elements to flow into an HTML table. I start with an expanded root rule, as shown here:

```
<rule>
  <root/>
  <HTML>
   <HEAD>
    <TITLE>Example 7</TITLE>
   </HEAD>
   <BODY>
    <TABLE BORDER="1" WIDTH="100%">
     <children/>
    </TABLE>
   </BODY>
  </HTML>
</rule>
```

Note how the table to hold the PC details is opened *prior* to telling the XSL processor to process the children and closed afterwards. This ensures that all output triggered by processing the children will find its way into the table. Next I need a rule to tell the XSL processor to slot each PC element into its own row in the table:

```
<rule>
 <target-element type = "PC"/>
  <TR>
   <children/>
  </TR>
</rule>
```

I use a target-element element to specify that this rule should trigger whenever a **PC** element is encountered in the XML. As before, the elements in uppercase are HTML elements and are directly transmitted to the output. I open a row with a **TR** prior to walking through the children nodes, and close the **TR** afterwards.

Next I need a rule to specify that **name**, **capacity**, and **price** should be slotted into individual table cells. Given that the rule is the same for all three elements, I can express this succinctly in XSL as follows:

```
<rule>
 <target-element type = "NAME"/>
 <target-element type = "CAPACITY"/>
 <target-element type = "PRICE"/>
 <TD>
   <children/>
 </TD>
</rule>
```

A rule can have more than one target-element, thus allowing it to be triggered for multiple elements. These changes completed the stylesheet cat1.xsl. I can invoke the msxsl processor like this:

```
C>mxsml -i cat.xml -s cat1.xsl -o cat.htm
```

The resultant HTML document looks like Figure 6-8 in Internet Explorer.

6.2.3 *Example 8—Performing calculations on XML data with XSL*

XSL incorporates an internationally standardized version of JavaScript known as ECMAScript (ECMA-262). In this example, I use ECMAScript to perform the same calculation performed earlier using XMLDSO. Namely, I plan to output the name and price of the dearest PC in the catalog beneath the table of PC information. The approach I take is as follows:

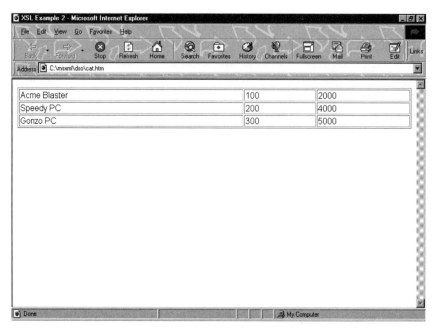

Figure 6–8   Example 7 output in Internet Explorer

- I will initialize global variables in the script to track the dearest PC information.
- Whenever I trigger on a PC rule, I will update the global variables, if required.
- When I reach the end of the XSL processing, I will output a paragraph containing the dearest PC information.

I start with the ECMAScript functions. I can incorporate scripts into XSL using the **define-script** element.

```
<define-script><![CDATA[
// Global Variable to track the name of the
// Dearest PC encountered
var DearestName = "";
// Global Variable to track the price of the
// Dearest PC encountered
var DearestPrice = -1;

// Function to update the dearest PC information
// Based on price and name of the current PC
function UpdateDearest(price,name)
{
        p = parseInt(price)
        if (p > DearestPrice) {
                DearestName = name;
                DearestPrice = p;
            }
}

// Function to call at the very end to create
// the paragraph after the table of PCs

function ShowDearest()
{
return ("Dearest PC is " + DearestName +
   " costing " + DearestPrice);
}

]]></define-script>
```

Note that the entire script is wrapped in a CDATA section, in order to avoid confusing the XML parser with characters such as "<" that can occur in JavaScript.

The root processing rule is the same as before, with the exception that I call the ShowDearest() function to generate the final paragraph.

```
<rule>
  <root/>
  <HTML>
   <HEAD>
    <TITLE>Example 7</TITLE>
   </HEAD>
   <BODY>
    <TABLE BORDER="1" WIDTH="100%">
     <children/>
    </TABLE>
    <P>
    <eval>ShowDearest()</eval>
    </P>
   </BODY>
  </HTML>
</rule>
```

Note the use of the **eval** element of XSL, which signals to the XSL processor that it should evaluate the ECMAScript contents of the element. The final change is to the PC rule, which needs to call Update-Dearest() for every PC.

```
<rule>
 <target-element type = "PC"/>
  <eval>UpdateDearest
  (children.item("PRICE",0).text,
       children.item("NAME",0).text)</eval>
  <TR>
   <children/>
  </TR>
</rule>
```

Note that ECMAscript has access to the XML document in the form of a set of properties and functions, just like in the XMLDSO examples. These changes complete the stylesheet cat2.xsl. The HTML document produced by running MSXSL with it and the cat.xml document appears in Figure 6-9.

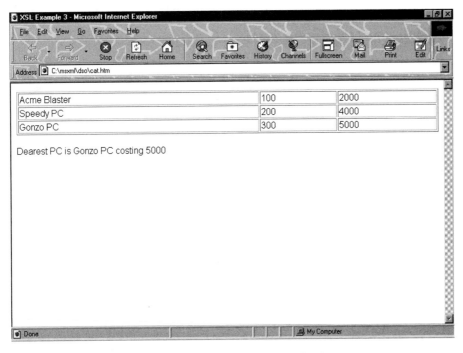

Figure 6–9   XSL Example 8 output in Internet Explorer

Database Publishing with XML

- Options for Database Publishing with XML
- Generating XML from a database
- Serving XML to a Web browser

One of the great advantages of the way the Web is designed is that Web browsers do not need to know or care how the HTML pages they view come into being on the server. This presents great scope for developing server-side applications that intercept browsers' requests for traditional database data and process them into pure HTML on the fly. This is illustrated in Figure 7–1.

This approach has been used to great effect in a variety of commercial applications such as Lotus Notes (Domino), Folio Views (Site Director) and Cold Fusion (Allaire Corp.).

Now that browsers such as Internet Explorer V4.0 can manipulate XML on the client side, there is another option—convert data to XML on the server and let the browser work directly with it as opposed to first dumbing it down to HTML. This is illustrated in Figure 7–2.

To illustrate database publishing using XML, I use a scenario from www.acmepc.com. One of their hard disk vendors, AcmeDisk Inc., has supplied a Microsoft Access database that lists all their hard disk offerings. Management at acmepc.com would like to make this data-

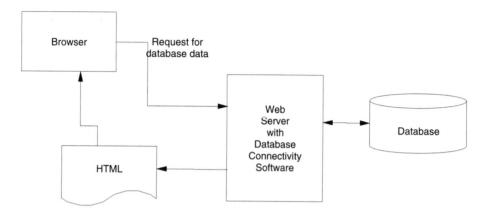

Figure 7-1   Traditional Database Publishing on the Web via HTML

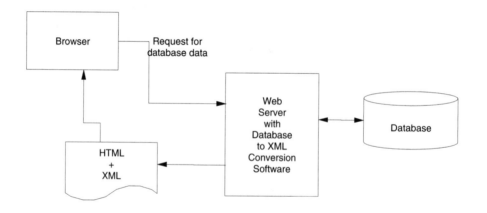

Figure 7-2   Database Publishing on the Web via XML

base available to customers on their Web site. Figure 7–3 shows how the database looks in Microsoft Access.

The developers have four main options:

1. Convert the data to HTML as a once-off conversion operation
2. Convert the data to HTML on the fly

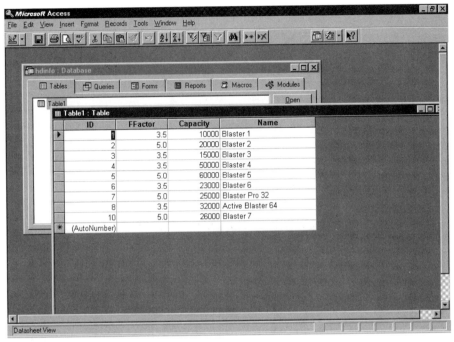

Figure 7–3 The hard disk database in Microsoft Access

3. Convert the data to XML as a once-off conversion operation

4. Convert the data to XML on the fly

Options 1 and 2 are easily dispatched! As you saw in Chapter 6, having XML on the client-side opens up all sorts of interesting possibilities for client side interaction, calculations and so on. Option 3 has the disadvantage that user requests for data from the database are not "live." Option 4 is therefore the most appealing and in a real world application this is the option I would tend to opt for. However, illustrating such an on-the-fly conversion to XML would involve using technology specific to a particular database and/or a particular Web server. Thus, in the interests of generality and simplicity we will opt for the third option—a once-off conversion process to convert the database to XML on the server side.

7.1 | Generating XML from a database

We will avoid introducing any database specific code in the XML conversion by picking up a simple line-oriented, tab-delimited table structure—the sort of export notation many database packages support. Here is the Access Database is this line-oriented, export notation:

```
C>type table1.txt

"ID"    "Name"              "Capacity"    "FFactor"
1       "Blaster 1"          10000         3.50
2       "Blaster 2"          20000         5.00
3       "Blaster 3"          15000         3.50
4       "Blaster 4"          50000         3.50
5       "Blaster 5"          60000         5.00
6       "Blaster 6"          23000         3.50
7       "Blaster Pro 32"     25000         5.00
8       "Active Blaster 64"  32000         3.50
10      "Blaster 7"          26000         5.00
```

A very convenient aspect of this notation is the first line which lists the field names in the order in which they occur on the following lines. We can use this first line to generate element names in the XML like this:

```
<Records>
<Record>
    <ID>1</ID>
    <Name>Blaster 1</Name>
    <Capacity>10000</Capacity>
    <FFactor>3.50</FFactor>
</Record>
...
</Records>
```

The conversion script is easily developed in many languages. Here we will use Python:

```
C>type hd.py

# Python script to convert flat ASCII database
# with tab delimited fields to XML

import sys, string
```

```
sep = '\t'
fp = open('table1.txt')

line = fp.readline()[:-1]# Field names
line = string.replace( line, '"', '' )

# Create list of field names
fldnames = string.splitfields( line, sep )

# XML declaration
print "<?xml version = '1.0'?>"

# Root element
print "<Records>"
line = fp.readline()[:-1]
while line:
   print "\t<Record>"
   line = string.replace( line, '"', '' )
   fieldvalues = string.splitfields( line, sep )
   for i in range( len(fieldvalues) ):
      print "\t\t<"+fldnames[i]+">"
+ fieldvalues[i]
+ "</"
+ fldnames[i]
+">"
   print "\t</Record>"
   line = fp.readline()[:-1]
print "</Records>"
```

The result of executing this script is shown here:

```
C>python hd.py

<?xml version = '1.0'?>
<Records>
  <Record>
    <ID>1</ID>
    <Name>Blaster 1</Name>
    <Capacity>10000</Capacity>
    <FFactor>3.50</FFactor>
  </Record>
  <Record>
    <ID>2</ID>
    <Name>Blaster 2</Name>
    <Capacity>20000</Capacity>
```

```
          <FFactor>5.00</FFactor>
       </Record>
       <Record>
          <ID>3</ID>
          <Name>Blaster 3</Name>
          <Capacity>15000</Capacity>
          <FFactor>3.50</FFactor>
       </Record>
       <Record>
          <ID>4</ID>
          <Name>Blaster 4</Name>
          <Capacity>50000</Capacity>
          <FFactor>3.50</FFactor>
       </Record>
       <Record>
          <ID>5</ID>
          <Name>Blaster 5</Name>
          <Capacity>60000</Capacity>
          <FFactor>5.00</FFactor>
       </Record>
       <Record>
          <ID>6</ID>
          <Name>Blaster 6</Name>
          <Capacity>23000</Capacity>
          <FFactor>3.50</FFactor>
       </Record>
       <Record>
          <ID>7</ID>
          <Name>Blaster Pro 32 </Name>
          <Capacity>25000</Capacity>
          <FFactor>5.00</FFactor>
       </Record>
       <Record>
          <ID>8</ID>
          <Name>Active Blaster 64</Name>
          <Capacity>32000</Capacity>
          <FFactor>3.50</FFactor>
       </Record>
       <Record>
          <ID>10</ID>
          <Name>Blaster 7</Name>
          <Capacity>26000</Capacity>
          <FFactor>5.00</FFactor>
       </Record>
     </Records>
```

7.2 | Serving up the XML to a Web browser

So far so good. We have a script that will take an arbitrary table from this flat database format and produce well-formed XML. In order to serve this up over the Web we can use ordinary CGI scripting with some HTML wrapping around the XML text. In Chapter 6 I illustrated how XML text can be encapsulated in an HTML **applet** element and then accessed via XMLDSO in Internet Explorer 4.

Here is the wrapping HTML we need to generate:

```
C>type hd.htm

Content-type: text/html

<HTML>
<HEAD>
<TITLE>Database Test</TITLE>
</HEAD>
<BODY>
<H1>AcmeDisk Inc. Disk Drive Selection</H1>
<applet code=com.ms.xml.dso.XMLDSO.class
width=100%
height=25
id=xmldso mayscript=true>
<?xml version = '1.0'?>
<Records>
  <Record>
    <ID>1</ID>
    <Name>Blaster 1</Name>
    <Capacity>10000</Capacity>
    <FFactor>3.50</FFactor>
  </Record>
    <!-- other records here -->
</Records>
</applet>
<table id=table
border=2
width=100%
datasrc=#xmldso
cellpadding=5>
```

```
<thead>
<th> ID
<th> Name
<th> Capacity
<th> FFactor
</thead>
<tr>
<td align=center valign=top>
<div datafld= ID   dataformatas=HTML>
</td>
<td align=center valign=top>
<div datafld= Name   dataformatas=HTML>
</td>
<td align=center valign=top>
<div datafld= Capacity   dataformatas=HTML>
</td>
<td align=center valign=top>
<div datafld= FFactor   dataformatas=HTML>
</td>
</tr>
</table>
</BODY>
</HTML>
```

Converting the Python script to include this wrapping HTML markup is quite straightforward. Note how the functionality of the earlier script has become a subroutine that returns a list of the field names. This is used to establish table column headers and bind the table cells to the various elements that XMLDSO will provide access to. Here is the modified script, which is now ready for activation via CGI:

```
C>type hd.py

# Python script to convert flat ASCII database
# with tab delimited fields to XML

import sys, string

def printtable():
  sep = "\t"

  fp = open('table1.txt')
  line = fp.readline()[:-1]# Field names
  line = string.replace( line, '"', '' )
  fldnames = string.splitfields( line, sep )
```

```
    print "<?xml version = '1.0'?>"
print "<Records>"
    line = fp.readline()[:-1]
    while line:
        print "\t<Record>"
        line = string.replace( line, '"', '' )
        fieldvalues = string.splitfields( line, sep )
        for i in range( len(fieldvalues) ):
            print "\t\t<"+fldnames[i]
+">"
+fieldvalues[i]
+"</"
+fldnames[i]+
">"
        print "\t</Record>"
        line = fp.readline()[:-1]
    print "</Records>"
    return fldnames

# HTML response header
print "Content-type: text/html"
print
print "<HTML><HEAD><TITLE>Database Test</TITLE>
    </HEAD><BODY>"
print "<P>Here is the table.</P>"
print "<applet code=com.ms.xml.dso.XMLDSO.class
    width=100% height=25 id=xmldso mayscript=true>"
fldnames = printtable()
print "</applet>"
print "<table id=table border=2 width=100%
    datasrc=#xmldso cellpadding=5>"
print "<thead>"
for fn in fldnames:
    print "<th>", fn
print "</thead>"
print "<tr>"
for fn in fldnames:
    print "<td align=center valign=top>"
print "<div datafld=", fn, " dataformatas=HTML>
    </td>"
print "</tr>"
print "</table>"
print "</BODY>"
print "</HTML>"
```

Invoking this CGI script is simply a matter of creating an input form to POST a request to invoke the CGI script on the server. Here is a very simple HTML document that achieves this:

```
C>type hd.htm

<HTML>
<HEAD><TITLE>AcmeDisk Inc. Disk Selector
   </TITLE></HEAD>
<BODY>
<H1>AcmeDisk Inc. Disk Selector</H1>

<CENTER>
<FORM ACTION="../scripts/db.py" METHOD=post>
<INPUT Type="Submit" Value="Get info">
</FORM>
</CENTER>
</BODY>
</HTML>
```

Figure 7–4 shows how the form looks in Internet Explorer 4.0 like this:

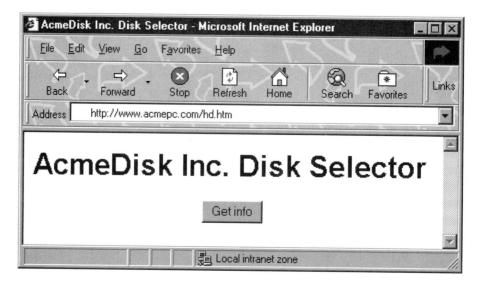

Figure 7–4   The AcmeDisk Inc CGI script activation form in Internet Explorer

Clicking the button activates the Python script and returns the following HTML document to the browser:

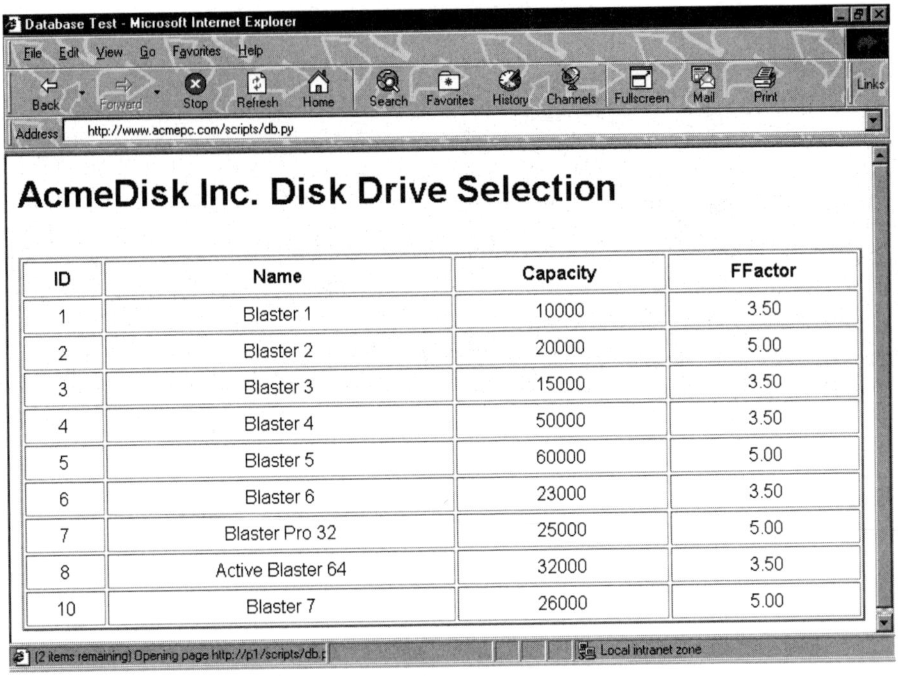

ID	Name	Capacity	FFactor
1	Blaster 1	10000	3.50
2	Blaster 2	20000	5.00
3	Blaster 3	15000	3.50
4	Blaster 4	50000	3.50
5	Blaster 5	60000	5.00
6	Blaster 6	23000	3.50
7	Blaster Pro 32	25000	5.00
8	Active Blaster 64	32000	3.50
10	Blaster 7	26000	5.00

Figure 7–5 XML from AcmeDisk Inc. Access Database displayed in HTML via XMLDSO

Web Automation with WIDL (Web Interface Definition Language)

- Advantages of Web Automation
- Creating the WIDL document
- Advantages of the WIDL approach
- Further capabilities of WIDL

The Web Interface Definition Language (WIDL) is a freely available XML application developed by WebMethods (http://www.webmethods.com) to allow normally interactive Web activities to be batch automated. Perhaps the most common example is a Web service where the user is expected to fill in some fields, submit the form, and then wait for the results to come back as an HTML page. Using WIDL, such conversations can be automated so that no human intervention—indeed no browser—is required. The WIDL-based definition of a Web conversation can be used to generate code in any language you like. The Web Automation Toolkit from WebMethods supports Java, JavaScript, C++, and Visual Basic.

WIDL relates to XML in two distinct ways. Firstly, it uses XML as its notation for describing Web conversations. Secondly, the technology is equally applicable to batch automating access to XML-based resources on the Web. The advent of XML and, in particular, XML-based metadata opens up a rich vein of potential applications for the WIDL concept. The WebMethods Toolkit is included on the accompanying CD.

191

To illustrate WIDL's automation abilities, I will use a variation of the AcmeDisk Inc. Disk Selector developed in Chapter 7. This service will allow the user to specify a threshold value for hard disk size. The HTML table that is created by the form will list only the hard disks with capacities greater than or equal to the specified threshold value. Here is the modified HTML form:

```
<HTML>
<HEAD><TITLE>AcmeDisk Inc. Disk Selector </TITLE></HEAD>
<BODY>
<H1>AcmeDisk Inc. Disk Selector</H1>
<CENTER>
<FORM ACTION="../scripts/db.py" METHOD=post>
<INPUT Type="Submit" Value="Select a minimum hard disk size">
<INPUT Type="String" Name = "Hdcapacity" value = "10000">
</FORM>
</CENTER>
</BODY>
<HTML>
```

8.1 | Creating the WIDL document

The first thing I need to do is to analyze the structure of the HTML document containing the interaction I wish to automate. The Web-Methods Toolkit does this analysis for me. When asked to open the URL http://www.acmepc.com/hd.htm, the Toolkit breaks the HTML down and isolates the parts that require interaction. These component parts are known in WIDL as *bindings*. The interaction component of my application consists of a single-input field. The form input binding has a single entry, as you see in Figure 8-1.

In the WIDL document that the WebMethods Toolkit is accumulating as I do this, the following entry is generated:

```
<BINDING NAME="HdInput" TYPE="INPUT">
 <VARIABLE
  NAME    = "HdCapacity"
  TYPE    = "String"
  FORMNAME = "HdCapacity" USAGE="DEFAULT"
  COMMENT=">" />
 </BINDING>
```

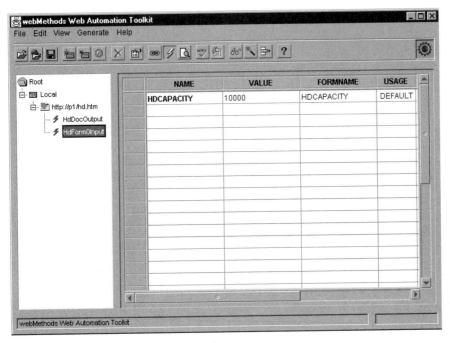

Figure 8–1   The form input binding

The other binding generated by the WebMethods Toolkit at this point lists all the component parts of the service HTML page. It has a lot more entries than the form input binding as the WebMethods Toolkit chops up the entire HTML page into its component parts and assigns *references* to each of them. These references can be used in code to locate each of the pieces. (The reference is simply the JavaScript object model syntax for accessing the component parts of an HTML document.) In the future, these references will be in the form standardized in the DOM (Document Object Model—see Chapter 15).

Figure 8–2 shows this binding displayed in the WebMethods Toolkit.

Next I need to create a *service* out of this HTML. I do so by selecting the lightning bolt icon from the Toolkit menu (see Figure 8–3).

The Toolkit can now perform an analogous job to generate an output binding. The following entry is added to the WIDL document.

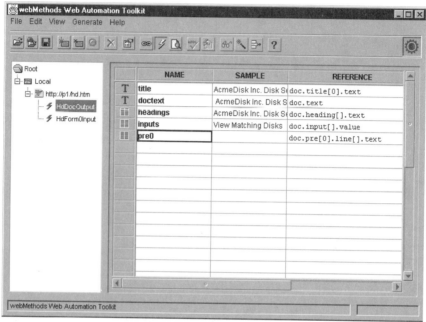

Figure 8–2   The full HTML document binding

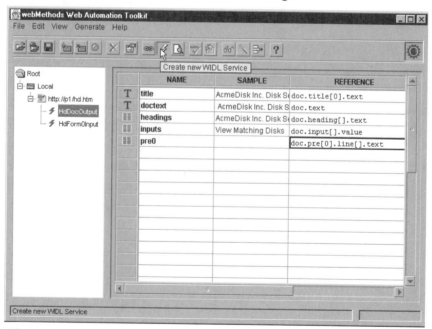

Figure 8–3   Creating a service

```
<BINDING NAME="HdOutput" TYPE="OUTPUT">
 <VARIABLE
  NAME     = "title"
  TYPE     = "String"
  REFERENCE= "doc.title[0].text"
  USAGE    = "DEFAULT" />
 <VARIABLE
  NAME     = "doctext"
  TYPE     = "String"
  REFERENCE= "doc.text"
  USAGE    = "DEFAULT" />
 <VARIABLE
  NAME     = "paragraphs"
  TYPE     = "String[]"
  REFERENCE= "doc.p[].text"
  USAGE    = "DEFAULT" />
 <VARIABLE
  NAME     = "table0"
  TYPE     = "String[][]"
  REFERENCE= "doc.table[0].tr[].th|td[].text"
  USAGE="DEFAULT" />
 </BINDING>
```

Notice how the HTML returned by activating the service has been analyzed and broken down into its constituent parts. Our primary interest will focus on the last variable above—the table of hard disk information returned by the service.

At this point, the Toolkit is all set to generate code. Having specified a name for the service and selected Java as the language, the Toolkit produces five files:

- A readme for the service
- A WIDL document describing the service
- A stand-alone Java program
- A Java applet
- An HTML document containing the Java applet

Once the Java programs are compiled into class files with a Java compiler, I can proceed directly to run the programs. Here is the command-line version in action:

```
C>jvc P1Hd
C>jview P1Hd 30000


************* Inputs ****************
HDCAPACITY = 30000
************* Outputs ***************
title = Selected Hard Disks
doctext =  Selected Hard Disks
headings =
  [0] Selected Hard Disks
table0 =
  [0][0] Name
  [0][1] Capacity
  [0][2] FFactor
  [1][0] Blaster 4
  [1][1] 50000
  [1][2] 3.5
  [2][0] Blaster 5
  [2][1] 60000
  [2][2] 5.0
  [3][0] Active Blaster 64
  [3][1] 32000
  [3][2] 3.5
```

I now have the shell of a stand-alone application for performing the interaction with the Hard Disk Selector. I can proceed to modify the program directly to, for example, simply list the hard disk data in some pretty format. More importantly, I can use Java's Object Oriented features to leave the generated program alone and develop a derived class with the required modifications. This option has the benefit that I can regenerate service code from the Toolkit without affecting my derived class.

The WebMethods Toolkit has generated code for this service as a Java applet. It has also created a little HTML document to host the applet for us. The generated HTML looks like Figure 8-4 prior to submitting a value for HDCAPACITY.

When the form is submitted, exactly the same output in Figure 8-4 appears in the applet window. The complete generated source code for this Java application is included at the end of this chapter.

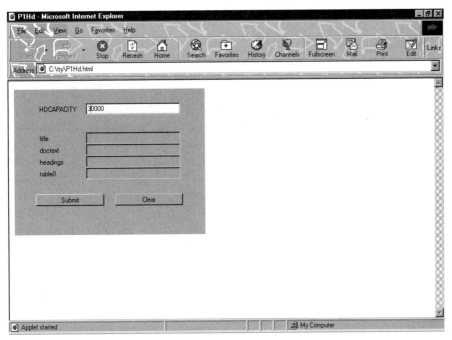

Figure 8–4   The HTML and applet generated by the WebMethods Toolkit

8.2 | The WIDL service definition document

You have already seen some snippets of the WIDL document generated by the Toolkit to describe the service. The full document appears here:

```
<?xml VERSION="1.0"?>
<!DOCTYPE WIDL SYSTEM "widl.dtd">
<WIDL NAME="P1" VERSION="2.0">
<!-- -------------------------------------- -->
<SERVICE
  NAME    = "Hd"
  METHOD  = "POST"
```

```
      URL       = "http://www.acmepc.com/hd.cfm"
      SOURCE    = "http://www.acmepc.com/hd.htm"
      INPUT     = "HdInput"
      OUTPUT    = "HdOutput" />


   <!-- ------------------------------------- -->
   <BINDING
     NAME    = "HdInput"
     TYPE    = "INPUT">
    <VARIABLE
     NAME    = "HDCAPACITY"
     TYPE    = "String"
     FORMNAME= "HDCAPACITY"
     USAGE   = "DEFAULT" />
   </BINDING>

   <BINDING
     NAME    = "HdOutput"
     TYPE    = "OUTPUT">
    <VARIABLE
     NAME    = "title"
     TYPE    = "String"
     REFERENCE= "doc.title[0].text"
     USAGE   = "DEFAULT" />
    <VARIABLE
     NAME    = "doctext"
     TYPE    = "String"
     REFERENCE= "doc.text"
     USAGE   = "DEFAULT" />
    <VARIABLE
     NAME    = "headings"
     TYPE    = "String[]"
     REFERENCE= "doc.heading[].text"
     USAGE   = "DEFAULT" />
    <VARIABLE
     NAME    = "table0"
     TYPE    = "String[][]"
     REFERENCE= "doc.table[0].tr[].th|td[].text"
     USAGE   = "DEFAULT" />
   </BINDING>
   <!-- ------------------------------------- -->
   </WIDL>
```

8.3 | Advantages of the WIDL approach

The most obvious advantage of the WIDL approach is *batch automation*. Even the little example in this chapter illustrates how WIDL can be used to quickly progress from an understanding of the requirements of an interactive Web-based service to a stand-alone program that automates interaction with the service. A number of other benefits are worth noting.

- **Browser independence:** Applications generated from WIDL specifications are independent of any one Web browser. Web automation can also be achieved by programmatically calling a Web browser, using OLE or DDE, for example. This approach ties the application to one browser and can limit performance as the entire interactive apparatus of the browser needs to be loaded into memory.

- **Dynamic loading of service information:** The WIDL notation captures information about a service—details such as where the service is, what the required input variables are, and so on. The applications generated using the WebMethods Toolkit load the WIDL definitions at run-time. Thus, if a service changes slightly, perhaps moving to a different URL, a simple modification to the WIDL document is all that is required. The application code does not need to be altered.

- **Protocol Transparency:** The WebMethods libraries look after all the details to do with implementing the HTTP protocol. Developers do not need to worry about manually implementing GET and POST, dealing with errors, and so on.

8.4 | Further capabilities of WIDL

I have only scratched the surface of WIDL here. Some of the other major features of WIDL include:

- **Error recovery:** Using condition elements, WIDL allows you to specify which set of output bindings to use for a successful interaction and a failed interaction. If an interaction fails, you might, for example, seek to interact with a different service at some other Web address.
- **Service chains:** You can arrange for the output data generated by a service to form part of the input of another service. For example, the URLs returned by a search engine can be fed into the service that connects to each of these URLs.

8.5 | The complete Java program for the Disk Selector Service

Here is the full Java source code generated by the WebMethods Toolkit for the Disk Selector Service.

```
import java.io.*;
import watt.api.*;

public class P1Hd extends Object
{
 public String  HDCAPACITY;

 public  String  title;
 public  String  doctext;
 public  String[]  headings;
 public  String[][] table0;
```

```java
public void   setHDCAPACITY (String HDCAPACITY)
  { this.HDCAPACITY = HDCAPACITY; }
public String getHDCAPACITY() { return HDCAPACITY; }

public String  gettitle() { return title; }
public String  getdoctext() { return doctext; }
public String[]   getheadings() { return headings; }
public String[][] gettable0() { return table0; }

//
// DEPLOYMENT CONSTRUCTOR
//
// Use this constructor to deploy the service class.
//
// Invoke this constructor from your application
// after creating a "Context"
// object and setting the remote Server and port:
//
// Context context = new Context(true);
// context.connect("your.server.com:5555",
// UserID, UserPassword);
//
// The constructor assumes the WIDL document
// P1.widl is managed by the
// Web Automation Server to which you
// are connecting.
// However, you may load a local
// WIDL file, such as
//
// context.loadDocument("P1.widl");
//
// You may also read from a properties
// file by calling
//
// Config.loadProperties(
//     new FileInputStream(ConfigFilePath));
//
public P1Hd(
    Context context,
    String HDCAPACITY
    ) throws IOException, WattException,
    WattServiceException
{
 Result  result;
 String args[][] = {
```

```
 {"HDCAPACITY", HDCAPACITY}
 };
 result = context.invokeService("P1","Hd", args);
 getValues(result);
}


//
// DEVELOPMENT CONSTRUCTOR
//
// This constructor and main() may be used
// for command-line testing of this
// service class. The main() method
// allows you to specify command-line
// options, such as a remote Web Automation Server:
//
//    -server <your.server.com>:<port>
//
// If none is specified, the constructor
// attempts to connect to "localhost:5555".
// Use the constructor above to deploy the service class.
//
public P1Hd(
    String HDCAPACITY
) throws IOException, WattException, WattServiceException
{
 String args[][] = {
  {"HDCAPACITY", HDCAPACITY}
 };

 Context context = null;
 Result  result;
 String server = null;

 context = new Context(true);
 try {
  //
  // Connect to server
  //
  server = Config.getServer();
  if (server == null)
   server = "localhost:5555";
  context.connect(server, null, null);
 } catch (WattException e) {
  System.out.println("\n\tUnable to connect to server \""
     + server + "\"");
```

```
  System.exit(0);
 }

 context.loadDocument("P1.widl");
 result = context.invokeService("P1", "Hd", args);
 getValues(result);
 context.disconnect();
}

public static void main(String args[])
{
 int i = 0;
 String HDCAPACITY;

 // Server specified here
 args = Config.processCmdLine(args);

 if (args.length < 1)
 {
  System.err.println("\n\tYou must specify 1 arguments for
    this Service\n");
  System.exit(0);
 }

 HDCAPACITY = args[i++];

 try
 {
  P1Hd o = new P1Hd(
          HDCAPACITY
        );
  System.out.println("\n****** Inputs ******");
  System.out.println("HDCAPACITY = " + HDCAPACITY);
  System.out.println("\n****** Outputs *****");
  System.out.println("title = " + o.title);
  System.out.println("doctext = " + o.doctext);
  System.out.println("headings = ");
  printArray(o.headings);
  System.out.println("table0 = ");
  printTable(o.table0);
 } catch (IOException e) {
 System.err.println(e);
 } catch (WattServiceException e) {
 System.err.println(e);
```

```
 } catch (WattException e) {
 System.err.println(e);
 }
}

private void getValues(Result r) throws WattException
{
 title = r.getField("title");
 doctext = r.getField("doctext");
 headings  = r.getFieldArray("headings");
 table0   = r.getFieldTable("table0");
}

public static void printArray(String array[])
{
 if (array == null)
  return;
 for (int i=0; i < array.length; i++)
   System.out.println("\t[" + i + "] " + array[i]);
}

public static void printTable(String table[][])
{
 if (table == null)
  return;
 for (int i=0; i < table.length; i++)
  for (int j=0; j<table[i].length; j++)
   System.out.println("\t[" + i +"]" + "[" + j + "] "
   + table[i][j]);
 }
}
```

Push Publishing with CDF (Channel Definition Format)

- Creating a simple channel
- Adding items to a channel
- Channel scheduling
- Personalization

9

T he Channel Definition Format (CDF) for push publishing is an integral part of the Internet Explorer Version 4 browser from Microsoft. In this chapter, we will create a newswire push channel for acmepc.com. We will start with a simple channel and then expand it to include the Acme Hard Disk Selector developed in Chapter 7. As you saw in chapter 7, the hard disk selector is in fact a CGI application that dynamically queries a Microsoft Access database. However, as far as push publishing is concerned, it is just another resource that can be added to a channel.

9.1 | A simple channel

Our simple channel will consist of two HTML files. The first will be the main page for the channel, the second, will contain details of current special offers. We can create these completely independent of worrying about how they will be fused into a channel. The two HTML files are shown here:

```
C>type acmepc.htm

<HTML>
<HEAD>
<TITLE>The AcmePC Newswire</TITLE>
</HEAD>
<BODY>
<H1>The AcmePC Newswire</H1>
<P>
Need a faster PC? Check out the current special offers
<a href = "offers.htm">here</a>
</HTML>

C>type offers.htm

<HTML>
<HEAD>
<TITLE>Special Offers from AcmePC</TITLE
</HEAD>
<BODY>
<H1>Special Offers from AcmePC</H1>
<P>
Blaster 555. Only $955 dollars!
</HTML>
```

The description of a channel in CDF consists of the main Web page (the **channel** element) and zero or more subsidiary pages (known as **item** elements). We could just author a CDF file by hand using the DTD provided in the standard but there is an easier way. To create the simple channel for acmepc.com we will use the cdfgen editing tool from Microsoft (available on the accompanying CD). Selecting New from the File menu starts the channel creation wizard as shown in Figure 9–1.

The first task is to specify the top-level HTML file for the channel. The Wizard allows us to specify a title and an abstract for the channel as shown in Figure 9–2.

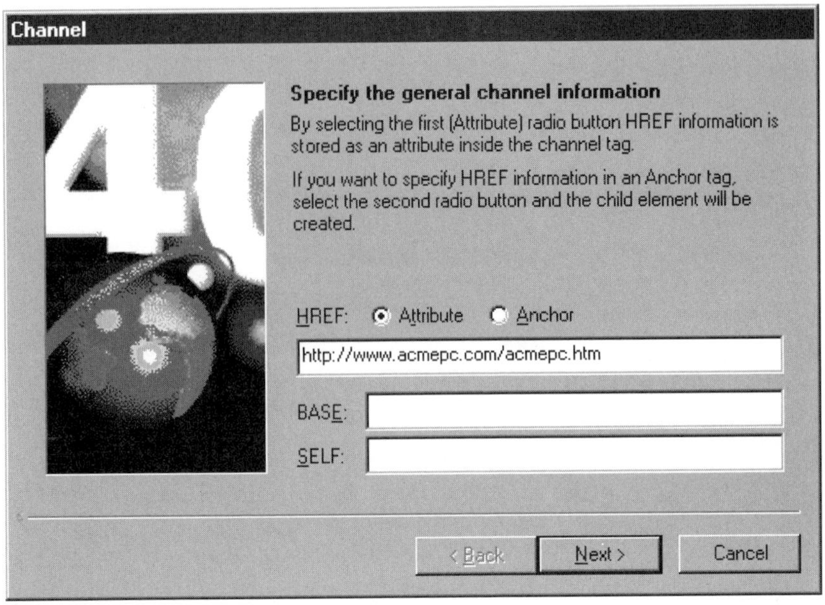

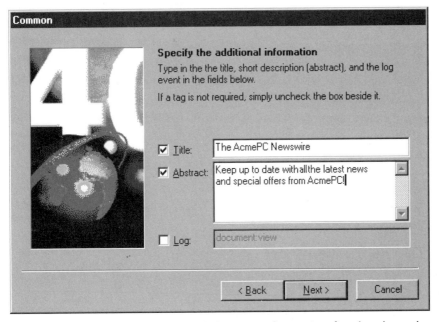

Figure 9–1   Creating a channel with the channel wizard

Figure 9–2   Specifying title and abstract information for the channel

Channels can have associated icons that will appear in the users channel lists. We will simply skip icons for our application by unchecking the icon box as shown in Figure 9–3.

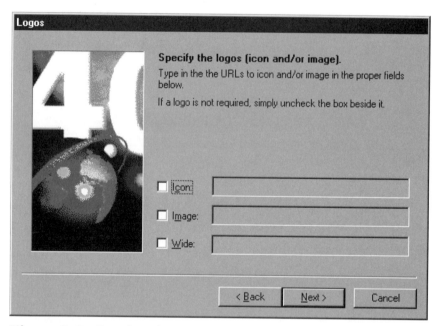

Figure 9–3   Specifying logos and background images for channels

Channels can have complex scheduling information associated with them to allow fine control over when and how a channel is updated. In our simple application we will simply disable scheduling as shown in Figure 9–4.

We can arrange that activity on the channel is logged to a specified filename. With Internet Explorer, this logging information can continue to be gathered even when the user is browsing the channel off-line. We will ask for a file called "log" to be created for this purpose (see Figure 9–5).

Finally, the wizard displays the CDF it has generated for us as shown in Figure 9–6.

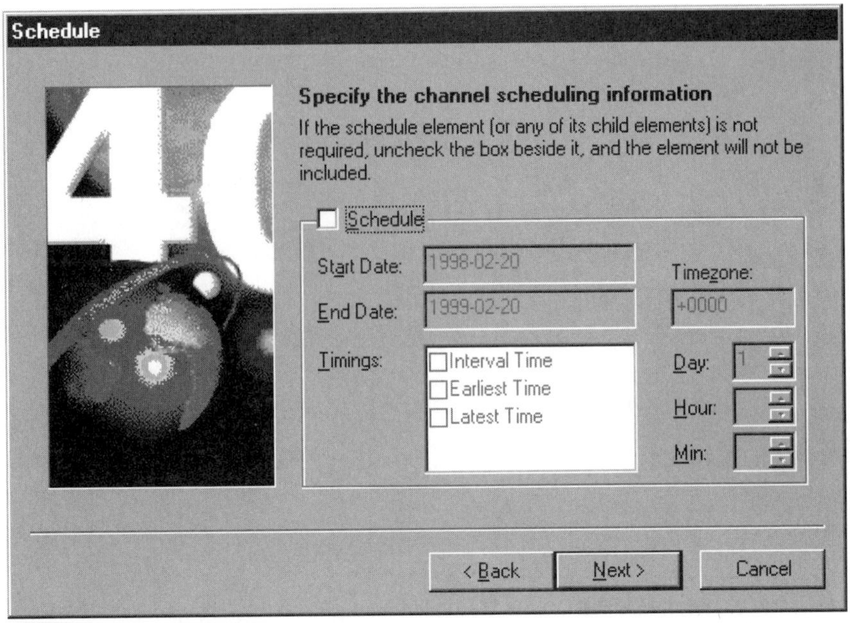

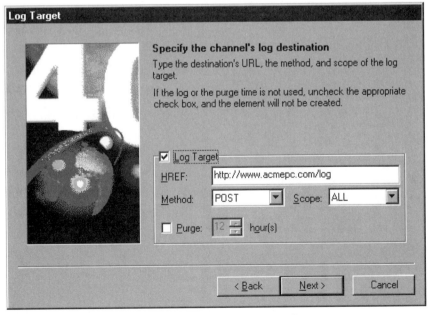

Figure 9–4 Specifying scheduling information for the channel

Figure 9–5 Specifying a log file for the channel

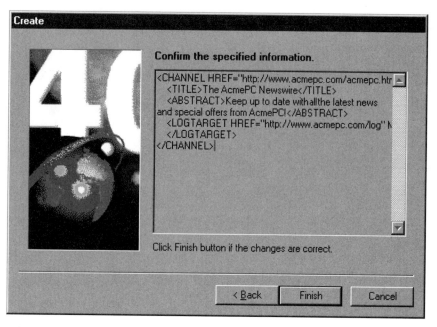

Figure 9–6   The CDF generated by the wizard

This completes the wizard and we can now look at the channel in a hierarchical view within the core cdfgen editing tool. The channel so far looks like Figure 9–7.

So far, the channel consists of a single HTML file http://www.acmepc.com/acmepc.htm. We need to insert the offers.htm HTML file. We do this by selecting the item element under the tag menu as shown in Figure 9–8.

This launches a second wizard for channel item creation. The first step is to specify the URL for the channel item as shown in Figure 9–9.

Items can have associated titles and abstracts. The next screen in the wizard allows us to fill them in as shown in Figure 9–10.

From here, the wizard prompts for icon information as before. We will simply disable the use of icons. When the wizard finishes, the hierarchical view of the channel looks like Figure 9–11.

That is about it! We can now save this CDF file. We will call it acmepc.cdf. Here it is as saved out of the cdfgen editing tool with the exception of some pretty printing on my part:

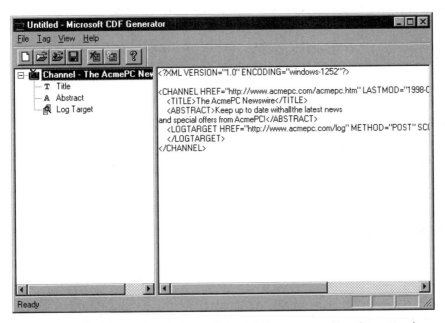

Figure 9–7   Hierarchical view of the CDF generated by the wizard

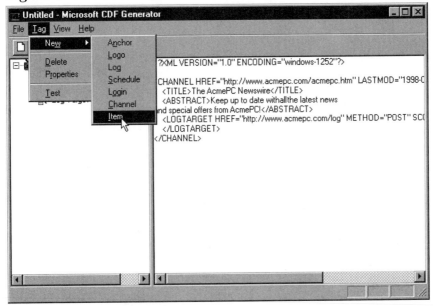

Figure 9–8   Creating an item within a channel

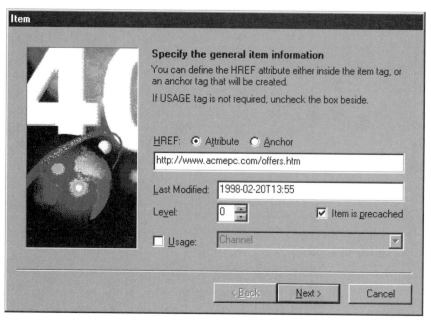

Figure 9–9 Specifying a URL for an item within a channel

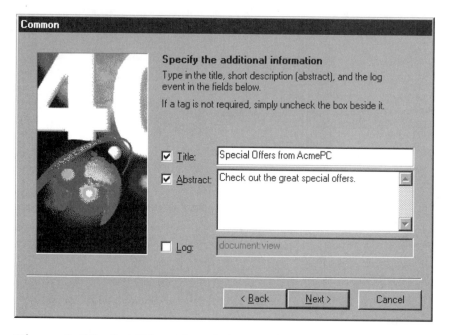

Figure 9–10 Specifying title and abstract information for a channel item

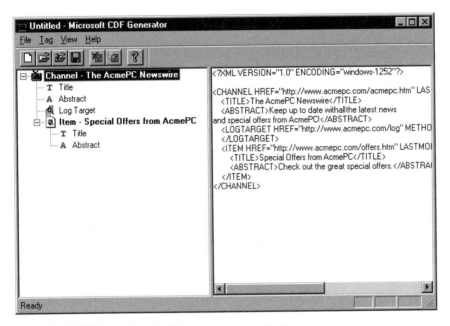

Figure 9–11   Hierarchical view of the full channel

```
C>type cdfgen.cdf

<?XML VERSION="1.0" ENCODING="windows-1252"?>

<CHANNEL
 HREF    = "http://www.acmepc.com/acmepc.htm"
 LASTMOD = "1998-02-20T13:32"
 PRECACHE= "YES"
 LEVEL   = "0">
<TITLE>The AcmePC Newswire</TITLE>
<ABSTRACT>
Keep up to date with all the latest news
and special offers from AcmePC!
</ABSTRACT>
<LOGTARGET
 HREF    = "http://www.acmepc.com/log"
 METHOD = "POST" SCOPE="ALL">
</LOGTARGET>
<ITEM
 HREF    = "http://www.acmepc.com/offers.htm"
 LASTMOD= "1998-02-20T13:55"
```

```
PRECACHE= "YES"
LEVEL   = "0">
<TITLE>Special Offers from AcmePC</TITLE>
<ABSTRACT>
Check out the great special offers.
</ABSTRACT>
 </ITEM>
</CHANNEL>
```

All that remains to do be done is to store this file on the http://www.acmepc.com Web site. Figure 9–12 shows what happens when the URL for the cdf file is entered into the address box in Internet Explorer 4.

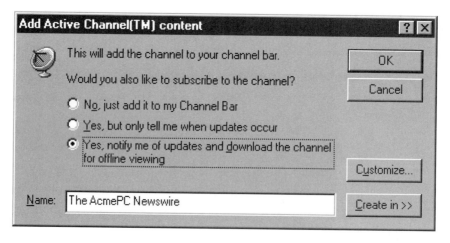

Figure 9–12   Hierarchical view of the full channel

Note the options that allow you to control how and when the channel is updated. We will run with the default option. Clicking OK causes the AcmePC channel to be added to the list of channels as shown in Figure 9–13.

Note how the special offers item appears as a child of the main channel of the left. Clicking the item has exactly the same effect as clicking the hypertext link. The special offers page will be loaded (Figure 9–14).

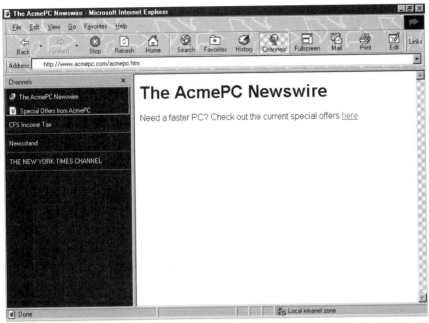

Figure 9–13   The AcmePC Channel installed in Internet Explorer 4

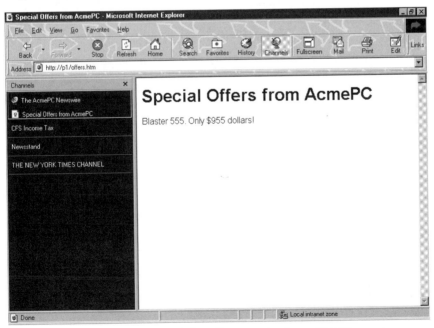

Figure 9–14   The Special Offers Page in the AcmePC Channel

9.2 | Adding a new item to the channel

Adding a new HTML page to the channel is as as simple as adding a
new item element to the CDF file. To show how easy it is we will do it
here directly with the CDF file as opposed to using cdfgen. For fun, we
will add the database publishing CGI script developed in Chapter 7 to
the channel. The new channel item is shown in bold below.

```
C>type acmepc.cdf

<?XML VERSION="1.0" ENCODING="windows-1252"?>

<CHANNEL
  HREF    = "http:www.acmepc.com/acmepc.htm"
  LASTMOD = "1998-02-20T13:32"
  PRECACHE= "YES"
  LEVEL   = "0">
<TITLE>The AcmePC Newswire</TITLE>
<ABSTRACT>
Keep up to date with all the latest news
and special offers from AcmePC!
</ABSTRACT>
<LOGTARGET
  HREF  = "http://www.acmepc.com/log"
  METHOD= "POST"
  SCOPE = "ALL">
</LOGTARGET>
<ITEM
  HREF    = "http://www.acmepc.com/offers.htm"
  LASTMOD = "1998-02-20T13:55"
  PRECACHE= "YES"
  LEVEL   = "0">
<TITLE>Special Offers from AcmePC</TITLE>
<ABSTRACT>Check out the great special offers.</ABSTRACT>
</ITEM>
<ITEM
  HREF="http://www.acmepc.com/scripts/hd.py">
<TITLE>AcmeDisk Inc Hard Disks</TITLE>
<ABSTRACT>
AcmeDisk Inc Hard Disks
</ABSTRACT>
</ITEM>
</CHANNEL>
```

By choosing the channel refresh option in Internet Explorer we can get the browser to connect to acmepc.com and download the updated CDF file. The result is an extra item beneath the AcmePC channel. Clicking this page shows all the hard disks from AcmeDisk Inc.

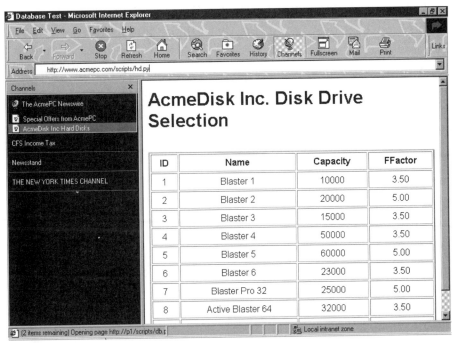

Figure 9–15   Using a CGI Script within channel

Whenever a user who has subscribed to this channel updates their content, it will cause a fresh invocation of the CGI script which will convert the flat database to XML and via the magic of XMLDSO, generate an HTML table of hard disk data.

9.3 | Scheduling

Using the **schedule** element in CDF, publishers can exert fine control over how Internet Explorer determines that the content of a channel needs to be updated. The schedule shown below tells Internet Explorer that the channel needs to be updated once every seven days. The actual time Internet Explorer performs the update will be somewhere between 1 and 5 a.m. The actual time is picked at random within the specified time range in order to ensure that the server does not get update requests from multiple subscribers all at the same time.

```
<SCHEDULE>
<IntervalTime Day  = "7"/>
<EarliestTime Hour = "1"/>
<LatestTime   Hour = "5"/>
</SCHEDULE>
```

Channels can be made to automatically expire by adding a STOP-DATE attribute. In this example the channel is updated every four hours at some random time between the first and fourth hour. Updates to the channel stop completely on new years eve, 1999.

```
<SCHEDULE STOPDATE = "1999-12-31">
 <IntervalTime Hour = "4"/>
 <EarliestTime Hour = "1"/>
 <LatestTime Hour   = "4"/>
</SCHEDULE>
```

9.4 | Personalization

Channels can easily be customized for individual users using server-side scripting and cookies. Instead of simply returning a CDF file when the user tries to subscribe to a channel, a form could be generated allowing the user to provide their personal information and preferences. A CDF file can then be generated based on these preferences and returned to the browser.

Note also, that a channel is simply a collection of Web pages. Anything you can do on a Web page you can do in a channel page. For example, instead of running a noninteractive CGI application to return hard disk information we could present the user with an interactive HTML form as part of the channel.

Developing XML Utility Programs

XML documents lend themselves to automated processing of all kinds. In an environment with perhaps many hundred of megabytes of XML, being able to quickly develop utility programs is very important to help manage the documents. Some examples include:

- Generating a report with just the invoice date and amount, sorted by amount
- Counting the number of times the **warning** element is used in the technical manuals
- Changing all the telephone numbers with the "01" prefix to the new prefix "071"
- Dropping all the prices for hard disks quoted in the catalog by 10%

In this chapter, I look at some tools and techniques for developing such utility programs. They can be broadly categorized into two classes: utilities that need to change the information in XML docu-

ments (read/write utilities) and those that do not (read-only utilities).
Different approaches are called for in each case.

10.1 | The ESIS parser output format

In this chapter and throughout the later chapters of the book, you
come across the EsisDemo application that ships with the Ælfred
parser. The word "ESIS" officially stands for "Element Structure
Information Set" and is defined as part of the SGML standard. In
practice, ESIS usually refers to a particular representation of the standard ESIS that can be produced by some SGML parsers (such as nsgmls) from SGML documents. That is how I use the term in this book.
The EsisDemo application produces a similar output notation from
XML documents that nsgmls produces from SGML documents.

ESIS is a very simple, line-oriented format, that is convenient for
viewing the effects of the SGML/XML parsing process and also for
feeding input into SGML/XML utility programs.

```
C>type invoice.xml

<!-- This is an invoice -->
<invoice>
<?progress "processing invoices"?>
<name id = "A1234">Joe Bloggs</name>
</invoice>

C>jview EsisDemo invoice.xml

(invoice
-\n
?progress "processing invoices"
-\n
A idA1234
(name
-Joe Bloggs
)name
-\n
)invoice
```

Some things to note about the output format:

- Each important "event" in the XML, such as starting at element, ending an element, etc., appears as a single line of output.
- Lines starting with "(" denote the start of an element
- Lines starting with ")" denote the end of an element
- Lines starting with "A" denote an attribute and its value
- Lines starting with "-" denote character data
- Lines starting with "?" denote a processing instruction
- Some markup constructs such as comments are not part of the output at all.
- Special characters such as newlines are escaped, i.e., the newline character appears as "\n."

10.2 | To parse or not to parse—that is the question

The plain-text nature of XML documents makes them very easy to work with using a whole variety of tools, from editors to pattern matchers to scripting languages. For example, a great convenience is being able to use command-line utilities such as grep to do simple searches and counts of patterns in XML documents. Some care needs to be taken to ensure that such tools do not produce erroneous answers. To illustrate the issues, consider the task of counting **name** elements in the following document:

```
C>type cat.xml

<?xml version = "1.0"?>
<PCS>
 <PC>
    <NAME>Acme Blaster</NAME>
    <CAPACITY>100</CAPACITY>
```

```
        <PRICE>2000</PRICE>
    </PC>
    <PC>
        <NAME>Speedy PC</NAME>
        <CAPACITY>200</CAPACITY>
        <PRICE>4000</PRICE>
    </PC>
    <PC>
        <NAME>Gonzo PC</NAME>
        <CAPACITY>300</CAPACITY>
        <PRICE>5000</PRICE>
    </PC>
</PCS>
```

Using the ubiquitous grep utility, you might count the name elements like this:

```
C>grep -c "<NAME>" cat.xml

File cat.xml:
3 lines match
```

This is the right answer. However, a variety of markup variations that can legitimately appear in an XML document can lead to problems with the simple grep approach. Consider this document:

```
C>type cat1.xml

<?xml version = "1.0"?>
<PCS>
 <PC>
    <!-- The <NAME> element contains the name of the
    PC -->
    <NAME>Acme Blaster</NAME>
    <CAPACITY>100</CAPACITY>
    <PRICE>2000</PRICE>
 </PC>
 <PC>
    <NAME    >Speedy PC</NAME>
    <CAPACITY>200</CAPACITY>
    <PRICE>4000</PRICE>
 </PC>
 <PC>
    <NAME>Gonzo PC</NAME>
    <CAPACITY>300</CAPACITY>
    <PRICE>5000</PRICE>
```

```
</PC>
</PCS>

C>grep -c "<NAME>" cat.xml

File cat.xml:
3 lines match
```

Again we get three lines that match, but this grep has arrived at the right answer for the wrong reasons. The first hit on the pattern, "<NAME>," has come about due to the string occurring within an XML comment—a false positive hit. The start-tag with the trailing white space "<NAME >," is missed—a false negative hit.

The use of entities in XML documents can further complicate matters for simple-minded pattern matching. Consider the following document:

```
C>type cat3.xml

<?xml version = "1.0"?>
<!DOCTYPE PCS [
<!ENTITY cap100 "<CAPACITY>100</CAPACITY>">
]>
<PCS>
 <PC>
    <NAME>Acme Blaster</NAME>
    &cap100;
    <PRICE>2000</PRICE>
 </PC>
 <PC>
    <NAME>Speedy PC</NAME>
    &cap100;
    <PRICE>4000</PRICE>
 </PC>
 <PC>
    <NAME>Gonzo PC</NAME>
    <CAPACITY>300</CAPACITY>
    <PRICE>5000</PRICE>
 </PC>
</PCS>

C>grep "<CAPACITY>" cat3.xml

File cat3.xml:
2 lines match
```

The problem here is caused by the fact that the replacement text of entities can contain markup. Here is another example. The following XML catalog document contains a PC named "<CAPACITY> Max":

```
C>type cat4.xml

<?xml version = "1.0"?>
<PCS>
<PC>
<NAME>
<![CDATA[ <CAPACITY> Max]]>
</NAME>
<CAPACITY>300</CAPACITY>
<PRICE>5000</PRICE>
</PC>
</PCS>
```

As a final example of a "gotcha," remember that many utilities in the grep category work on a line-by-line basis. Consider the following document:

```
C>type cat6.xml

<?xml version = "1.0"?>
<PCS>
<PC>
<NAME>Foo PC</NAME><PRICE>5000</PRICE><NAME>Bar PC
</NAME>
<PRICE>6000</PRICE>
</PC>
</PCS>

C>grep "<NAME>" cat6.xml

File cat6.xml:
1 lines match
```

This grep has registered the two occurrences of the **name** element on one line as a single hit. Also, some grep programs have limits on the lengths of lines they process. Remember that XML documents can have arbitrarily long lines!

The bottom line is that if you are going to process XML with non-XML-aware tools such as grep in this fashion, you need to examine carefully your XML for problem areas such as the ones I have illustrated in this section. The problem with examining the XML is that it is rather time consuming when you have hundreds of megabytes of it! Even if visual inspection leads you to believe that none of these scenarios are relevant, who knows what perfectly valid constructs might appear in your XML in the future, thus silently breaking your programs?

The moral of the story is this: "if in doubt, parse it out." All of the problems illustrated earlier in this section go away if the XML is parsed *prior* to processing with grep-like tools. Here is a version of the catalog that combines all the earlier problem scenarios into a single document:

```
C>type cat7.xml

<?xml version = "1.0"?>
<!DOCTYPE PCS [
<!ENTITY cap100 "<CAPACITY>100</CAPACITY>">
]>
<PCS>
<PC>
<!-- The <NAME> element contains the name of the PC -
  -->
<NAME    >Foo PC</NAME>
<CAPACITY>300</CAPACITY><PRICE>5000</PRICE>
<NAME>Bar PC</NAME>&cap100;<PRICE>10</PRICE></
   PC><PC><NAME>
<![CDATA[ <CAPACITY> Max]]>
</NAME>
</PC>
</PCS>
```

The output of the EsisDemo example application of the Ælfred parser for this document looks like this:

```
C>jview EsisDemo cat7.xml
(PCS
-\n
(PC
-\n\n
(NAME
-Foo PC
)NAME
```

```
-\n
(CAPACITY
-300
)CAPACITY
(PRICE
-5000
)PRICE
-\n
(NAME
-Bar PC
)NAME
(CAPACITY
-100
)CAPACITY
(PRICE
-10
)PRICE
)PC
(PC
(NAME
-\n <CAPACITY> Max\n
)NAME
-\n
)PC
-\n
.)PCS
```

Now, getting correct answers with grep is straightforward. Here is the command to find the number of **name** elements:

```
C>jview EsisDemo cat7.xml | grep -c "^\(NAME$"
File STDIN:
3 lines match
```

Note the use of the "^" and "$" characters, which, in my version of grep, restrict the pattern to match only at the start and end of a line. The EsisDemo application outputs each event communicated to it from the parser as a single line, the first character of which indicates what type of event it is. The "(" character will only ever appear at the start of a line when the line represents a start-element event. Hooking these start-of-line characters with grep is thus guaranteed to produce the right answer.

10.3 | Read-only utilities

Suppose the developers at acmepc.com have been asked by the marketing department for a spreadsheet listing the names of all PCs selling for less than $5000 in the acmepc catalog. How would they proceed? I illustrate four ways:

- The XSL style sheet language
- The Perl scripting language
- The Python scripting language
- Java using the Ælfred XML parser

For ease of reference, here is the XML document with which I work:

```
C>type cat.xml

<?xml version = "1.0"?>
<PCS>
 <PC>
    <NAME>Acme Blaster</NAME>
    <CAPACITY>100</CAPACITY>
    <PRICE>2000</PRICE>
 </PC>
 <PC>
    <NAME>Speedy PC</NAME>
    <CAPACITY>200</CAPACITY>
    <PRICE>4000</PRICE>
 </PC>
 <PC>
    <NAME>Gonzo PC</NAME>
    <CAPACITY>300</CAPACITY>
    <PRICE>5000</PRICE>
 </PC>
</PCS>
```

10.3.1 *The XSL style sheet language*

XSL incorporates ECMAScript, which, in the Microsoft implementation, has been extended with a useful **println** function that can be used to generate output directly to the screen rather than into, say, an HTML page. This output can be easily redirected into a file or piped into another application. At the moment, this is the only way to do plain-text output with XSL. In the future, I hope that XSL will provide a plain-text flow object that can be used instead of the println extension. Replacing println with a plain-text flow object has the added benefit of avoiding some rather technical "gotchas" that can occur when output is created other than via a flow object construction.

These caveats aside, I believe XSL will prove very useful for developing XML utility applications. In the absence of a plain-text flow object from the current XSL proposal, I use the **println** function in this section.

The following style sheet does not generate any HTML or other form of typeset output. Your sole interest is in the screen output it generates with the **println** function.

```
C>type report.xsl

<xsl>
<rule>
  <target-element type = "PRICE"/>
  <eval><![CDATA[
  if (parseInt(this.text) < 5000)
    {
    println (this.text + ":" + this.parent.chil-
  dren.item ("NAME",0).text)
    }
  ]]></eval>
</rule>
</xsl>
```

This style sheet produces no output whatsoever other than lines on standard output. The command to invoke the style-sheet processing looks like this:

```
C>msxsl -i cat.xml -s report.xsl

2000:Acme Blaster
4000:Speedy PC
```

Note that the output contains only details on PCs selling for less than 5000 dollars, as desired. Note also that I have chosen to output the data with ":" characters to separate the fields. This notation is readily imported into spreadsheet programs. You will readily appreciate that the power inherent in XSL for specifying *context* can be very useful in this sort of reporting application. For example, expressing "do this when a **foo** element occurs within a **bar** element with an attribute named **baz** set to 42" is trivially easy in XSL.

Note also that the plain-text generating capability means I can also use XSL as a data-harvesting application for generating more XML. This little style sheet outputs an XML document in which all the **price** elements from the original reappear as empty **cost** elements with a value attribute set to the original price.

```
C>type report1.xsl

<xsl>
<rule>
        <target-element type = "PRICE"/>
        <eval><![CDATA[
        println ("<COST dollars = " + "\"" +
this.text + "\">")
        ]]></eval>
</rule>
</xsl>
```

Here is the command to apply this style sheet to the catalog, as well as the output generated:

```
C>msxsl -i cat.xml -s report11.xsl

<COST dollars = "2000">
<COST dollars = "4000">
<COST dollars = "5000">
```

In the future, XSL may well have an XML *flow object*. This will allow us to avoid the plain-text output phase and proceed directly to creating an XML tree as the output of the "formatting" process.

10.3.2   *The Perl scripting language*

Perl is arguably the world's most popular general-purpose, text-processing language. Fully fledged XML parsers can, and doubtless will, be developed in Perl. However, the line-oriented notation output by the EsisDemo application of the Ælfred parser is very well suited for processing in Perl. Here is a Perl script that will generate the required spreadsheet report by processing the output produced by EsisDemo:

```
C>type report.pl

while (<STDIN>) {
        if (/^\(NAME/) {
                $name = substr(<STDIN>,1);
                chop ($name);
        }
        elsif (/^\(PRICE/) {
                $price = substr(<STDIN>,1);
                chop ($price);
                if ($price < 5000) {
                        print $price,":",$name,"\n"
                }
        }
}

C>jview EsisDemo cat.xml  | perl report.pl

2000:Acme Blaster
4000:Speedy PC
```

In this example, I have processed the ESIS notation from Ælfred directly. You can straightforwardly develop a general-purpose ESIS-handling library in Perl that deals with a lot of the ESIS housekeeping chores and allows you to concentrate on the task at hand. I show how to develop such an ESIS handling library in Perl, Python and C++ programming languages in my book *ParseMe.1st: SGML for Software Developers.*[1] One very popular technique for processing XML is to use an event-driven style in which handler functions are declared that are

---

1. ISBN 0-13-488967-3

called for particular events such as the start of an element, the end of an element, and so on. This little event-driven application outputs only the data content that occurs beneath **name** elements. It uses a little ESIS processing library I discuss a little later:

```
C>type report1.pl
require 'esis.pl';

$Output = 0;

sub start_NAME {
        $Output = 1;
}

sub end_NAME {
        $Output = 0;
}

sub data {
        if ($Output eq 1) {
                print "$_\n";
        }
}

&esis();
```

The ESIS library included on line 1 looks after interpreting the ESIS output. When it sees a start-element event for an element **foo,** it looks to see whether a function has been provided to handle it named **start_foo**. A similar process occurs for an end-element event. When it encounters data, it calls the **data** function if one has been defined. Here is how this application works:

1. The ESIS handling library is loaded.
2. Handler functions are defined for the start and end of **name** elements. When a **name** element starts, the $Output flag is set to true. When a **name** element ends, the $Output flag is set to false.

3. A data event handler is defined. It uses the value of the $Output flag to determine whether it should print the chunk of data.

4. The library is invoked by the code "&esis();". This causes the ESIS input to be processed and function calls dispatched to the relevant handler functions.

The ESIS library is very straightforward. Here it is:

```
C>type esis.pl

# Simple ESISDemo Event Dispatcher
sub esis {
  while (<STDIN>) {
      chop;
      $command = substr($_, 0, 1);
      substr($_, 0, 1) = "";
      if ($command eq '(') {
    $call = "start_".$_;
    if (defined &$call) {
       &$call($_,@Attributes);
    }
    @Attributes=();
      }
      elsif ($command eq ')') {
    $call = "end_".$_;
    if (defined &$call) {
       &$call($_);
    }
      }
      elsif ($command eq '-') {
    if (defined &data) {
       &data($_);
    }
      }
      elsif ($command eq 'A') {
    push (@Attributes , $_);
      }
      else {
    warn "Unknown ESIS Event $command\n";
      }
  }
}
1;
```

This little library is particularly useful for handling attributes as it accumulates the attributes for an element and passes them in an array structure into the start-element event handlers. To illustrate attribute handling, consider the task of generating a report of all customer **id** attributes from the following XML document:

```
C>type cust.xml

<?xml version = "1.0"?>
<Customers>
<Customer id = "c124">
 <Name>Joe Bloggs</Name>
 <Reference id = "abcd"/>
</Customer>
<Customer id = "c567">
 <Name>A. Another</Name>
 <Reference id = "efgh"/>
</Customer>
</Customers>
```

A simple grep treatment of the id attributes will not work because both **Reference** and **Customer** elements have **id** attributes. Here is the perl script that does the job:

```
C>type report3.pl

require 'esis.pl';

sub start_Customer {
        print "$_[1]\n";
}

&esis();

C>jview EsisDemo cust.xml | perl report3.pl

id      c124
id      c567
```

Note that this script works because **Customer** elements have a single attribute. If they had multiple attributes, we would have to be more careful, because the order in which attributes are assigned values in XML documents is never significant. That is, the **id** attribute could appear first in the array or third in the array, depending on the number of attributes and the order in which they appear in the XML document. A more robust approach would be to use Perl's powerful associative array capabilities to store the attributes. That way an attribute can be referenced directly using something like $_[1]{"id"}. Implementing this is left as a fun exercise for the Perl hackers out there!

10.3.3   *Using Python as a reporting tool*

Python (http://www.python.org) is a very easy-to-use, freely available programming language that is well suited to developing XML processing utilities. Direct support for XML in Python is currently under development. As is the case with Perl, Python is well suited to processing ESIS style information. Here is a Python script that generates the required spreadsheet report form cust.xml:

```
C>type report.py
NamePattern  = re.compile ("^\(NAME")
PricePattern = re.compile ("^\(PRICE")

l = sys.stdin.readline()
while (l):
        if NamePattern.match (l):
                l = sys.stdin.readline()
                Name = l[1:-1]
        elif PricePattern.match (l):
                l = sys.stdin.readline()
                Price = l[1:-1]
                if string.atoi(Price) < 5000:
                        print "%s:%s" % (Price,Name)
        l = sys.stdin.readline()

C>jview EsisDemo cust.xml | python report.py

2000:Acme Blaster
4000:Speedy PC
```

10.3.4   *Using Java as a reporting tool*

The EsisDemo application of the Ælfred XML parser that I have used throughout this chapter is a very simple event-driven application built on top of the core XML parser. Here it is in its entirety:

```
C>type EsisDemo.java

import com.microstar.xml.*;
import java.io.*;
import java.util.*;

public class reporter extends XmlApp {
  public static void main (String args[])
    throws Exception
  {
    doParse(args[0], new reporter());
  }

  public void attribute (XmlParser p, String aname,
        String value, boolean isSpecified)
  {
    displayText("A " + aname + '\t' + value);
  }

  public void startElement (XmlParser p, String name)
  {
    displayText("(" + name);
  }

  public void endElement (XmlParser p, String name)
  {
    displayText(")" + name);
  }

  public void charData (XmlParser p, char ch[], int
  length)
  {
    displayText("-" + escape(ch, length));
  }

  public void processingInstruction (XmlParser p,
  String target,
              char ch[], int length)
```

```
      {
        displayText("?" + target + ' ' +
      escape(ch,length));
      }
    }
```

Even if you do not naturally think of Java as a language in which you would develop XML reporting applications, you may well be surprised how easy it can be. Here is the report generator for cust.xml in Java using the Ælfred parser:

```
C>type reporter.jav

import com.microstar.xml.*;
import java.io.*;
import java.util.*;

public class reporter extends XmlApp {
  boolean InName = false;
  boolean InPrice = false;
  String CurrentName = "";
  int CurrentPrice = 0;

  public static void main (String args[])
    throws Exception
  {
    doParse(args[0], new reporter());
  }

  public void startElement (XmlParser p, String name)
  {
    if (name.equals ("NAME"))
  InName = true;
    if (name.equals ("PRICE"))
  InPrice = true;
  }

  public void endElement (XmlParser p, String name)
  {
    if (name.equals ("NAME")==true)
  InName = false;
    if (name.equals ("PRICE")==true)
  InPrice = false;
    if (name.equals ("PC")==true) {
  if (CurrentPrice < 5000)
    displayText (CurrentPrice + ":" + CurrentName);
```

```
        }
    }
    public void charData (XmlParser p, char ch[], int
    length)
    {
      if (InName == true)
      CurrentName = escape(ch, length);
      if (InPrice == true)
      CurrentPrice = Integer.parseInt(escape(ch,
    length));
    }
}
```

Unlike Perl and Python, Java programs need to be compiled before they are executed. Here I use Microsoft's Visual J++ Java compiler to compile the program and then execute it with jview.

```
C>jvc reporter.jav

C>jview reporter cat.xml

2000:Acme Blaster
4000:Speedy PC
```

10.4 | Read/Write Utilities

Often, performing batch modifications of XML documents is convenient. I mentioned some examples in the introduction to this chapter:

- Change all the telephone numbers with the "01" prefix to the new prefix "071"
- Drop all the prices for hard disks quoted in the catalog by 10%

The key difference between these problems and the ones so far discussed is that we are required to generate modified XML as the output. All the arguments supporting an "if in doubt parse it out" strategy are doubly applicable to this class of application. However, the set of events communicated to an application by an XML parser typically falls well short of what would be required in order to allow an application to process arbitrary XML, perform some form of batch modification, and write the XML out again.

Broadly speaking, XML parsers seek to shield the user from the physical structure of the XML document and just communicate information about logical structures. Entities are the classic example. If an XML document is physically contained in a collection of entities chained together with entity declarations and entity references, this information would need to be communicated to an application in order to allow it to be recreated on the output side. Consider the following little XML document that is physically spread across two entities:

```
C>type complex.xml

<!DOCTYPE complex [
<!ENTITY hello "Hello World">
<!ENTITY chap1 SYSTEM "chap1.xml">
]>
<complex greeting = "&hello;">
&chap1;
</complex>

C>type chap1.xml

I am chap 1
```

This document is parsed with EsisDemo here to see the events communicated by the parser:

```
C>jview EsisDemo complex.xml

A greeting       Hello World
(complex
-\n
-I am chap 1\n
-\n
)complex
```

Note that all the entity-level structure has been resolved into a single logical structure and that only information about the logical structure appears as part of the EsisDemo output.

If you plan to write utilities to change XML documents and wish to keep the entity structure intact, a parser communicating logical events only is not the way to go! In the future, XML parsing technologies will likely emerge that can cope with preserving XML's entity structure and yet be easy to use for writing utility programs (the DOM is one such technology—see Chapter 15). In the mean time, read/write utilities for XML that need to maintain entity structure need to process the XML directly—that is to say, without using an XML parser to deal with correctly interpreting the XML constructs. The lack of an XML parser as a safety net means all due care must be taken! The Perl script below operates directly on the cat.xml document to drop the prices of all PCs by 10%. This program works, but is highly dependent on assumptions about how the price elements appear in the XML document.

```
C>type cut.pl

while (<STDIN>) {
        if (/<PRICE>(.*)<\/PRICE>/) {
                $price = $1;
                $price = $price * 0.9;
                print $`,"<PRICE>$price</PRICE>",$';
        }
        else {
                print;
        }
}

C>perl cut.pl < cat.xml

<?xml version = "1.0"?>
<PCS>
 <PC>
    <NAME>Acme Blaster</NAME>
    <CAPACITY>100</CAPACITY>
    <PRICE>1800</PRICE>
 </PC>
 <PC>
    <NAME>Speedy PC</NAME>
    <CAPACITY>200</CAPACITY>
    <PRICE>3600</PRICE>
 </PC>
```

```
<PC>
    <NAME>Gonzo PC</NAME>
    <CAPACITY>300</CAPACITY>
    <PRICE>4500</PRICE>
</PC>
</PCS>
```

Various steps can be taken to extend the simple patterns I have used here to make them more robust. However, extending them to cope with the full generality of XML is tantamount to writing an XML parser!

Part Three

A Close Look at XML and Related Standards

The XML Standard

- Design goals
- Markup declarations
- Element type content models
- Start-tags, end-tags and empty elements
- Attributes
- Entities
- Marked sections

11

I n this chapter, I take a close look at all the principle components of the XML standard and provide worked examples of how the various features are used. This chapter builds on the overview treatment presented in Chapter 5. Please read Chapter 5 before tackling this chapter. The full text of the XML standard version 1.0 is available in HTML on the accompanying CD.

This chapter is intended to serve as a handy reference to the main features of the XML standard. It is intended to be sufficiently detailed to be useful as a reference yet not sufficiently detailed to replace reading the standard itself for the finer points. Also, some details have been deferred to Appendix A. As you read through this chapter, you may well come across references to terms that are explained later on in the chapter. Be prepared to jump around the various sections as required!

11.1 | Design goals

The design goals of XML, stated very early on in the development of the standard, have been of paramount importance in its development. They are paraphrased here from the XML standard document.

1. XML shall be straightforwardly usable over the Internet
2. XML shall support a wide variety of applications
3. XML shall be compatible with SGML
4. Writing programs that process XML documents shall be easy
5. The number of optional features in XML is to be kept to the absolute minimum, ideally zero
6. XML documents should be human-legible and reasonably clear
7. The XML design should be prepared quickly
8. The design of XML shall be formal and concise
9. XML documents shall be easy to create
10. Terseness in XML markup is of minimal importance

11.2 | The big picture

XML documents consist of one or more *entities,* which are the basic storage units of XML. Entities can contain XML text that is intended to be parsed for XML markup. Entities can also contain non-XML data, such as graphics, video, and so on. Part of the task in constructing an XML document is to construct a hierarchy of entities that is rooted in a top-level entity known as the *document entity.* The document entity is the entity that is fed into an XML parser.

An entity that contains XML markup is made up of *characters.* Some of these will belong to the data proper (known as *character data*) and some will belong to the XML markup that annotates the data. The purpose of the markup is threefold:

- To indicate how the character data is structured into a hierarchy of elements and associated attributes
- To indicate how the entities knit together to form the full XML document
- To provide syntax to allow entities, elements, etc., to be *declared* and thus interpreted correctly by an XML processor

Prior to looking at the details of individual markup constructs, I look at some of the (potentially confusing) terminology used to describe particular types of markup or collections of markup (see Figure 11–1).

11.2.1 *The prolog*

The part of an XML document that precedes the first start-tag is collectively known as the *prolog*. It can be completely empty but should at least contain an *XML declaration* processing instruction. The simplest XML declaration looks like this:

```
<?xml version = "1.0"?>
```

If the XML document is going to be associated with a *Document Type Definition,* then the prolog will contain a *Document Type Declaration* (see the next section).

11.2.2 *The Document Type Declaration*

The term Document Type Declaration is the (optional) area of the prolog used to declare element types, attributes, entities, and so on. It takes the following general form:

```
<!DOCTYPE ...>
```

The Document Type Declaration can be entirely self-contained, as in the following document.

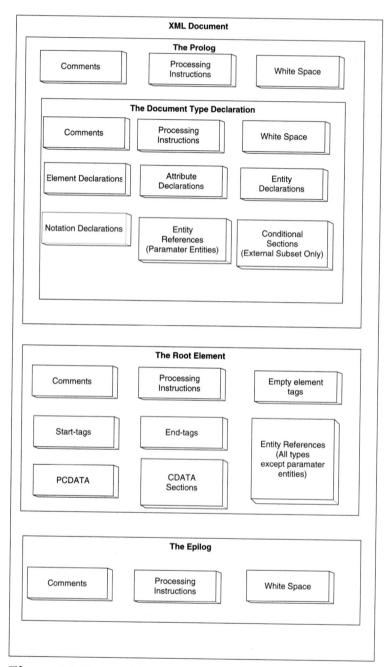

Figure 11–1   The big picture

```
<?xml version = "1.0"?>
<!DOCTYPE invoice [
<!ELEMENT invoice (#PCDATA)>
]>
<invoice>
...
</invoice>
```

The area shown in bold above is known as the *internal subset* of the Document Type Declaration. It is called a *subset* because all or part of the overall Document Type Declaration can be housed externally, as illustrated here:

```
<?xml version = "1.0"?>
<!DOCTYPE invoice SYSTEM "invoice.dtd">
<invoice>
</invoice>
```

In this example, the entity invoice.dtd is the *external subset* of the Document Type Declaration. A full Document Type Declaration can have both internal and external subset components, as illustrated here:

```
<?xml version = "1.0"?>
<!DOCTYPE invoice SYSTEM "invoice.dtd" [
<!ATTLIST invoice InvoiceID CDATA #REQUIRED>
]>
<invoice>
...
</invoice>
```

In this example, the InvoiceID attribute list declaration makes up the internal subset. The entity "invoice.dtd" makes up the external subset.

Taken together, element type declarations, attribute list declarations, entity declarations, and so on in the Document Type Declaration declare the *grammar* to which the document must conform. This grammar is known as the *Document Type Definition* (see the next section).

11.2.3 *The Document Type Definition*

The Document Type Definition (DTD) is the name given to the over-all grammar defined by the constructs that appear in the *Document Type Declaration.* If you like, the DTD is what results when the parser has processed all the declarations housed in the Document Type Declaration internal and external subsets. The fact that both terms have the same acronym (DTD) is regularly a source of confusion!

11.2.4 *The root element*

The root element of an XML document is the element that contains all other elements in the document. In this example it is **book**:

```
C>type simple.xml

<?xml version = "1.0"?>
<book>
.. other elements go here...
</book>
```

The root element can be empty (not a particularly useful XML document!):

```
C>type simple1.xml

<?xml version = "1.0"?>
<book/>
```

You can have only one root element:

```
C>type error.xml

<!-- invalid document -->
<?xml version = "1.0"?>
<book>
.. other elements go here...
</book>
<memo>
...
</memo>
```

11.2.5 *The epilog*

Although the term is not officially used in the XML standard, some markup constructs are allowed to occur after the root element has ended. The word *epilog* is used here to name that area which can contain processing instructions, comments, or white space.

11.2.6 *In summary*

The terminology in the preceding sections doubtless takes some time to sink in. Let me summarize before moving on.

- XML documents have both a *logical* and a *physical* structure.
- The physical structure is formed by the knitting together of various *entities,* which are typically files of some sort. The top-level entity is known as the *document entity.* It is the entity that is fed into an XML processor.
- The logical structure is a layer above the physical structure. At this level, an XML document consists of an optional prolog, a root element, and an optional epilog.
- The **prolog** is everything that occurs before the root element starts.
- The **epilog** is everything that occurs after the root element ends.
- The first start-tag in an XML document begins the root element.
- The **Document Type Declaration** is the part of the prolog that defines the grammar of the document. It takes the form "<!DOCTYPE ...>."
- The Document Type Declaration can be made up of an internal and/or an external component. The internal component is known as the internal subset. The external component is known as the external subset.

- The Document Type Definition is the term for the grammar described by the Document Type Declaration.

11.3 | Some more terminology!

Parsing is the fundamental task of an XML processor, and refers to the process whereby the characters that make up the XML document are categorized as either markup or character data.

Well-formed XML Documents are documents that meet all the so-called *well-formedness constraints* in the XML specification.

Valid XML Documents are documents that are *well formed* and additionally meet all the so-called *validity constraints* in the XML specification. Validity constraints detail how an XML document must behave with respect to the structural rules specified in the DTD.

A **Fatal error** is an error that an XML Processor **must** detect and report to the application. Once a fatal error is encountered, no further parsing can be performed. That is to say, the processor must stop differentiating between character data and markup. It can, if it so chooses, continue to look for more errors, however.

An **error** is a violation of a rule in the XML specification that an XML processor may choose to detect, report, and recover from if it can.

11.4 | Constraints on special characters

Certain characters are allowed to appear directly only in a limited set of circumstances, in order to make XML processors' jobs easier. The most constrained characters are "&" and "<." Some other characters and character sequences are also somewhat constrained in the interests of simpler parsing. These are:

- The double quote character (")
- The single quote character (')
- The greater than sign (>)
- The percent sign (%)
- The string (]]>)

The most common situations in which occurrences of these characters must be shielded from the attentions of the parser are listed in Table 11.1.

Table 11.1   The Most Important Character Usage Constraints in XML

Constrained Character	*Constraints*	*Escape Mechanisms*
&	Represents itself only in: Comments Processing Instructions CDATA sections	& & (hex) & (decimal)
<	Represents itself only in: Comments Processing Instructions CDATA sections	< < (hex) < (decimal)
>	Represents itself everywhere except where you need the string "]]>"	> > (hex) > (decimal)
"	Cannot appear in an attribute value if the " character is being used to demarcate the value	" " (hex) 4 (decimal)
'	Cannot appear in an attribute value if the ' character is being used to demarcate the value	' ' '

11.5 | White space handling

In XML, the term "white space" refers to one or more space, tab, carriage return, or line feed characters. The Unicode (and US ASCII) numbers for these are 32, 9, 13, and 10 respectively.

Often, especially when authoring XML by hand, using white space is convenient to show the hierarchical structure of the XML:

```
c>type invoice.xml

<!-- This is an invoice.
Creator : SMG
-->
<?xml
  version = "1.0"
?>
<invoice>
  <from>Joe Bloggs</from>
  <to
    CreditAccountHolder = "TRUE">
    Fred Bloggs
  </to>
  <items>
   <item>AcmeBlaster PC 555
         with Turbo mode</item>
   <item>Go Faster Modem XXX</item>
  </items>
</invoice>
<!-- End of Invoices
SMG -->
```

This use of white space for layout purposes presents a problem for the XML Processor. What whitespace in the invoice document has been added for layout purposes, and what whitespace is actually *part* of the document content? We can use the EsisDemo application of the Ælfred parser to find out:

```
C>jview EsisDemo invoice.xml

(invoice
-\n
(from
-Joe Bloggs
```

```
)from
-\n
A CreditAccountHolderTRUE
(to
-\n      Fred Bloggs\n
)to
-\n
(items
-\n
(item
-AcmeBlaster PC 555\n           with Turbo mode
)item
-\n
(item
-Go Faster Modem XXX
)item
-\n
)items
-\n
)invoice
```

Note that almost *all* the whitespace in the root element has been preserved by the parser and passed on to the application. The only exception is the white space present in the **to** start-tag. The general rule for the root element is that any white space that occurs *outside* a markup construct such as a start-tag is considered significant and is passed to the application. White space is not significant in the epilog or prolog.

In a valid document, a validating XML processor must pass whitespace that occurs in element content to the application and signal that it is not significant (see Appendix A).

11.6 | Comments

Comments take the following general form. The bold text indicates the character strings that signal the start and end of a comment.

```
<!-- I am a comment -->
```

The string "--" is not allowed to occur within a comment. Apart from that, anything goes, including newlines. In general, comments can appear anywhere outside other markup, i.e., a comment can appear in the prolog, the root element, or the epilog.

Here is a comment spanning two lines:

```
<!-- This is a perfectly
legal comment spanning two lines -->
```

Here is an illegal comment:

```
<!-- this comment is not legal
<!element apple #PCDATA> <!-- the apple element -->
because it is trying to wrap itself around another
comment -->
```

Here is a comment occurring within the Document Type Declaration:

```
<?xml version = "1.0"?>
<!DOCTYPE apple [
<!-- This DTD is for apples -->
<!ELEMENT apples (#PCDATA)>
]>
<apples>12</apples>
```

Here is a comment occurring within the epilog:

```
<?xml version = "1.0"?>
<!DOCTYPE apple [
<!ELEMENT apples (#PCDATA)>
]>
<apples>12</apples>
<!-- End of apples -->
```

Here is an illegal comment (comments cannot occur within other markup):

```
<!-- Illegal document -->
<?xml version = "1.0"?>
<!DOCTYPE apple [
<!ELEMENT apples (#PCDATA) <!-- Apples contain pcdata
  -->
]>
<apples>12</apples>
<!-- End of apples -->
```

Comments are not considered part of the logical structure of an XML document. XML processors can choose whether or not to communicate comments through to the XML application.

11.7 | Processing instructions

Processing instructions provide an "escape hatch" to allow information specific to a particular application to be embedded in an XML document. Processing instructions take the following general form (bold text indicates the character strings used to signal the start and end of a processing instruction:

```
<?troff .br ?>
```

In this example, a command ".br" is aimed at a *target* application called troff. The processing instruction target **xml** (and case variations thereof) are reserved for use in XML and related standards. In particular, the **xml** target is used in the processing instruction known as the *XML declaration,* which is described in the section "the XML declaration" later on. You have already seen numerous examples of the simplest XML declaration:

```
<?xml version = "1.0"?>
```

Processing instructions are not considered to be part of the character data content of an XML document, but they are always passed on to the application by the parser. The contents of a processing instruction (the part between the two "?" characters) is passed directly through to the application.

Applications that use processing instructions typically monitor them, looking to match the target string against their particular target and ignore the rest. Processing instructions can occur essentially anywhere outside of other markup constructs. In this example, a mythical processing target **foo** is used:

```
C>type foo.xml

<?xml version = "1.0"?>
<!DOCTYPE apple [
<?foo Do this?>
<!-- This DTD is for apples -->
<!ELEMENT apples (#PCDATA)>
]>
<apples>12
<?foo Do that?>
</apples>
<?foo Do the
other?>
```

The slightly edited output of the eventdemo sample application of the Ælfred XML processor appears here:

```
C>jview eventdemo foo.xml

Starting entity:  file://localhostC:\af/foo.xml
Processing Instruction:  foo Do this
Doctype declaration:  apple
Start element:  name=apples
Character data:  "12\n"
Processing Instruction:  foo Do that
Character data:  "\n"
End element:  apples
Processing Instruction:  foo Do the\nother
Ending entity:  file://localhostC:\af/foo.xml
End document:  errors=0
```

11.8 | CDATA Sections

A CDATA Section is used in XML to shield a body of text from the attentions of the XML Processor. Once in a CDATA Section, the only markup the XML Processor will attach special meaning to is the "]]>" string that ends the CDATA Section. You can see the general form of a CDATA section here (bold text indicates the character strings used to start and end the CDATA section):

```
<![CDATA [This is not an <apple> start-tag]]>
```

CDATA Sections can occur anywhere character data can occur. Note that because the first occurrence of "]]>" will terminate the CDATA Section, CDATA sections cannot be nested.

Here is an example of a valid CDATA Section:

```
C>type foo.xml

<?xml version = "1.0"?>
<apples><![CDATA[
This in not an </apple> end-tag and this is not an
   &entity; reference
]]></apples>
```

Note the shielding effect of the CDATA section, which protects what looks like an apple end-tag and what looks like an entity reference.

```
C>jview EsisDemo foo.xml

(apples
-\nThis in not an </apple> end-tag and this is not an
   &entity; reference\n
)apples
```

11.9 | The XML declaration

All XML Documents should begin with the XML declaration processing instruction. It can have up to three component parts:

- Version information
- Character set encoding information
- Stand-alone document declaration

11.9.1 *Version information in the XML declaration*

An XML declaration containing version information appears here:

```
<?xml version = "1.0"?>
```

The intent of the version information is to capture the version of the XML standard to which a document conforms. As the standard evolves, numbers higher than 1.0 will be used, and XML processors can use this information to determine whether they are capable of processing XML documents.

11.9.2 *Character set encoding information*

The character set of XML documents is Unicode. Unicode has a number of encodings that allow Unicode characters (16 bits) to be encoded in 7/8 bits for compatibility with systems that can only work with 7/8 bit characters (see Chapter 14 for details). By default, an XML processor will assume that one of these, known as UTF-8, is being used, i.e., the following encoding declaration is assumed.

```
encoding = "UTF-8"
```

All XML processors are required to be able to read two of these encodings. The other one is UTF-16. A document in UTF-16 should use the following encoding declaration.

```
encoding = "UTF-16"
```

XML processors can *optionally* support other encodings. If some other encoding is required that is not mandated in the standard, it must be specified with a character encoding like this:

```
<?xml version = "1.0" encoding = "ISO-8859-1"?>
```

Some further details of how XML deals with character set encoding can be found in Chapter 14 and also in Appendix A.

11.9.3 *Stand-alone document declaration*

Certain markup declarations that may be stored in the external subset of the Document Type Declaration can affect the information sent by an XML processor to an XML application. The most common example is when *Attribute Defaults* are specified externally, as you see here:

```
C>type people.xml

<?xml version = "1.0"?>
<!DOCTYPE people SYSTEM "people.dtd">
<people>
<person>
Joe Bloggs
</person>
</people>


C>type people.dtd

<!ELEMENT people (person+)>
<!ELEMENT person (#PCDATA)>
<!ATTLIST person ShoeSize CDATA #FIXED "12">


C>jview EsisDemo people.xml

(people
A ShoeSize      12
(person
-\nJoe Bloggs\n
)person
)people
```

Both validating and nonvalidating parsers are required to pass attribute default information through to the application. In order to do so in the above example, the parser must process the external subset. If you know that no such declarations are stored externally, communicating that fact to the XML processor can be useful. An XML processor that is nonvalidating can then safely ignore these external declarations in the interests of a speedier parse. An XML declaration containing a stand-alone document declaration appears here:

```
<?xml version = "1.0" standalone="yes"?>
```

The value "yes" asserts that this document is stand-alone. In the absence of a standalone declaration, an XML Processor assumes a value of "no." Consult the XML specification for other requirements of stand-alone documents.

11.10 | Start-tags, end-tags, and empty elements

In XML, elements come in two main flavors: those that contain some mixture of markup and/or character data, and those that do not. The latter are known as *empty* elements. (It does not matter whether their declarations require them to be empty). Empty elements can have attributes. In the following examples, bold text indicates the character strings that open and close the empty element tag:

```
<foo/>
<foo happy="TRUE"/>
<foo
/>
```

Note that in the last example, the newline will be ignored as it occurs within markup.

Elements that contain some mixture of markup/character data must have matching start- and end-tags, as the following examples illustrate:

```
<person>
Sean McGrath
</person>

<fruit type = "apple">
Granny Smith
</fruit>

<address>
<street>Main St.</street>
<country>Tumbolia</country>
<business type = "retail"/>
</address>
```

```
<printer
 name = "Acme"
 type = "laser"
>
<description>
Bright pink and noisy
</description>
</printer>
```

The newlines surrounding the printer attributes above are ignored as they occur in markup.

Empty elements can also have matching start- and end-tags as the following examples illustrate:

```
<foo></foo>

<foo
></foo>
```

In a *valid* XML document (as distinct from a merely well formed XML document), the name used in the Document Type Declaration must match the name of the root element. This document is valid:

```
<!DOCTYPE fruit [
<!ELEMENT fruit (apple|orange)+>
<!ELEMENT apple  EMPTY>
<!ELEMENT orange EMPTY>
]>
<fruit>
<apple/>
</fruit>
```

This document is well formed but not valid because its document type name does not match the name of the root element:

```
<!DOCTYPE fruit [
<!ELEMENT fruit (apple|orange)+>
<!ELEMENT apple  EMPTY>
<!ELEMENT orange EMPTY>
]>
<apple/>
```

11.11 | Attributes

Attributes can be associated with an element by attaching them to a start-tag or an empty element tag. They always take the form of an assignment of an attribute value (in quotes) to an attribute name with "=" in between.

```
<fruit type = "apple">
<table border = "1">
```

Attribute values can be delimited by either matching double quotes or matching single quotes.

```
<person name = "Sean O'Dear">
<quotation text = 'He said "Hello" to Fred'>
```

Attribute values can contain entity references but cannot contain other forms of markup such as start-tags, comments, CDATA sections, and so on. Here is an example of an attribute value specification that contains an entity reference.

```
C>type blurb.xml

<!DOCTYPE blurb [
<!ENTITY company "AcmePC Inc">
]>
<intro title = "&company; will solve all your prob-
   lems"/>

C>jview EsisDemo blurb.xml

A title AcmePC Inc will solve all your problems
(intro
)intro
```

11.12 | The Document Type Declaration

The Document Type Declaration is the construct in which any element type declarations, attributes list declarations, entities declarations, and notations declarations are housed. The overall structure appears here (bold text indicates the strings used to start and end the Document Type Declaration):

```
<!DOCTYPE ... >
```

The Document Type Declaration can have an internal and/or an external component known as the internal and the external subset respectively.

11.12.1 *Internal subset*

The internal subset, if present, is delimited by angle brackets as shown here:

```
<!DOCTYPE ... [
<!-- Internal Subset -->
]>
```

An XML document with an internal subset only is shown here:

```
<!DOCTYPE apples [
<!ELEMENT apples [#PCDATA]>
]>
<apples>12</apples>
```

11.12.2 *External subset*

The external subset, if present, consists of a reference to an external entity following the DOCTYPE keyword as illustrated here:

```
C>type apples.dtd

<!ELEMENT apples (#PCDATA)>

C>type apples.xml
<!DOCTYPE SYSTEM "apples.dtd">
<apples>12</apples>
```

A document with both an internal and an external document type declaration subset is shown here:

```
C>type apples.dtd

<!ELEMENT apples (#PCDATA)>

C>type apples.xml

<!DOCTYPE SYSTEM "apples.dtd"[
<!ATTLIST apples color CDATA #REQUIRED>
]>
<apples color = "green">12</apples>
```

Note that the term "external subset" refers solely to the external entity following the DOCTYPE keyword. The following document has the same logical structure as the previous document but has no external subset. All the declarations are considered to be housed in the internal subset, including those in apples.dtd:

```
C>type apples.dtd

<!ELEMENT apples (#PCDATA)>

C>type apples.xml

<!DOCTYPE SYSTEM [
<!ENTITY % apples SYSTEM "apples.dtd">
%apples;
<!ATTLIST apples color CDATA #REQUIRED>
]>
<apples color = "green">12</apples>
```

11.13 | Element type declarations

Element type declarations allow an XML application to constrain the elements that can occur in the document and to specify the order in which can occur. The general form of an element type declaration appears here (bold text indicates the character strings used to delimit the start and end of an element type declaration).

```
<!ELEMENT ...>
```

The ellipsis above is a placeholder for the *content specification* of the element type. The three variations that exist are illustrated in detail later.

```
<!ELEMENT foo EMPTY>
```

Declares **foo** elements to be *empty* elements.

```
<!ELEMENT foo ANY>
```

Declares that a **foo** element can contain any mixture of character data and other elements as long as those element types have been declared in the DTD.

```
<!ELEMENT foo (apple|orange|banana)>
```

Declares that the element **foo** can contain exactly one **apple**, one **orange,** or one **banana** element. The part between the parenthesis is known as the *content model* of the element. See below for a full description of content model variations.

11.14 | Element Type Content Models

XML allows element types to be declared that can contain other elements, the order and occurence of these elements can be constrained in various ways as the examples below illustrate.

11.14.1 *A sequence of elements, one after another*

```
<!ELEMENT person (name,address,telephone)>
```

This declaration says, "a person element consists of a name element, an address element, and a telephone element, in exactly that order." An example appears here:

```
<person>
<name>...
<address>...
<telephone>...
</person>
```

You can see an invalid example of a person element here (all items in the sequence must be provided).

```
<!-- invalid person element -->
<person>
<address>...
<telephone>...
</person>
```

The following example is also invalid (all sequence items must appear in the specified order).

```
<!-- invalid person element -->
<person>
<name>...
<telephone>...
<address>...
</person>
```

11.14.2 A selection from a list of elements, only one allowed

```
<!ELEMENT fruit (apple|orange|bannana)>
```

This declaration says, "a fruit consists of either an apple element, an orange element, or a banana element." An example appears here:

```
<fruit>
<apple>...
</fruit>
```

This example is invalid (only one allowed).

```
<!-- invalid fruit element -->
<fruit>
<apple>...
<orange>...
</fruit>
```

11.14.3 *An element occurring once or not at all*

```
<!ELEMENT person (name,address,telephone?)>
```

This declaration says, "a person element consists of a name element followed by an address element, optionally followed by a telephone element." Here is an example of a valid person.

```
<person>
<name>...
<address>...
<telephone>...
</person>
```

This example is also valid (telephone is optional).

```
<person>
<name>...
<address>...
<telephone>...
</person>
```

This example is invalid (telephone can occur only once or not at all).

```
<person>
<name>...
<address>...
<telephone>...
<telephone>...
</person>
```

11.14.4 *An element occurring zero or more times*

```
<!ELEMENT person (name,address,telephone*)>
```

This declaration says, "a person element consists of a name element followed by an address element followed by zero or more telephone elements." Here is an example of a valid person (okay to have no telephone elements).

```
<person>
<name>...
```

```
<address>...
</person>
```

This example is also valid (okay to have as many telephone elements as you like).

```
<person>
<name>...
<address>...
<telephone>...
<telephone>...
<telephone>...
<telephone>...
</person>
```

11.14.5 *An element occurring one or more times*

```
<!ELEMENT person (name,address,telephone+)>
```

This declaration says, "a person element consists of a name element followed by an address element followed by one or more telephone elements." Here is an example of a valid person (okay to have lots of telephone elements).

```
<person>
<name>...
<address>...
<telephone>...
<telephone>...
<telephone>...
<telephone>...
</person>
```

Here is an example of an invalid person element (must have at least one telephone element).

```
<!-- invalid person -->
<person>
<name>...
<address>...
</person>
```

11.14.6 *An element containing any other element(s) in any order*

```
<!ELEMENT person ANY>
```

This declaration says, "a person element consists of any combination of elements in any order. It can also contain character data anywhere." A validating XML parser will accept any mixture of elements and/or data characters as the content of an element of this type as long as all the elements have been declared.

11.14.7 *Some more complex examples*

The various occurrence indicators (zero or one, zero or more, one or more) can be combined with sequence and selection specifications to build up complex models. Table 11.2 lists some examples.

Table 11.2   Some XML Content Models

Content Model	*Interpretation*
<!ELEMENT invoice (from,to,item+)>	An **invoice** element consists of a **from** element followed by a **to** element followed by one or more **item** elements.
<!ELEMENT invoice (from,to?,item+)>	An **invoice** element consists of a **from** element, optionally followed by a **to** element and one or more **item** elements.
<!ELEMENT invoice (from,to*,item+)>	An **invoice** element consists of a **from** element followed by zero or more **to** elements, followed by one or more **item** elements.

Table 11.2   Some XML Content Models *(continued)*

Content Model	Interpretation
<!ELEMENT invoice (from,to,(item+|batch*))>	An **invoice** element consists of a **from** element followed by a **to** element. This is followed either by one or more **item** elements *or* zero or more **batch** elements.
<!ELEMENT invoice ANY>	An **invoice** element consists of any combination of elements and character data, in any order.
<!ELEMENT invoice (((from,to)|(to,from)),item?)>	An **invoice** element consists of the elements **from** and **to** in any order, followed by an optional item element.
<!ELEMENT invoice (from,to,item|batch?)>	An **invoice** element consists of a **from** element followed by a **to** element followed by either one or more **item** elements or an optional **batch** element.

11.14.8 *Character data*

The term *character data* describes the content of an XML document that occurs outside any markup (with the exception of CDATA sections). In element type content models, the keyword "#PCDATA" denotes character data. In this example, a **para** element is declared to contain zero or more **quotation** elements or character data in any order.

```
<!ELEMENT para (#PCDATA|quotation)*>
<!ELEMENT quotation #PCDATA>
```

Here is an example of this **para** element.

```
C>type simple.xml

<para>
As someone once said
<quotation>Cogito ergo sum</quotation>
</para>
```

```
C>jview EsisDemo simple.xml

(para
-\nAs someone once said\n
(quotation
-Cogito ergo sum
)quotation
-\n
)para
```

Note that #PCDATA means "zero or more characters," and so this example is perfectly valid.

```
C>type simple.xml

<para>
<quotation><quotation>
</para>

C>jview EsisDemo simple.xml

(para
-\n
(quotation
)quotation
-\n
)para
```

If a content model includes the #PCDATA keyword, the element type is said to have *mixed content*. If the content model consists purely of element type names, the element is said to have *element content*. Validating XML processors treat white space differently, depending on whether the element has mixed content or element content. Specifically, a validating XML parser must flag as ignorable, white space that occurs in element content.

Experience with mixed content in SGML has shown that a number of complex parsing issues result if #PCDATA is allowed to occur as part of sequence or selection content models. XML avoids these issues by allowing #PCDATA to occur in a content model *only* in the following forms:

```
<!ELEMENT foo (#PCDATA)>

<ELEMENT foo (#PCDATA|bar|...)*>
```

11.15 | Attribute List Declarations

Attribute list declarations serve to specify the name, type, and option-ally the default value of the attributes associated with an element. The general form of an attribute list declaration for an element type **foo** appears here:

```
<!ATTLIST foo ...>
```

Ten attribute types exist:

- String
- Enumerated
- ID
- IDREF
- IDREFS
- ENTITY
- ENTITIES
- NMTOKEN
- NMTOKENS
- NOTATION

11.15.1 *String attributes*

A string attribute bar for the element type foo looks like this:

```
<!ATTLIST foo bar CDATA ...>
```

String attributes can contain essentially an arbitrary collection of characters of any length as long as any occurrence of "<" or "&" is escaped with entity references

11.15.2 *Enumerated attributes*

An enumerated attribute is one that can take on one of a fixed set of values supplied as part of its declaration. An enumerated attribute **quality** for the element **apple** looks like this:

```
<!ATTLIST apple quality (GOOD|BAD|INDIFFERENT) ... >
```

In this example, the quality attribute is declared to have three permissible values "GOOD," "BAD," and "INDIFFERENT." Here is a valid apple element, according to this declaration:

```
<apple quality = "GOOD">
```

Here is an example of an invalid apple element (enumerated values are case-sensitive).

```
<!-- incorrect -->
<apple quality = "good">
```

11.15.3 *ID/IDREF/IDREFS*

These three attribute types are treated together as they are strongly interrelated. Any ID attributes occurring in an XML document must be unique in order for the document to be valid (as distinct from merely well formed). Attributes of type ID thus provide a handy way of assigning a name to an element to uniquely identify it. IDs must begin with a letter, a "_", or a ":" character (although ":" should not ordinarily be used as it has been earmarked for special meaning in future XML extensions.). In this example, a **UniqueName** attribute is attached to **foo** elements:

```
<!ATTLIST foo UniqueName ID ...>
```

An example foo element might look like this:

```
<foo UniqueName = "P1234">
```

IDREF attributes are the flip side of the coin. Any IDREF attributes assigned values in a valid XML document must match the value assigned to an ID attribute somewhere in the document.

```
<!ATTLIST bar Reference IDREF ...>
```

Here is an example of a bar element using its IDREF attribute to point to the foo element of the last example.

```
<bar Reference = "P1234">
```

IDREFS is a variation on IDREF in which an attribute is allowed to contain multiple referenced IDs. So given this declaration:

```
<!ATTLIST bar References IDREFS ...>
```

a bar element might look like this:

```
<bar References = "P1234 Q5678">
```

11.15.4 *ENTITY/ENTIIES*

Attributes of type ENTITY or ENTITIES are treated together because they are strongly related. An attribute of type ENTITY must have a value corresponding to the name of an unparsed entity declared somewhere in the Document Type Declaration. In this snippet, an external data entity, bob, is declared, and the salutation attribute of the letter element is declared to be of type ENTITY.

```
<!ENTITY bob SYSTEM "bob.gif" NDATA gif>
<!ATTLIST letter salutation ENTITY...>
```

Given these declarations, a letter element might look like this:

```
<letter salutation = "bob">
```

Like IDREFS above, ENTITIES is a variation on ENTITY that allows an attribute to contain one or more entity names in its value.

11.15.5 *NMTOKEN/NMTOKENS*

Attributes of type NMTOKEN or NMTOKENS are treated together because they are strongly related. Essentially, an NMTOKEN attribute is restricted to contain characters allowed in a name: any combination of letters, digits, and some punctuation characters ".", "-", "_", and ":". Note that this list does not contain any white space characters. This is the principle practical use of NMTOKEN—to allow the XML processor to catch values that contain erroneous spaces. An NMTOKENS attribute is one that can contain one or more NMTOKENs, separated by white space.

```
<!ATTLIST product code NMTOKEN ...>
```

Given this declaration, product elements might look like this:

```
<product code = "Alpha-123">
<product code = "333">
```

Here is an example of an invalid NMTOKEN attribute.

```
<!-- Incorrect -->
<product code = "A 123">
```

11.15.6 *NOTATION*

An attribute list declaration of type NOTATION must specify one or more notations declared somewhere in the Document Type Declaration. Its value is constrained to match one of those notations. In this snippet, a notation EDIFACT is declared, and the format attribute of the **invoice** element is declared to be of type NOTATION.

```
<!NOTATION EDIFACT SYSTEM "EDIFACT Format">
<!ATTLIST invoice format NOTATION (EDIFACT)>
...
<invoice format = "EDIFACT">
```

In this example, two notations are declared, and the format attribute of the invoice element is allowed to contain either one.

```
<!NOTATION EDIFACT SYSTEM "EDIFACT Format">
<!NOTATION ANSIX12 SYSTEM "ANSI X.12 Format">

<!ATTLIST invoice format NOTATION
   (EDIFACT|ANSIX12)>
...
<invoice format = "EDIFACT">
```

11.16 | Attribute defaults

An attribute list declaration includes information about whether or not a value must be supplied for it and, if not, what the XML processor should do. There are three variations:

- Required—a value must be supplied.
- Implied—the XML processor tells the application that no value was supplied. The application can decide what best to do.
- Fixed—A value is supplied in the declaration. No value need be supplied in the document, and the XML processor will pass the specified fixed value through to the application. If a value is supplied in the document, it must exactly match the fixed value.

11.16.1 *Required attributes*

In this example, the type attribute of the fruit element is declared to be required.

```
C>type fruit.xml

<!DOCTYPE fruit [
<!ELEMENT fruit EMPTY>
<!ATTLIST fruit type CDATA #REQUIRED>
]>
<fruit type = "apple"/>
```

A validating XML processor would thus reject the following document.

```
C>type fruit.xml

<!DOCTYPE fruit [
<!ELEMENT fruit EMPTY>
<!ATTLIST fruit type CDATA #REQUIRED>
]>
<fruit/>


C>jview msxml fruit.xml

Attribute 'type' is required.
Location: file:/C:/msxml/fruit.xml(6,-1)
Context: <fruit>
```

11.16.2 *Implied attributes*

These are attributes that can be left unspecified if desired. The XML processor passes the fact that the attribute was unspecified through to the XML application, which can then choose what best to do.

```
C>type fruit.xml

<!DOCTYPE fruit [
<!ELEMENT fruit EMPTY>
<!ATTLIST fruit type CDATA #IMPLIED>
]>
<fruit/>
```

The EsisDemo application signifies that the value of type has been implied by giving it a null value

```
C>jview EsisDemo fruit.xml

A type  null
(fruit
)fruit
```

11.16.3 *Fixed Attributes*

These are attributes that have their value fixed in the DTD.

```
C>type fruit.xml

<!DOCTYPE fruit [
<!ELEMENT fruit EMPTY>
<ATTLIST fruit edible CDATA #FIXED "YES">
]>
<fruit/>

C>jview EsisDemo fruit.xml

A edible YES
(fruit
)fruit
```

11.17 | Entity declarations

Entities come in two main flavors:

- Parameter entities are entities used solely within the DTD
- General entities are entities used within the root element

The two types of entities are distinguished by a slight difference in the way they are declared. A parameter entity **foo** is declared in the following general form:

```
<!ENTITY % foo ...>
```

A general entity **foo** is declared in the following general form:

```
<!ENTITY foo ...>
```

11.17.1 *Parameter entities*

In this example, parameter entities "ProductIdType" and "string" are declared to have the values "NMTOKEN" and "CDATA," respectively. These are then used in attribute list declarations to make them easier to read and easier to modify in the event that their types need to change.

```
C>type products.xml

<!DOCTYPE products [
<!ENTITY % ProductIdType "NMTOKEN">
<!ENTITY % string "CDATA">
<!ELEMENT products (product)+>
<!ELEMENT product EMPTY>
<!ATTLIST product
        type %ProductIdType; #REQUIRED
        name %string; #REQUIRED>
]>
<products>
<product type = "PC" name = "Master Blaster"/>
</products>

C>jview EsisDemo products.xml

(products
A type  PC
A name  Master Blaster
(product
)product
)products
```

11.17.2 *General entities*

In this example, two general entities are declared, and their use indicates some important points about general entities.

- Entities can contain references to other entities (see **compname** in **Disclaimer** below).
- Entities can contain markup (see the p element in the Disclaimer entity below).

```
C>type manual.xml

<!DOCTYPE manual [
<!ENTITY Disclaimer "<p>This product is provided as is
  by &compname;, so there.</p>">
<!ENTITY compname "Acme PC Inc.">
<!ELEMENT manual (p)+>
<!ELEMENT p (#PCDATA)>
]>
```

```
<manual>
<p>This is a manual from &compname;</p>
&Disclaimer;
</manual>
```

Applications such as EsisDemo expand all entities prior to passing information on to the application, as you see here:

```
C>jview EsisDemo manual.xml

(manual
(p
-This is a manual from Acmepc Inc.
)p
(p
-This product is provided as is by Acmepc Inc., so
   there.
)p
)manual
```

11.17.3 *External entities*

The entity examples in the previous two sections are examples of *internal entities*. An internal entity is one in which the *replacement text* for the entity is provided as part of the declaration. Entities can house their replacement text externally to the declaration. Such entities are known as *external entities*. Both parameter and general entities can be external entities.

11.17.3.1   External general entities

External general entities are illustrated in this example:

```
C>type manual.xml

<!DOCTYPE manual [
<!ENTITY chapter1 SYSTEM "chap1.sgm">
<!ENTITY chapter2 SYSTEM "chap2.sgm">
<!ELEMENT manual (chapter+)>
]>
```

```
<manual>
&chapter1;
&chapter2;
</manual>
```

In this XML document, two external general entities have been declared—**chapter1** and **chapter2**. The keyword **SYSTEM** indicates that the delimited string that follows is to be interpreted as a URI at which the entity replacement text can be found. In this case, the file-names are chap1.sgm and chap2.sgm.

Just as with internal entities, applications like EsisDemo resolve the entities prior to passing data through to the application.

```
C>jview EsisDemo manual.xml

(manual
(chapter
-This is chapter 1
)chapter
(chapter
-This is chapter 2
)chapter
)manual
```

11.17.3.2 External parameter entities

In this example, a parameter entity is used to import some DTD declarations stored externally in address.dtd into the documents DTD. Using parameter entities in this fashion can be a useful way to share DTD components amongst a number of XML DTDs.

```
C>type person.xml

<!DOCTYPE person [
<!ELEMENT person (name,address)>
<!ELEMENT name (#PCDATA)>

<!ENTITY % address SYSTEM "address.dtd">
%address;

]>
<person>
<name>Sean McGrath</name>
```

```
<address>Enniscrone, County Sligo, Ireland
</address>
</person>
```

Note that the content model for person above uses the address element and that the element type is not defined directly in the internal subset. It is housed in the external entity stored in the file address.dtd.

```
C>type address.dtd
```

```
<!ELEMENT address (#PCDATA)>
```

An XML processor resolves the reference to the address entity and loads the declarations from address.dtd.

```
C>jview EsisDemo person.xml
```

```
(person
(name
-Sean McGrath
)name
(address
-Enniscrone, County Sligo, Ireland
)address
)person
```

11.18 | Notation declarations

The purpose of notation declarations is to allow XML documents to refer to external, often non-XML information in a consistent way. Additionally, a notation declaration allows a "helper application" to be specified, which can be used by an XML application to process data represented using the notation.

```
<!NOTATION DSIG SYSTEM
"http://www.acmepc.com/dsig.exe">
```

This notation declaration declares "DSIG" to be a notation and specifies a program on http://www.acmepc.com that can be used to view data in the DSIG notation. An XML document wishing to use data in this notation can reference it via an External Entity or include it directly in the data content of an element that exhibits "DSIG" as the value of a NOTATION attribute type.

11.18.1   *External data entities*

An external general entity declaration can allow XML documents to make explicit that the contents of an external entity is not XML-text.

```
<!DOCTYPE person [
<!NOTATION DSIG SYSTEM "Digital Signature
Notation">
<!ENTITY sig SYSTEM "mysig.dsg" NDATA DSIG>
<!ELEMENT person (name)>
<!ATTLIST person signature ENTITY #REQUIRED>
<!ELEMENT name (#PCDATA)>
]>
<person signature = "sig">
<name>Sean McGrath</name>
</person>
```

Because NDATA signifies that an entity contains non-XML data, NDATA entities cannot be referenced from an element's content— they can only be referenced as the value of an attribute of type ENTITY or ENTITIES.

11.19 | Conditional sections

A conditional section is a mechanism used to allow portions of a document type declaration subset to be included or excluded from the DTD. Conditional sections may appear only in the external subset of the Document Type Declaration. Conditional sections have been used extensively over the years in SGML applications. Supporting them in XML allows SGML DTDs to be adapted for use with XML. An included conditional section takes the following general form:

```
<![INCLUDE[
...
]]>
```

An excluded conditional section takes the following general form:

```
<![EXCLUDE[
...
]]>
```

Unlike CDATA sections, conditional sections are allowed to nest within each other. In this example, the GovernmentCode attribute of the fruit element is ignored by the parser and therefore the attribute does not appear anywhere in the output communicated to the XML Application.

```
C>type fruit.xml

<!DOCTYPE fruit [
<!ELEMENT fruit EMPTY>
<!ATTLIST fruit type CDATA #IMPLIED>
<![IGNORE[
<!ATTLIST fruit GovernmentCode CDATA #IMPLIED>
]]>
]>
<fruit/>

C>jview EsisDemo fruit.xml

A type  null
(fruit
)fruit
```

If the IGNORE is replaced by INCLUDE, the parser will process the GovernmentCode attribute declaration:

```
C>type fruit.xml

<!DOCTYPE fruit [
<!ELEMENT fruit EMPTY>
<!ATTLIST fruit type CDATA #IMPLIED>
<![INCLUDE[
<!ATTLIST fruit GovernmentCode CDATA #IMPLIED>
]]>
]>
<fruit/>

C>jview EsisDemo fruit.xml

A type null
```

```
A GovernmentCode null
(fruit
)fruit
```

A parameter entity is often used instead of direct use of the INCLUDE/EXCLUDE keyword. This substitution makes switching between including and ignoring sections in large DTDs easier.

```
C>type fruit.xml

<!DOCTYPE fruit [
<!ENTITY % GovernmentStuff "IGNORE">
<!ELEMENT fruit EMPTY>
<!ATTLIST fruit type CDATA #IMPLIED>
<![%GovernmentStuff;[
<!ATTLIST fruit GovernmentCode CDATA #REQUIRED>
]]>
]>
<fruit/>

C>jview fruit.xml

A type  null
(fruit
)fruit
```

Switching over to include GovernmentCode is achieved by just changing the parameter entity.

```
C>type fruit.xml

<!DOCTYPE fruit [
<!ENTITY % GovernmentStuff "INCLUDE">
<!ELEMENT fruit EMPTY>
<!ATTLIST fruit type CDATA #IMPLIED>
<![%GovernmentStuff;[
<!ATTLIST fruit GovernmentCode CDATA #REQUIRED>
]]>
]>
<fruit/>

C>jview EsisDemo fruit.xml

A type  null
A GovernmentCode        null
(fruit
)fruit
```

XML Hypertext Linking with XLL

- Hypertext terminology
- Link recognition
- Simple links
- Extended links
- XPointers

In this chapter, I look at Version 1.0 of the XLL proposal, which aims to provide a standard way of achieving powerful hypertext linking effects with XML. In a fixed tag-set (properly, "element tyope set") language such as HTML, achieving hypertext is straightforward. You simply use the predefined element type(s) provided for that purpose, principally the **<A>** element. Moreover, in HTML, the *meaning* of the <A> element is predefined. If it has a name attribute, it serves to name a location in a document (a hypertext anchor). If it has an href attribute, it serves to specify that clicking on its content causes the link to be traversed.

In XML, things are somewhat different. No predefined element types exist, and thus neither do predefined hypertext elements. A mechanism is required to allow arbitrary XML elements to take part in hypertext links without forcing them to use any particular predefined name. The goals of XLL can be summed up like this:

- To provide a mechanism for signaling the presence of a link (link recognition)

- To define, at least partially, what the intended behavior of the link is (link behavior)
- To extend the types of hypertext links than can be used beyond the simple hypertext model of HTML

12.1 | Some hypertext terminology

When one looks beyond the simple hypertext linking capabilities of HTML (essentially "link this object to that object"), terminology can become a real problem. Before you look at the specifics, nail down some of that terminology:

- A **resource** is anything that participates in a link. A resource can be as simple as an HTML document on the Web or as complex as a program that queries a database and returns a set of results.
- To **traverse** a link is to cause the link to be activated. In the most common type of hypertext, a user will traverse a link by clicking something.
- A **linking element** is an XML element that takes part in a link in some form or other. Linking elements need to signal the fact that they take part in a link. They may also need to specify how the link should behave, i.e., should the link be traversed when the document is loaded or when the user actions the link, and so on.
- A **locator** is a character string associated with a linking element that can be used to locate a resource, for example, the href attribute of the HTML A element.
- An **in-line link** is a type of link that is specified as part of the resources taking part in the link. The A element of HTML, for example, is an in-line link because the link

machinery (href, name attributes, and so on) is stored within the A element itself.

- An **out-of-line** link is a type of link that is specified completely *independently* of the resources that take part in the link. Out-of-line links can be used to attach hypertext to XML documents without modifying the XML documents themselves. Such links are particularly useful for attaching hypertext to documents stored on read-only media such as CD-ROM and also for attaching hypertext to documents that cannot be modified in any way for legal reasons.

12.2 | Relationship to existing standards

The XLL proposal has been heavily influenced by a number of existing hypertext technologies, most notably:

- **HTML**—perhaps more than any other hypertext system, HTML has shown the great power of hypertext. In HTML, hypertext is very simple, so simple in fact that hypertext theorists have been somewhat taken aback at how popular and useful such a simple hypertext technology has become! XLL seeks to keep the essential simplicity of HTML linking in XML yet allow room for expansion into more powerful hypertext concepts.
- **TEI**—The Text Encoding Initiative is a long-standing SGML initiative to capture literature of all forms in a machine-understandable format. It makes extensive use of hypertext to faithfully capture source documents. The diversity of data captured in the TEI initiative has led to an extensive body of knowledge about real-world requirements for hypertext.

■ **HyTime**—HyTime is the international standard for hypertext linking with SGML. Many of the ideas for layering hypertext onto SGML have been brought over to XML.

12.3 | Link recognition

XLL uses a reserved attribute name **XML-LINK** to allow elements to signal that they are link resources. The value of the attribute is used to specify what type of link the element is taking part in. The type of link exemplified by the A element in HTML is known as a SIMPLE link in XLL. To allow an XLL processor to correctly interpret the HTML A element, all that is needed is the XML-LINK attribute, as you see here:

```
<A
 XML-LINK = "SIMPLE"
     HREF = "http://www.acmepc.com/">
Click here for great deals on Personal Computers
</A>
```

Note that the XML-LINK attribute, not the element type name, is important as far as XLL is concerned. The following XML snippet will have exactly the same meaning to an XLL processor.

```
<CrossReference
 XML-LINK = "SIMPLE"
     HREF = "http://www.acmepc.com/">
Click here for great deals on Personal Computers
</CrossReference>
```

Other values for XML-LINK are used for more complex types of linking, as you see later on in this chapter.

12.4 | LINK information attributes

A variety of other attributes can be associated with XML elements.

- **Role**. A linking element can have a ROLE attribute that specifies what each resource's involvement in a link is. For example, if you wish to capture information about employees and who employs them, you could assign "Employee" and "EmployedBy" as roles. An XLL processor can then use that information, perhaps to display it to the user, making the intention of the link more obvious.
- **HREF**. A linking element must specify each resource by means of an HREF attribute.
- **Title**. Locators may have an associated title. This could be used, for example, to display information about the link when the user hovers the mouse over the link text.
- **INLINE**. This attribute is used to specify whether the link is in-line or out-of-line.
- **SHOW**. This attribute is used to specify how a link is presented. It is further explained in the next section.
- **ACTUATE**. This attribute is used to specify how a link is traversed. It is further explained in the next section.

12.5 | The show and actuate attributes

The show attribute can take three values. A value of **EMBED** indicates that the resource traversed to should be embedded for display purposes at the point where the link started. For example, a document containing a simple link with the embed attribute set to "EMBED" might look like this:

```
<CrossReference
 XML-LINK = "SIMPLE"
      SHOW = "EMBED"
      HREF = "http://www.acmepc.com/resourceb.xml">
click me</CrossReference>
```

This scenario is illustrated in Figure 12–1.

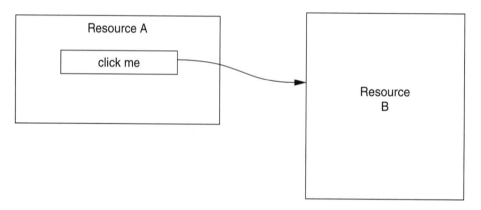

Figure 12–1   A simple EMBED link prior to activation

When activated, the display of Resource A might look like Figure 12–2.

Setting the value of the SHOW attribute to **"REPLACE"** indicates that the resource specified should replace the resource currently displayed. This is the familiar default behavior of most HTML browsers.

Setting the value of the SHOW attribute to **"NEW"** indicates that the resource specified should be displayed in a new display area without affecting the one currently displayed. In many Web browsers, this effect is achieved by opening a new browser window.

The actuate attribute takes one of two values:

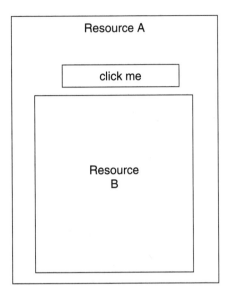

Figure 12–2   A simple EMBED link
after activation

- AUTO indicates that the link should be traversed when encountered, perhaps as part of loading the XML document that contains the link
- USER indicates that the link should not be traversed until some external command (such as a mouse click) requests the link to be traversed

The full set of attributes associated with a simple link is illustrated below using an XREF element:

```
<!ELEMENT XREF ANY>
<!ATTLIST XREF
  XML-LINK       CDATA #FIXED "SIMPLE"
  ROLE           CDATA #IMPLIED
  HREF           CDATA #REQUIRED
  TITLE          CDATA #IMPLIED
  INLINE               (TRUE|FALSE)  "TRUE"
  CONTENT-ROLE   CDATA #IMPLIED
  CONTENT-TITLE  CDATA #IMPLIED
  SHOW                 (EMBED|REPLACE|NEW)  "REPLACE"
  ACTUATE              (AUTO|USER)  "USER"
  BEHAVIOR       CDATA #IMPLIED
  >
```

12.6 | Specifying the addresses of resources

A locator always contains a URL. XLL supports the common HTML practice of allowing the URL to contain a query component (denoted by a "?" character) and also a fragment identifier (denoted by a "#" character). These can be used to reference HTML documents from XML documents.

Here is an example of a locator using a fragment identifier.

```
href = "http://www.acmepc.com/products.htm#blasterpc"
```

This informs the XLL processor that the designated resource is identified by the "blasterpc" identifier.

Here is an example of a locator with a query component.

```
href = "http://www.acmepc.com/prod-
ucts.htm?name==blasterpc"
```

In this example, the designated resource is the result of executing the query "name==blasterpc."

When the locator references a resource that is part of an XML document, the fragment identifier takes a different form, known as an XPointer. XPointers are discussed in the following section.

12.7 | XPointers

An XPointer is a sequence of location terms, each of which specifies a location, typically relative to the previous location terms. Each term has a keyword such as CHILD, ANCESTOR, and so on, that can be used in conjunction with element types, attributes, and location numberings to zoom in on a particular resource. Here are some examples:

- **CHILD (2,INVOICE):** The second invoice element
- **CHILD (2,INVOICE)(1,DATE):** The first date element in the second invoice element

An XPointer locator can contain two XPointers separated by ".." to specify begin and end points for the resource. The keywords provided by XPointer syntax appear in Table 12.1.

Table 12.1 XPointer Keywords

Keyword	Interpretation	Absolute/Relative
ROOT	The root element of the source XML document. This keyword is actually implicit in an XPointer, i.e., the XPointer "ROOT()CHILD(1)" is the same as "CHILD(1)."	Absolute
HERE	The location of the linking element. Using HERE in XPointers allows XPointers to be constructed that are relative to the point where the XPointer occurs, i.e., "The paragraph before the one containing this linking element."	Absolute
DITTO	Can be used in the second of a pair of XPointers. It specifies that the location source for its first term is equal to the resource pointed to by the first XPointer.	Absolute
ID(foo)	The element that has an attribute of type ID with the value **foo**.	Absolute
HTML(**foo**)	Selects the first A element whose NAME attribute is set to **foo.**	Absolute

Table 12.1   XPointer Keywords *(continued)*

Keyword	Interpretation	Absolute/Relative
CHILD(N)	The Nth child.	Relative
DESCENDANT	The descendants of the location.	Relative
PRECEDING	All elements preceding the location.	Relative
PSIBLING	All sibling elements preceding the location.	Relative
FOLLOWING	All elements following the location.	Relative
FSIBLING	All sibling elements following the location.	Relative
STRING(n,s,i)	The *i*th character of the *n*th occurrence of the string s.	Relative

12.7.1 *Arguments to relative location terms*

The entries in Table 12.1 that are marked as *relative* can take a variety of arguments to fine tune the selection. The arguments are illustrated in Table 12.2.

Table 12.2   Arguments to relative XPointer keywords

Example	Interpretation
CHILD(ALL)	All children of current location
CHILD(4)	Fourth child of current location
CHILD(3,SECT)	The third child of type SECT

Table 12.2   Arguments to relative XPointer keywords *(continued)*

Example	Interpretation
DESCENDANT(-1,DATE)	The last date element beneath the current location
CHILD(2,*)	The second child of the current location, irrespective of its type (it may be data content rather than an element)
CHILD(1,INVOICE,STATUS,DUE)	The first child of the current location that is of type INVOICE on which the STATUS attribute has been assigned the value "DUE"
CHILD(2,*,STATUS,DUE)	The second child of the current element that has a STATUS attribute set to the value "DUE"
CHILD(1,*,STATUS,*)	The first child of the current element that has a STATUS attribute set to any value
STRING(1,"Hello",1)	The first character in the first occurrence of the string "Hello" within the current element

12.8 | Extended links

An extended link is a link that can involve any number of resources and can be stored completely separately from any of the linked resources if required. Because an arbitrary number of locators can exist, they are housed as child elements of the linking element. Each locator can have its own set of attributes. In this example, a document is created that contains an extended link. It links hard disk technical data from one source with a manufacturer's description from another source. The link will be automatically actuated when the document is loaded, and the resultant data will display in a new window.

```
<PC
 XML-LINK = "EXTENDED"
 ACTUATE="AUTO"
 SHOW="NEW">
<HardDiskData
ROLE     = "Hard Disk Techincal Data"
XML-LINK = "LOCATOR"
href = " http://www.acmepc.com/harddisks.xml#CHILD(3,DISK)"
<Description
ROLE = "Manufacturers Description"
XML-LINK = "LOCATOR"
 = " http://www.acmepc.com/descrip.xml#ID(BLASTER)"
</PC>
```

Note the use of XPointers in the two locators. The first serves to designate the third child of type DISK within the harddisks.xml document as the linked resource. The second serves to designate the element with an ID attribute set to "BLASTER" as the linked resource.

The full set of attributes associated with extended links is illustrated here for elements nominally called CleverLink and Locator:

```
<!ELEMENT CleverLink ANY>
<!ELEMENT LOCATOR ANY>
<!ATTLIST CleverLink
  XML-LINK      CDATA #FIXED "EXTENDED"
      ROLE      CDATA #IMPLIED
     TITLE      CDATA #IMPLIED
    INLINE (TRUE|FALSE) "TRUE"
  CONTENT-ROLE CDATA #IMPLIED
      SHOW  (EMBED|REPLACE|NEW)  "REPLACE"
   ACTUATE  (AUTO|USER) "USER"
  BEHAVIOR      CDATA #IMPLIED
     >
```

```
<!ELEMENT LOCATOR
 XML-LINK CDATA #FIXED "LOCATOR"
 ROLE CDATA #IMPLIED
 HREF CDATA #REQUIRED
 TITLE CDATA #IMPLIED
 SHOW (EMBED|REPLACE|NEW) "REPLACE"
 ACTUATE (AUTO|USER) "USER"
 BEHAVIOR CDATA #IMPLIED
>
```

12.9 | Using fixed attributes

In earlier examples, I have shown how the XML-LINK attribute and others can be specified for each element that represents a link. In many cases, elements with the same name have the same hypertext interpretation wherever they occur in a document. To take a simple example, assume you have an element type CrossReference that is used like this:

```
<CrossReference href = "http://www.acmepc.com/blaster.xml">
See Blaster for details.
</CrossReference>
```

To expose this element as a hypertext-linking element to an XLL processor, you can simply add the XML-LINK attribute like this:

```
<CrossReference
XML-LINK = "SIMPLE"
href = "http://www.acmepc.com/blaster.xml">
See Blaster for details.
</CrossReference>
```

An alternative is to omit the XML-LINK attribute entirely from the instance and create a *fixed* attribute for the element type in the

DTD. This is most conveniently done in the internal document type declaration subset:

```
C>type cross.xml

<!DOCTYPE cross [
<!ATTLIST CrossReference XML-LINK CDATA #FIXED "SIM-
   PLE">
]>
<?xml version = "1.0">
<CrossReference
href = "http://www.acmepc.com/blaster.xml">
See Blaster for details.
</CrossReference>
```

12.10 | Attribute mapping

As you can see elsewhere in this chapter, XLL uses certain attribute names to specify aspects of hypertext such as XML-LINK. XML documents may already use these attribute names to mean other things and thus cause problems for an XLL-aware application. To cater for this possibility, arbitrary user-defined attribute names can be used instead of the ones used in the specification. This result is achieved using the XML-ATTRIBUTES attribute. In this document, the **to** attribute of an xref element serves as the locator.

```
C>type xref.xml

<!DOCTYPE xref [
<!ELEMENT xref (#PCDATA)>
<!ATTLIST xref to CDATA #REQUIRED>
]>
<xref to = "chap1">I am a link to chap 1</xref>
```

The locator is known in XLL as the HREF attribute. You can arrange for an XLL processor to treat the to attribute as if it were an HREF attribute as follows:

```
C>type xref.xml
<!DOCTYPE xref [
<!ATTLIST xref (#PCDATA)>
<!ATTLIST xref
  to CDATA #REQUIRED
  XML-ATTRIBUTES "HREF to">
<xref to = "chap1">I am a link to chap 1</xref>
```

XML Formatting with XSL

- Purpose of XSL
- Relationship to existing standards
- XSL Architecture
- Construction Rules
- Style Rules
- Scripting with JavaScript

13

In August of 1997, Microsoft, Inso, Arbortext, and others made a preliminary draft specification for a style language for XML known as XSL—eXtensible Style Language— available for discussion. Although the document is only at the working draft stage, interest in XSL has been very high, with at least three partial implementations of the working draft in existence. You can see some examples of XSL, based on Microsoft's partial implementation, in Chapter 6. In this chapter, I present more details from the draft, which, at the rate XSL development is going, may well all be implemented by the time you read this!

13.1 | The purpose of XSL

The purpose of XSL is to provide a powerful, yet easy-to-use style sheet syntax for expressing how XML documents should be rendered.

XSL is intended to be independent of any one output format. That is to say, a single XSL style sheet could be used to format XML for RTF today, TeX tomorrow, and HTML the day after, by using different XSL-aware tools, as illustrated in Figure 13-1.

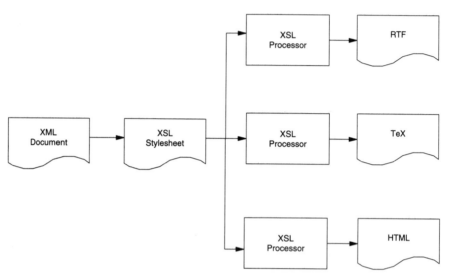

Figure 13–1   A single XSL style sheet can generate multiple output formats

Moreover, multiple style sheets can be de–eloped so that the same XML document can be presented in many different ways. XSL is powerful enough to cope with deleting, rearranging, and generating content "on the fly" during the formatting process.

13.2 | The need for a scripting language

No style sheet language, no matter how comprehensive, can ever hope to satisfy everyone's needs unless it provides the features of a programming language, i.e., branching, looping, variables, and so on. In recognition of this fact, XSL incorporates the internationally standardized version of JavaScript known as ECMAScript (ECMA-

262). From the style sheet language, you can "escape" into JavaScript to perform complex calculations and so on as required.

13.3 | Relationship to CSS

The Cascading Style Sheet (CSS) specification was developed in recognition of the fact that even a fixed tag-set language such as HTML can benefit from separating out the presentation information from the content of the document itself. As a style sheet language, CSS has a number of important limitations that XSL overcomes. With XSL, rearranging content is possible, for example—something that is impossible to do with CSS.

Having said that, the designers of XSL have incorporated many features of CSS into XSL in order to reduce the learning curve of those coming from a CSS background to XSL. Also, the designers of XSL have taken pains to ensure that existing CSS style sheets can be automatically translated into equivalent XSL style sheets.

13.4 | Relationship to DSSSL

DSSSL (Document Style and Semantics Specification Language: ISO/IEC 10179) is an international standard style-sheet language for formatting SGML. DSSSL, like SGML, is big and powerful. With that power comes a degree of complexity! From the early days of the XML initiative, the parties involved agreed that DSSSL would act as the role model on which a simple style-sheet language for XML would be based. In those early days, it was known as DSSSL-O.

DSSSL style sheets are written using a variant of a programming language called Scheme, which is from the Lisp family of languages.

XSL has incorporated a lot of the ideas of DSSSL but has eschewed the Scheme syntax in favor of a simple XML-based syntax.

Many of the developers of XSL are also heavily involved in DSSSL, and work is ongoing to introduce a modification to DSSSL in the future so that the XML-based syntax of XSL will be a conformant syntax within the DSSSL standard. Even in the absence of such a change to the DSSSL standard, you can mechanically convert any XSL style sheet into its big-brother DSSSL equivalent. I take a brief look at DSSSL in Chapter 16.

13.5 | Relationship to HTML

Although intended to allow style sheets to be completely independent of a particular output format, XSL recognizes the great importance of allowing easy generation of HTML from XML. Facilitating HTML output leverages the huge installed base of HTML-aware browsers and other tools. To this end, XSL incorporates a number of extensions (known as *flow objects*) that are specific to HTML output generation.

13.6 | Design principles

Just as with XML, the designers of XSL worked with a set of core design principles in mind. They are reproduced here directly from the draft submission.

1. XSL should be straightforwardly usable over the Internet.
2. XSL should be expressed in XML syntax.
3. XSL should provide a declarative language to do all common formatting tasks.

4. XSL should provide an "escape" into a scripting language to accommodate more sophisticated formatting tasks and to allow for extensibility and completeness.

5. XSL will be a subset of DSSSL with the proposed amendment.

6. A mechanical mapping of a CSS stylesheet into an XSL stylesheet should be possible.

7. XSL should be informed by user experience with the FOSI stylesheet language.

8. The number of optional features in XSL should be kept to a minimum.

9. XSL stylesheets should be human legible and reasonably clear.

10. The XSL design should be prepared quickly.

11. XSL stylesheets shall be easy to create.

12. Terseness in XSL markup is of minimal importance.

13.7 | XSL architecture

An XSL style sheet consists of a set of rules known as *construction rules,* which specify how a source XML document is converted into a hierarchy of formatting objects known as *flow objects.* The concept of a text flow is fundamental to all forms of digital typesetting. A typesetting program pours text into a flow object, working out where each character should appear and wrapping text as necessary to stay within the boundaries of the flow object. Common flow objects include the concept of a page, a paragraph, a table cell, and so on. Flow objects can nest within each other, i.e., a page flow object might contain a table flow object that itself contains cell flow objects, and so on. XSL defines a core set of these flow objects that will be common to all XSL implementations.

Flow objects have associated properties known in XSL as *character-istics* that provide control over the exact workings of the flow object. Examples of characteristics include page width (for a page flow object), justification (for a paragraph flow object), and so on.

As well as the core flow objects that are independent of any one output device, XSL includes flow objects specifically for targeting HTML output. Examples include HTML, HEAD, TABLE, and so on.

As well as construction rules, XSL provides *style rules* that provide a convenient shorthand way of specifying formatting characteristics. In keeping with CSS tradition, these style rules *cascade*. That is to say, multiple style rules can be applied to the same element in the source XML document.

An XSL style sheet is itself an XML document based on a small and simple DTD with a handful of element types such as **<xsl>**, **<rule>**, and so on. The HTML flow objects in XSL are also represented by tags such as <HTML>, <P>, <TABLE>, and so on. These flow object tags are always in uppercase, whereas XSL style sheet tags are always in lowercase.

13.8 | Construction rules

A construction rule may take the following general form.

```
<rule>
  [ pattern ]
  [ action ]
</rule>
```

The pattern part of the rule serves to specify which elements in the source XML document should *trigger* this rule. The action part specifies what to do once the rule triggers.

A simple construction rule pattern appears here:

```
<rule>
  <target-element type = "foo"/>
  [ action ]
</rule>
```

The **target-element** element is used to specify the element type—in this case, **foo**—that will trigger the rule. You see a simple action here:

```
<rule>
  <!-- Pattern -->
  <target-element type = "foo"/>
  <!-- Action -->
  <P>
   <children/>
  </P>
</rule>
```

This rule will cause the construction of a P flow object, into which the results of triggering rules for all the children on the **foo** element will be put. The P element is then closed. Note the difference in case. The uppercase P is a flow object (an HTML paragraph). The lower-case <children/> element is from the XSL tag set and means "process all children of this element now."

A complete XSL style sheet to generate a very unexciting but complete HTML page appears here:

```
<xsl>
 <rule>
  <target-element type = "foo"/>
   <HTML>
    <BODY>
     <children/>
    </BODY>
   </HTML>
 </rule>
</xsl>
```

13.9 | The root rule

The top-level element (the root element) of an XML document can be referred to in the pattern part of a rule using the **<root/>** tag. The following complete XSL style sheet will convert arbitrary XML documents into complete (but unexciting) HTML.

```
<xsl>
 <rule>
  <root/>
   <HTML>
    <BODY>
     <children/>
    </BODY>
   </HTML>
 </rule>
</xsl>
```

13.10 | Multiple target element patterns

The pattern part of a construction rule must contain at least one **target-element** element unless it uses the **<root/>** tag to specify its target. Multiple target-element elements cause the rule to trigger for multiple elements in the source XML document. The following rule will trigger on both apple and orange elements, causing P elements to be constructed for all apples and oranges:

```
<rule>
 <target-element type = "apple"/>
 <target-element type = "orange"/>
 <P>
   <children/>
 </P>
</rule>
```

13.11 | Ancestor patterns

Patterns can be used to trigger rules when an XSL processor finds elements with elements of specified types as their ancestors. The following pattern will trigger when the **pipcount** element is encountered immediately beneath an **apple** element.

```
<element type = "apple">
 <target-element type = "pipcount"/>
</element>
```

Any number of ancestors can be specified starting with parent, then grandparent, then great-grandparent, and so on. This pattern will trigger when a **name** element is encountered within a **person** element that is itself within an **employee** record:

```
<element type = "employee">
 <element type = "person">
  <target-element type = "name"/>
 </element>
</element>
```

13.12 | Descendant patterns

Descendants can be specified in patterns in an analogous way to ancestors. This pattern will trigger on a **fruit** element that has an **apple** element immediately below it.

```
<target-element type = "fruit"/>
 <element type = "apple"/>
```

13.13 | Combined ancestor/descendant patterns

Ancestor and descendant patterns can be combined. This pattern triggers on **person** elements that have an **employee** as parent and **name** as a child.

```
<element type = "employee">
 <target-element type = "person"/>
  <element type = "name"/>
</element/>
```

13.14 | Wildcard patterns

You can specify "one or more ancestors" and "one or more descendants" using the XSL **<any>** tag. This pattern triggers on any invoice
element that has an element **overdue** anywhere in its list of ancestors.

```
<element type = "overdue">
 <any>
 <target-element type = "invoice"/>
</element>
```

13.15 | Attributes

Attributes of an element can also be used to trigger rules. This rule
triggers on **list** elements with the symbol attribute set to "bullet."

```
<target-element type = "list">
 <attribute name = "symbol" value = "bullet"/>
```

Attributes can also be specified as part of the element context. This
rule triggers on any **amount** elements that have a parent element
invoice with the attribute **state** set to the value "overdue."

```
<element type = "invoice">
 <attribute name = "state" value = "overdue"/>
  <target-element type = "amount">
```

You can also simply check that an attribute has a value, without
regard to what that value is using the has-value attribute. This rule
triggers on any **item** element that has a value supplied in its **marker**
attribute.

```
<target-element type = "item">
 <attribute name = "marker" has-value = "yes"/>
```

13.16 | The position qualifier

XSL allows patterns to contain qualifiers specifying the relative position of elements among its siblings. This qualification is done with a position attribute that can have four values:

- **first-of-type**. The element must be the first sibling of its type
- **last-of-type**. The element must be the last sibling of its type
- **first-of-any**. The element must be the first sibling, irrespective of its type
- **last-of-any**. The element must be the last sibling, irrespective of its type

This pattern triggers for an **author** element as long as it is the first **author** element within a **writers** element.

```
<element type = "writers">
 <target-element type = "author" position = "first-of-
type"/>
```

This pattern triggers for an **author** element as long as it is the last **author** element within a **writers** element.

```
<element type = "writers">
 <target-element type = "author" position = "last-of-
type"/>
```

This pattern triggers for a **para** element as long as it is the first child of a **section** element.

```
<element type = "section">
 <target-element type = "para" position = "first-of-
any"/>
```

This pattern triggers for a **para** element as long as it is the last child of a **section** element.

```
<element type = "section">
 <target-element type = "para" position = "last-of-
   any"/>
```

13.17 | Solitary element qualifier

XSL allows a pattern to trigger on elements that have no siblings at all, or that are the only sibling of their type. This qualification is done with the **only** qualifier, which can have two values:

- **of-type**. The element must be the only sibling of its type
- **of-any**. The element must the only element sibling

This pattern will trigger for **item** elements within **list** elements in which only one **item** exists.

```
<element type = "list">
 <target-element type = "item" only = "of-type"/>
```

This pattern will trigger for **emphasis** elements within **para** elements in which the **emphasis** element is the only element beneath the **para.**

```
<element type = "para">
 <target-element type = "emphasis" only = "of-any"/>
```

13.18 | Multiple elements in any order

Multiple element tags can be placed in a target element. The pattern triggers as long as all the specified elements appear as children—irrespective of the order in which they appear. The following pattern triggers as long as both an **apple** and an **orange** element appear somewhere beneath a **fruit** element.

```
<target-element type = "fruit"/>
 <element type = "apple"/>
 <element type = "orange"/>
```

13.19 | Style rules

Style rules allow characteristics of flow objects to be set. Like construction rules, they take the basic pattern/action form:

```
<style-rule>
  [ pattern ]
  [ action ]
</style-rule>
```

Unlike construction rules, any number of style rules can be applied to an element from the XML source document. In this example, all **foo** elements in the XML source document are rendered in italic text

```
<style-rule>
 <target-element type = "foo"/>
 <apply font-weigth="bold"/>
</style-rule>
```

13.20 | Style macros

In a style sheet, a number of flow objects may share the same characteristics. XSL allows groups of style characteristics to be defined in a *style macro.* The macro can then be invoked from multiple style rules. Note in the second example how extra characteristics are also applied with the same apply element.

```
<define style
  name = "Warning"
  font-weight = "bold"
```

```
     color = "red">
<style-rule>
 <target-element type = "Caution"/>
  <apply use = "Warning"/>
</style-rule>

<style-rule>
 <target-element type = "Caution"/>
  <apply use = "Warning" quadding = "center"/>
</style-rule>
```

13.21 | Actions

When a pattern triggers in a rule, the action part of a rule is executed. The action part of the rule consists of *flow object* elements in the order in which they should be created in the output. Any attributes on these elements will specify *characteristics* of the flow object. Tags that appear in uppercase refer to HTML flow objects; all others refer to general-purpose flow objects that can be used to make a style sheet to target multiple output formats. Attributes that appear in uppercase are considered to be cascading style sheet properties.

Within an action, you can specify which source elements should be processed to produce flow objects. The **children** element can be used to specify that all elements in the immediate content of the source element should be processed. This is illustrated below where the children of a **section** element are processed and the resultant flow objects inserted into an HTML DIV element.

```
<rule>
 <target-element type = "section"/>
  <DIV>
   <children/>
  </DIV>
</rule>
```

The **children** element is provided as shorthand for the more general **select** element. The previous example is identical to this one.

```
<rule>
 <target-element type = "section"/>
  <DIV>
   <select from = "children"/>
  </DIV>
 </rule>
```

The **select** element can also specify "ancestors" or "descendants" as the value of its **from** attribute, indicating that all the ancestors/descendants of an element should be processed. In the following example, all elements beneath the **accounts** element are processed.

```
<rule>
 <target-element type = "accounts"/>
  <DIV>
   <select from = "descendants"/>
  </DIV>
 </rule>
```

The select element can itself contain *targets,* thus limiting the selection to elements of a particular type. In this example, all **date** elements beneath an **accounts** element are processed.

```
<rule>
 <target-element type = "accounts"/>
  <DIV>
   <select from = "descendants"/>
    <target-element type = "date"/>
   </select>
  </DIV>
 </rule>
```

Multiple select elements can appear in a single action, allowing quite powerful rearrangements of data to be achieved. In this example, two HTML tables are created, one containing all the male employees, and the other containing all the female employees.

```
<rule>
 <target-element type = "employee"/>
  <TABLE>
   <select from = "descendants">
    <element type = "person">
     <attribute name = "sex" value = "MALE">
    </element>
```

```
    </select>
   </TABLE>
   <TABLE>
    <select from = "descendants">
     <element type = "person">
      <attribute name = "sex" value = "FEMALE">
     </element>
    </select>
   </TABLE>
  </rule>
```

13.22 ⏐ The import element

An XSL style sheet can be imported into any other XSL style sheet using the import element, as you see here:

```
<import href = "http://www.acmepc.com/mystyle.xsl">
```

13.23 ⏐ The define-macro and invoke-macro elements

In larger XSL style sheets, the same collection of flow objects will often be constructed in different rules.

```
<define-macro name = "Blank">
 <P>
   This area intentionally left blank.
 </P>
</define-macro>
```

This macro can then be used in multiple actions using the invoke-macro element. In the example below, the macro is invoked for both **PlaceHolder** and **Deleted** elements.

```
<rule>
 <target-element type = "PlaceHolder"/>
```

```
    <invoke-macro name = "Blank"/>
  </rule>

  <rule>
   <target-element type = "Deleted"/>
     <invoke-macro name = "Blank"/>
  </rule>
```

13.24 | The default rule

In the event that an element is encountered for which no rule has been defined, the following rule is implicitly used.

```
    <rule>
     <target-element/>
     <children/>
    </rule>
```

For debugging style sheets, overriding this rule can be useful. In this example, elements that do not trigger rules are output in red and thus easily spotted in the output.

```
    <rule>
     <target-element/>
     <DIV COLOR = "red">
       <children/>
     </DIV>
    </rule>
```

13.25 | Scripting

XSL incorporates the international standard version of JavaScript (ECMAScript) as its scripting language. Global variable declarations and function definitions can be placed in the **define-script** element.

The functionality of the scripting language can be accessed in two ways:

- From attribute values via the "=" start character
- Via the **eval** element

In the example below, some global constants are defined and subsequently referenced from both attribute values and via the **eval** element.

```
<xsl>
<define-script><![CDATA[
 var MyName   = "Sean";
 var ShoeSize = 11;
]]></define-script>

<rule>
<target-element type = "foot"/>
<DIV font-size="=ShoeSize">
 <children/>
</DIV>
<eval><![CDATA[
if (ShoeSize > 12) "Big feet"; else "Small feet";
]]></eval>
</rule>
</xsl>
```

13.26 | Built-in functions

As well as all the functionality provided in the ECMAScript language, XSL implementations provide a collection of built-in functions specifically aimed at making writing style sheets easier. In this section I look at some of them.

13.26.1 *The formatNumber function*

This function converts numbers into a variety of string formats. It takes two parameters. The first is the number to format. The second is a string indicating how the number should be formatted.

```
formatNumber(3,"1") // "3"
formatNumber(3,"0") // "03"
formatNumber(3,"a") // "c"
formatNumber(3,"A") // "C"
formatNumber(3,"i") // "iii"
```

and so on.

13.26.2 *The formatNumberList function*

This function is similar to the formatNumber function but works on a list of numbers. It takes three parameters:

- The number to format
- A string specifying the format required (same as above); a list of strings can also be provided
- A string to use as a separator

Some examples:

```
formatNumberList((4,2,7),("1","a","i"),"-") // 4-b-vii
formatNumberList((1,2,3),"1","-") // 1-2-3
```

13.26.3 *The ancestor function*

This function returns the nearest ancestor of a specified starting location that is of the specified element type. If no such ancestor exists, it returns null. In this example, the ancestor function is used to navigate from the **amount** element back to the parent **invoice** element. From there, the contents of the **date** subelement are gathered and output.

```
C>type invoice.xml

<invoice>
 <date>1-1-2010</date>
 <amount>12.24</amount>
</invoice>

C>type invoice.xsl

<xsl>
<!-- no output from date elements -->
<rule>
<target-element type = "date"/>
</rule>

<rule>
<target-element type = "amount"/>
<P>
<!-- Output contents of amount element -->
<children/>
<!-- Output a line break -->
<BR/>
<!-- Navigate to find the date information -->
<eval><![CDATA[
"Date is " +
ancestor ("invoice",this).chil-
  dren.item("date",0).text
]]></eval>
</P>
</rule>
</xsl>

C>msxsl -i invoice.xml -s invoice.xsl -o invoice.htm

C>type invoice.htm

<P>
12.24
<BR>
Date is 1-1-2010
</P>
```

13.26.4   *The childNumber function*

This function returns the relative order number of an element. The number is relative to its siblings that have the same type. In this example, the function is used to add numbering to list items.

```
C>type list.xml

<list>
<item>Straight hair</item>
<item>Curly teeth</item>
</list>


C>type list.xsl
<xsl>
<rule>
<target-element type = "item"/>
<DIV>
<eval>"Number : " +
FormatNumber(ChildNumber(this),"1")</eval>
<children/>
</DIV>
</rule>
</xsl>


C>msxsl -i list.xml -s list.xsl -o list.htm
C>type list.htm

<DIV><DIV>
Number : 1
Straight hair
</DIV><DIV>
Number : 2
Curly teeth
</DIV></DIV>
```

13.26.5   *The ancestorChildNumber function*

This function is like childNumber, except it returns the number of a specified ancestor element. In this example, the function is used to produce numbering on nested list items.

```
C>type list.xml

<list>
 <list>
  <item>Blond Eyes</item>
  <item>Blue Hair</item>
 </list>
 <list>
  <item>Straight hair</item>
  <item>Curly teeth</item>
 </list>
</list>


C>type list.xsl

<xsl>
<rule>
<target-element type = "item"/>
<DIV>
<eval>"Number : " + FormatNumber (ancestorChildNum-
   ber("list",this),"1")
+ "." + FormatNumber(ChildNumber(this),"1")</eval>
<children/>
</DIV>
</rule>
</xsl>


C>msxsl -i list.xml -s list.xsl -o list.htm
C>type list.htm

<DIV><DIV>
Number : 1.1
Blond Eyes
</DIV><DIV>
Number : 1.2
Blue Hair
</DIV><DIV>
Number : 2.1
Straight hair
</DIV><DIV>
Number : 2.2
Curly teeth
</DIV></DIV>
```

13.26.6 *The path function*

This function returns an array of numbers. Each number represents an element in the list of ancestors of the starting location for the path function. Each number corresponds to the relative number of the ancestor element in its list of siblings.

```
C>type list.xml

<list>
 <list>
  <item>Blond Eyes</item>
  <item>Blue Hair</item>
 </list>
 <list>
  <item>Straight hair</item>
  <item>Curly teeth</item>
 </list>
</list>

C>type list.xsl

<xsl>
<rule>
<target-element type = "item"/>
<DIV>
<eval><![CDATA[
formatNumberList(path(this),"1",".")
]]></eval>
<children/>
</DIV>
</rule>
</xsl>

C>msxsl -i list.xml -s list.xsl -o list.htm
C>type list.htm

<DIV><DIV>
1.1.1
Blond Eyes
</DIV><DIV>
1.1.2
Blue Hair
</DIV><DIV>
```

```
1.2.1
Straight hair
</DIV><DIV>
1.2.2
Curly teeth
</DIV></DIV>
```

13.26.7 *The hierarchicalNumberRecursive function*

This function is similar to the path function, except that only the child numbers of elements matching the specified type are considered in the numbering. This function is very useful for generating nested section numbers, as the following example illustrates.

```
C>type chapter.xml

<chapter>
<sect>
<title>Engine</title>
 <sect><title>Sump</title></sect>
 <sect><title>Gasket</title></sect>
</sect>
<sect>
<title>Interior</title>
 <sect><title>Radio</title>
  <sect><title>On/Off button</title></sect>
  <sect><title>Tuner</title></sect>
 </sect>
 <sect><title>Gasket</title></sect>
</sect>
</chapter>

C>type chapter.xsl

<xsl>
<rule>
<target-element type = "title"/>
<DIV>
Section :
<eval><![CDATA[
```

```
formatNumberList (hierarchicalNumberRecur-
  sive("sect",this),"1",".")
]]></eval>
<children/>
</DIV>
</rule>
</xsl>

C>msxsl -i chapter.xml -s chapter.xsl -o chapter.htm
C>type chapter.htm

<DIV><DIV> Section : 1
Engine
</DIV><DIV> Section : 1.1
Sump
</DIV><DIV> Section : 1.2
Gasket
</DIV><DIV> Section : 2
Interior
</DIV><DIV> Section : 2.1
Radio
</DIV><DIV> Section : 2.1.1
On/Off button
</DIV><DIV> Section : 2.1.2
Tuner
</DIV><DIV> Section : 2.2
Gasket
</DIV></DIV>
```

13.27 | Linking an XML document to a style sheet

The draft proposes the use of a processing instruction to specify which style sheet should be used to render an XML document.

```
<?xml-stylesheet href = "mystyle.xsl" type = "text/
xsl"?>
```

13.28 | HTML flow objects

I list the HTML flow objects provided in XSL here:

    HTML
      TITLE
      META
      BASE
    BODY
    SCRIPT
    PRE
    DIV
    SPAN
    BR
    HR
    TABLE
      CAPTION
      COL
      COLGROUP
      THEAD
      TBODY
      TFOOT
      TR
      TD
    A
    FORM
      INPUT
      SELECT
      TEXTAREA
    IMG
      AREA
      MAP
    OBJECT
      PARAM
      FRAMESET

The Unicode Standard

The Web—and indeed computing in general—has a long-standing reputation for favoring the English language. Everything from programming languages to HTML element type names are defined using English. The English language uses very few symbols. The collection of letters, digits, punctuation, and so on that are required fit into the 128 codes available in what is known as 7-bit ASCII. Most machines use a byte (8 bits) as their basic unit of storage, and a large proportion of the world's software has been built on the premise that 1 byte holds 1 character.

Unfortunately, single byte characters are far from adequate to deal with the variety of languages and character sets in use throughout the world, a fact that is thrown into stark relief by the Web, which has wrapped the world in a single giant virtual printing press. You can just as easily point your Web browser at a pizza parlor on the far side of the world as you can point it at your local one. If you are using a browser that expects characters to fit into a single byte, you will most likely get some delightful rubbish on the screen if the page is in Chinese or Arabic, for example.

The Unicode standard is a way of handling character sets that over-come this problem. Unicode is a single, standardized character set that can be used to deal with English, Arabic, Chinese, and so on. Any system that is Unicode-compliant can display any Unicode-encoded information correctly, irrespective of the language in which it is written.

14.1 | The origins of Unicode

The Unicode standard has been developed and is actively maintained by a consortium founded in 1991 known as the Unicode Consortium (http://www.unicode.org). Its charter is to develop the standard and promote its use worldwide. Members of the Unicode consortium include Adobe, Apple, Novell, Lotus, and Unisys. The standard is not available electronically but is fully documented in The Unicode Standard Version 2.0, 1996, ISBN 0-201-48345-9.

14.2 | Unicode and the World Wide Web Consortium

Unicode has been the standard character set of all W3C specifications since 1997. Specifically, it is the base character set of both HTML version 4.0 and XML version 1.0.

14.3 | Unicode overview

Unicode is a 16-bit character set that assigns unique numbers to over 38,000 of the different characters used in the world's languages. Languages that can be encoded in Unicode include Arabic, Anglo-Saxon, Devanagari, Russian, Greek, Hebrew, Thai, and Sanskrit. Additionally, ideograph languages such as Chinese and Japanese are supported, with over 20,000 ideograph characters defined by standards bodies in China, Japan, Korea, and Taiwan. Of the 65,000 numbers available, some 18,000 are currently unassigned and available for future expansion.

Unicode can be viewed as a superset of the character sets commonly used in 8-bit systems such as ASCII, ISO-8859-1 (Latin 1), etc. (see Figure 141).

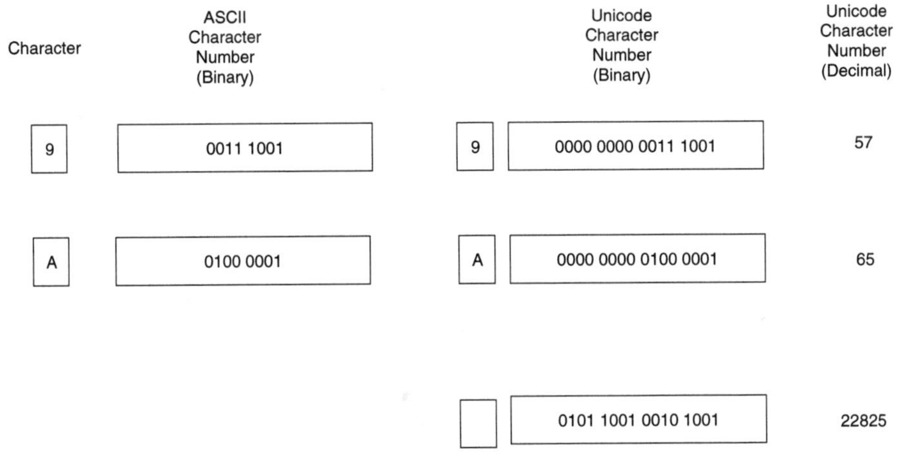

Character	ASCII Character Number (Binary)		Unicode Character Number (Binary)	Unicode Character Number (Decimal)
9	0011 1001	9	0000 0000 0011 1001	57
A	0100 0001	A	0000 0000 0100 0001	65
			0101 1001 0010 1001	22825

Figure 14–1 Comparing Unicode and ASCII

14.4 | Unicode and ISO 10646

The terms "Unicode" and "ISO 10646" are sometimes used inter-changeably. Although the characters assigned in Unicode are character for character identical to those in ISO 10646, the latter is a separate, ISO-developed standard. Until 1991, a number of independent efforts were underway to design a universal character set. In 1991, the Unicode consortium and the ISO 10646 committee joined forces, leading to a merger of their character repertoires in 1992.

ISO 10646 supports a 4-byte character set encoding known as UCS4 (UCS stands for Universal Character Set). At the present time, no characters have been assigned to the top two bytes. The bottom two are known as the BMP (Basic Multilingual Plane). Thus, the BMP component of ISO 10646 is character for character identical to Unicode, as you see in Figure 14–2.

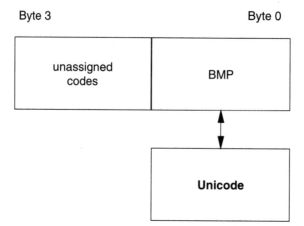

Figure 14–2   The Basic Multilingual Plane (BMP) in ISO 10646

14.5 | Design goals

The Unicode standard has the following main design goals.

- **Universal.** The repertoire of characters supported must be large enough to cover the majority of the interchange requirements of the most heavily used character sets from natural language and also specialized areas such as mathematics.
- **Efficient.** In Unicode, *all* characters are the same size, namely, 2 bytes. Writing systems to deal with this sort of character encoding is easier than dealing with schemes that use escape sequences and the like.
- **Unambiguous.** Any given 16-bit number always represents the same Unicode character.
- **One character. One number.** Often, the same character appears in different languages. In Unicode, each character has a single number irrespective of the number of languages in which it is used.

14.6 | Surrogates

The Unicode standard includes a provision for the use of two 16-bit values to represent a single Unicode character. This capability, known as *surrogates,* expands the range of characters that Unicode can handle into millions. No surrogate characters have so far been defined.

14.7 | Transformation formats

In order to allow systems that can deal only with 7- or 8-bit character sets to handle Unicode, two *transformation formats* are defined in the standard. Using these formats, you can convert 16-bit Unicode into an 8-bit equivalent and back again without loss of information. These transformation formats are know as UTF-8 and UTF-7.

- **UTF-8** is a transformation encoding that uses 8-bit codes to represent Unicode characters. In UTF8, all US ASCII characters have their normal interpretation. Unicode characters outside this range are encoded as a variable number of bytes (up to 6 bytes per character). When multiple bytes are required, the first byte indicates how many bytes will follow.
- **UTF-7** is a transformation encoding that uses 7-bit codes to represent Unicode.

A third transformation format, UTF-16 specifies how Unicode that may contain surrogates can be converted from/to ISO 10646.

14.8 | The Byte Order Mark

The fact that Unicode uses 2 bytes per character raises the question as to what happens when the 16-bit quantities are serialized into 8-bit quantities for storage on disk, transmission via modem, and so on. Some devices store 16-bit quantities such that the least significant byte is stored first (little-endian architectures). Other devices do it the other way around (big-endian architectures). Potential trouble results when, for example, a little-endian architecture receives 8-bit serialized Unicode from a big-endian architecture, as you see in Figure 14–3.

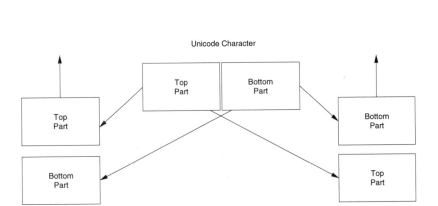

Figure 14–3   Big- and little-endian transmissions of the same Unicode character

To allow an application to detect in which order the bytes should be interpreted, the Unicode standard recommends prefixing the data stream with the Unicode character 0xFEFF. This code is known as the zero-width, non-breaking space character in Unicode. If a big-endian/little-endian mismatch occurs, this number arrives as 0xFFFE. This is not a valid character in Unicode! Consequently, software can be confident that the byte stream that follows will also have its Unicode characters "the wrong way around."

14.9 | Unicode and programming languages

Many of the world's programming languages originated in the 8-bit world. Languages such as ANSI C, Pascal, Cobol, Clipper, and so on are all 8-bit languages. Some languages such as C++ contain support for Unicode in the form of "wide character" libraries. Some more

modern languages such as Java contain direct support for wide characters. Operating systems with direct support for Unicode are also
becoming increasingly common. Examples include Windows NT,
AIX, and Plan 9.

14.10 | Unicode and XML

All conforming XML processors are required to be capable of reading
both the UTF-8 and UTF-16 transformation formats. If UTF-16 is
being used, the Byte Order Mark is required. Each entity in an XML
document is permitted to use either UTF-8 or UTF-16.

In addition, an XML processor may implement support for other
character encodings if it wishes. If other encodings are being used,
then an encoding declaration must be supplied for each entity; that is
to say:

```
<?xml encoding = "EUC-JP"?>
```

In the absence of an encoding declaration or a Byte Order Mark, an
XML Processor will assume that the data is in UTF-8 format.

Note that irrespective of the encoding specified in the encoding
declaration, any character references such as "A" *always* refer
to the Unicode character set.

14.11 | UTF-8

In the absence of instructions to the contrary, an XML processor
assumes that an entity has been encoded in UTF-8. If you have an
existing set of US ASCII files, they are automatically compatible with
XML because they are considered to be in the UTF-8 transformation
format. This fact requires some explanation.

UTF-8 was invented at Bell Labs by a team including the designers of the Unix and Plan 9 operating systems. The idea was to create a character encoding that would allow wide characters but not break the huge existing installed base of systems, protocols, and so on that expect 8-bit data.

UTF-8 is a multibyte encoding of Unicode. In other words, some characters are 1 byte long, some are 3 bytes long, and so on. Up to 6 bytes are used to represent a single character. If more than 1 byte is being used, part of the first byte indicates how many bytes follow. Single-byte characters correspond exactly to 7-bit ASCII. In the example below, "*" indicates a bit used to represent the character. The other "1" and "0" places are used to allow systems to decode the UTF-8 encoding.

```
0*** ****                   (7 bit ASCII)
110* **** 10** ****
1110 **** 10** **** 10** ****
1111 0*** 10** **** 10** **** 10** ****
1111 11** 10** **** 10** **** 10** ****
1111 111* 10** **** 10** **** 10** **** 10** **** 10** ****
```

The Document Object Model (DOM)

15

The Document Object Model (DOM) is a specification under development at the World Wide Web Consortium for a platform- and language-independent interface to the structure and content of XML and HTML documents. The DOM seeks to provide a single-standard model of how the various objects that make up XML and HTML document are organized. It also seeks to standardize an interface to these objects for navigation and document processing.

By using DOM, users benefit from a single homogenous interface to both HTML and XML. They also can move their applications to any DOM-compliant platform without having to make code changes.

The specification consists of a *core* DOM, which provides a low-level set of objects that can represent any sort of structured document. This is known as level 1 DOM. The vision is that additional layers will be added above the core DOM layer to simplify the interfaces to various specific document types and specific forms of processing, such as interactive documents (i.e., dynamic events), DTD manipulation, and style-sheet processing.

15.1 | Design goals

The main design goals of DOM are:

- To provide a set of objects and interfaces sufficient to represent the content and structure of HTML 4.0 and XML 1.0 documents without loss of significant information

- To do so in a platform- and language-independent way

- To provide sufficiently powerful object creation functionality to allow HTML and XML documents to be created from scratch entirely in DOM

- To allow a document to be written from the DOM objects that is structurally identical to the one read into DOM

- To provide a solid, extensible base on which further DOM layers can be added in the future

15.2 | The DOM specification language

In keeping with DOM's aim to be a platform- and language-independent specification, it uses the Object Management Groups IDL (Interface Definition Language—ISO 14750) to express its object types.

15.3 | DOM object types

In DOM, an HTML or XML document is represented as a hierarchical collection of *Node* objects. The node types form the following class hierarchy.

```
Node
    Document Node
    Element Node
    Attribute Node
    Text Node
    Comment Node
    Processing Instruction Node
```

Some *helper* object types are also defined

- **NodeList:** A read-only list of nodes
- **EditableNoteList:** A list of nodes that can be modified
- **NodeEnumerator:** An object used to iterate over a set of nodes
- **DocumentContext:** A (currently unspecified) holder for document metadata such as creation date, author, and so on
- **DOM:** An object providing access to functionality that is equally applicable to HTML and XML documents
- **DOMFactory:** An object used to create new DOM objects

15.4 | Node objects

Nodes are joined together in parent/child relationships as you see in Figure 15–1.

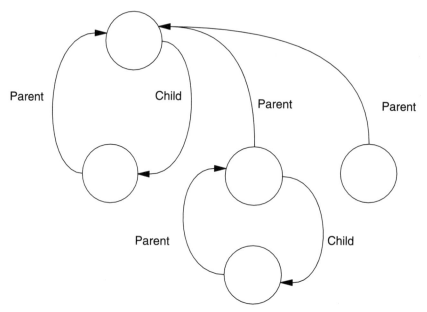

Figure 15–1   Parent/child relationship between nodes in DOM

A node can have zero or more child nodes. Every node, with the exception of the root node, has an associated parent node. Node objects provide the following basic functionality.

- **GetNodeType:** Returns the type of a node; possible return values include Element, Text, and so on, corresponding to the different node types defined in DOM

- **GetParentNode:** Returns the node that is the parent of the current node

- **GetChildren:** Returns a list of all child nodes of the current node

- **HasChildren:** Returns TRUE if the current node has children, FALSE otherwise

- **GetFirstChild:** Returns the first child node beneath the current node

- **GetPreviousSibling:** Returns the node immediately preceding the current node
- **InsertBefore:** Inserts a node into the tree directly preceding a specified node
- **RemoveChild:** Deletes the specified node from the tree

15.5 | Element objects

Element node objects represent elements from the source XML or HTML document. Everything occurring between the start-tag and end-tag appears as descendants of an element node object. The element type name associated with an element object can be retrieved with the **getTagName** method. An element node has a list of any attributes assigned to the element. This is available as the **attributes** property on the object.

15.6 | The document object

The document object is the top-level object for both XML and HTML documents. It has the following properties:

- **DocumentType:** For XML documents with DTDs, this provides access to the DTD. For XML documents without DTDs and for HTML documents, this property has the value **null**.
- **DocumentElement:** This object of type Element is the root element of the document. For HTML documents, this will always have the element type name "HTML" associated with it.

- **GetElementsByTagName:** This method returns a NodeEnumerator object listing all the element nodes in the document that match the specified element type name.

15.7 | The DOM object

This object has a single method getFactory() that returns an object that implements the DOMFactory interface. Future versions of DOM will use the DOM object to store version number information for XML.

15.8 | The DOMFactory object

This object allows users to programmatically create new DOM objects. DOMFactory can be used to add new objects to an existing document or create a document entirely from scratch. Some methods provided by DOMFactory are:

- **CreateElement:** Creates an Element node with the specified element type name and attributes
- **CreateTextNode:** Creates a Text node containing the specified text
- **CreateComment:** Creates a Comment node containing the specified text
- **CreatePI:** Creates a Processing Instruction node according to the specified PI Target and contents strings

15.9 | The NodeList object

Provides a data structure for storing and accessing a read-only list of nodes. The **item** method can be used to retrieve an item based on a specified offset from the beginning of the list. The **getLength** method returns the number of nodes in the list.

15.10 | The EditableNodeList object

This object is akin to a NodeList object but adds methods to allow the node list to be modified. The **replace** method will replace a given node in the list with another. The **insert** method will insert a node at the specified location. The **remove** method deletes the specified node.

15.11 | The NodeEnumerator object

This object provides a general-purpose iteration mechanism over arbitrary collections of nodes. The **getFirst** method returns the first node in a collection. The **getNext** method returns the next node in a collection, and so on.

15.12 | The AttributeList object

This type of object represents collections of attributes. Methods provided include **getAttribute**, **setAttribute**, **remove,** and **getLength**.

15.13 | The Attribute object

The Attribute object represents a single attribute. Methods provided include **getName,** which returns the attribute name, and **toString,** which converts the attribute value to a string. The value of the attribute is made available in the **value** property.

15.14 | The Comment object

This object represents a comment. It has a single property, **data,** which contains the text of the comment.

15.15 | The PI object

The PI object represents a processing instruction. It has two properties: **name,** the processing instruction target, and **data**, the contents of the processing instruction.

15.16 | The Text object

Text objects contain the character data chunks in a document. The data property contains the data itself.

15.17 | HTML-specific components of DOM

The HTML components of DOM add functionality and convenience functions specifically aimed at making life easier for HTML scripting applications. The capabilities are based on the models and functionality currently provided in leading browsers such as Netscape Navigator and Internet Explorer.

- The HTMLDocument object
- The HTMLElement object
- Special HTMLElements such as IMG, TABLE, and so on

15.17.1 *The HTMLDocument object*

This object represents the root of an HTML document tree. Some of its methods/properties are:

- **Images:** A collection of all the images (<img> elements)
- **Applets:** A collection of all the applets (<applet> and <object> elements)
- **Links:** A collection of all the links (<a> and <area> elements)
- **Forms:** A collection of all the forms (<form> elements)
- **Cookie:** A collection of cookies associated with the HTML document
- **Filesize:** The size of the HTML document in bytes
- **FileCreatedDate:** The date the document was created
- **Body:** The element containing the content of the document (for normal HTML, this corresponds to the <body> element; for frameset documents, it corresponds to the outermost <frameset> element)

15.17.2   *The HTMLElement object*

This object is used as the base object type for all HTML-specific objects. Some HTML elements such as head, strong, and address are provided as HTMLElement objects. Others are derived from HTML-Element into further classes. A few examples, which follow, serve to give a flavor of the full set of HTMLElement objects.

15.17.2.1   The A element

The A element has properties such as:

- **href:** The href attribute of the element
- **name:** The name attribute of the element
- **tabIndex:** The element's position in the tabbing order
- **charset:** The character set used by the linked resource

15.17.2.2   The IMG element

The IMG element has properties such as:

- **border:** Specification for the border to surround the image
- **alt:** A short description of the image
- **src:** The source URI for the image

15.17.2.3   The Script element

The Script element has properties such as:

- **src:** The URI of an externally stored script
- **language:** The name of the scripting language used

15.17.2.4   The Table element

This element is more complex in HTML and has a correspondingly larger DOM interface. Properties of the Table element include:

- cols
- border
- cellSpacing
- cellPadding
- align
- width

Methods of the table element include:

- getRows
- getTHead
- getCaption
- insertRow

15.18 | XML-specific components of DOM

The XML components of DOM add functionality on top of base DOM to allow all aspects of a parsed XML document to be represented, and to allow validating XML parsers to work with DOM objects. Specifically, the XML components add support for:

- Document Type Declarations
- Entities
- CDATA Marked Sections
- Conditional Sections

15.18.1 *The Document Type object*

This object provides access to all the declarations that make up the Document Type Declaration. Properties provided include:

- **externalSubset:** All declarations from the external subset
- **internalSubset:** All declarations from the internal subset
- **generalEntities:** All the general entity declarations
- **parameterEntities:** All the parameter entity declarations
- **notations:** All the notation declarations
- **elementTypes:** All the element definitions

15.18.2 *The Element Definition object*

This object represents the information contained in a single element type declaration. Properties include:

- **name:** The name of the element type.
- **contentType:** One of (EMPTY, ANY, PCDATA, or MODEL_GROUP). The MODEL_GROUP value signifies that the element type has a content model associated with it (i.e., it has element or mixed content). The full details of the content model are available via the contentModel attribute.
- **contentModel:** For element types with a content model, this property provides access to a hierarchy of information representing connectors (selection, sequence, etc.), occurrence indicators (+, *, or ?), and tokens such as PCDATA or ElementToken. An ElementToken can also have a name and an occurrence indicator.
- **AttributeDefinitions:** This property provides access to the list of attribute type declarations for the element type.

15.19 | Uses and users of DOM

Throughout this book, you can see examples of applications that will benefit from the standardization of a single, clean interface to XML and HTML documents. ECMAScript, XSL, XLL, WIDL, CFML, etc., all stand to benefit. Moreover, as DOM develops implementations scripting languages such as Perl, Python, and Visual Basic are sure to emerge. The fact that the DOM is a read/write interface means that it will be of use in creating documents from scratch as tree structures, rather than writing a mixture of tags and character data to a flat text file. Also, DOM promises to be very useful as a standard exposed interface for XML/HTML applications for, say, OLE automation on Windows platforms.

Raiding the SGML Larder

- Omitted tag minimization

- White space handling

- Conditional sections

- CDATA elements

- Converting SGML to XML

- SGML Viewers

- DSSSL

All XML Documents are SGML documents. They are simply limited in the features of SGML that they can use. Some of the features of SGML that do not appear in XML have been excluded because they are not used very much in practice—even by seasoned SGML users. Other features, however, have been excluded in order to make developing software for XML easier. Some of these features are very useful!

Thankfully, SGML vs. XML is not a "one or the other" choice. You can certainly mix the two. You can use SGML where SGML's extra functionality is of benefit and down translate to XML for delivery. Equally, you can use some of SGML's power to get your documents marked up in the first place and then convert to XML for production use.

Moreover, you can leverage SGML's power with freely available tools. All you need is some idea of what useful functionality lurks in SGML and how you can use it to your advantage. In this chapter, I look at some of the gems of functionality in SGML that can make life easier for deploying XML. I also look at some of the freely available tools that bridge the SGML and XML worlds. All the tools used in this chapter are available on the accompanying CD.

16.1 | Useful features of SGML not in XML (a personal choice)

SGML has many features not found in XML. Most seasoned SGML users have their own pet favorites and pet hates. Debates about the merits/demerits of various SGML features, such as the comp.text.sgml newsgroup on Usenet, have continued unabated for over ten years now.

Any list of "useful" features from the SGML standard that are not in the XML standard is therefore always a personal choice and bound to find disagreement from some quarter. With the caveat that this list is very much *personal,* here is my list of SGML features that can usefully be used in an environment targeting XML as the delivery/production format:

- Omitted tag minimization
- White space handling
- Conditional sections
- CDATA elements

16.1.1 *Omitted tag minimization*

You probably have noticed that XML documents typically contain more tags per square inch than HTML documents. The reason is that, as an SGML application, HTML takes advantage of a feature known as *omitted tag minimization.* In SGML, you can declare an element in such a way as to instruct the parser that either the start-tag or end-tag (or both!) can be missing from the SGML document. The parser then uses clever logic to *infer* the presence of the tags. This feature is of particular benefit when documents are being created by hand. When marking up large quantities of documents manually, the amount of tagging required significantly affects the effort involved (not to mention cost, if you are paying for data entry by the keystroke!).

16.1.2 *White space handling*

In XML, almost all white space is considered significant and passed on to the application. (I covered the details and nuances of this function in XML in Chapter 11.) SGML, by contrast, defines a number of situations in which white space is not significant and is not passed on to the application. Specifically, a general rule exists in SGML that a newline immediately following a start-tag or immediately preceding an end-tag will be eaten up by the parser and not passed on to the application. This feature can be useful when you wish to break up a document into multiple lines without causing those line breaks to appear in the parsed document.

16.1.3 *Conditional sections*

XML allows conditional sections to occur within the external entities in the document type declaration subset. This feature of XML allows SGML users to move their DTDs over to XML easily as conditional sections are used extensively in DTDs such as the TEI DTD. Unlike XML, full SGML also allows conditional sections to occur within the document instance. Thus you can have chunks of a document that appear/disappear in the output, depending on the way the conditional sections have been arranged. For situations in which slight variations in the content of a document are required for particular uses, conditional sections can be just the thing.

16.1.4 *CDATA elements*

In XML, you can *escape* a body of text from the attentions of the parser using a CDATA marked section. SGML provides an additional option for achieving this effect that requires less markup in the form of the CDATA elements.

16.2 | The NSGMLS parser

To illustrate these selected features of SGML, I employ the services of the famous NSGMLS SGML parsing application by James Clark (http://www.jclark.com).

Strictly speaking, the NSGMLS application is one particular application built on top of a comprehensive C++ based, SGML parsing core known as SP. NSGMLS uses SP to perform the core parsing tasks and generates an output notation known as ESIS. We have seen examples of ESIS, like output from the Ælfred XML parser. It is a line-oriented notation in which each line corresponds to an event communicated from the SGML parser. The ESIS output notation has been used extensively in building SGML applications over the years.

16.3 | A simple SGML document

Here is a very simple SGML document.

```
C>type simple.sgm

<!DOCTYPE simple [
<!ELEMENT simple - - (#PCDATA)>
]>
<simple>
Hello World
</simple>
```

The only syntactic difference between this document and a conformant XML document is the "- -" appearing to the right of the element type name in the declaration of the **simple** element type. This area is where SGML allows omitted tag minimization to be specified, as you can see a little later. For now, see how to parse this SGML document with NSGMLS:

```
C>nsgmls simple.sgm

(SIMPLE
-Hello World
)SIMPLE
C
```

You will note that the output looks very similar to the output you have seen from the EsisDemo application of the Ælfred XML parser. This is not an accident, because this application of Ælfred is modeled on the ESIS output from NSGMLS. Note also the "C" line at the very end. This stands for "Conforming" and indicates that the parse proceeded without a hitch. SGML parsers (unlike XML parsers) are permitted to attempt to recover from errors and continue to emit events. NSGMLS does a very good job of forging on in the face of errors but will not append the "C" record if errors occur. This feature can be useful when catching markup errors, because a single parse can often locate multiple errors that can then be fixed together.

16.4 | SGML-to-XML conversion

Just as NSGML is an application built on top of the core SP parser, SX is an application built on top of SP to adapt full SGML documents for processing by XML systems.<fn>The change is called an "adaptation" rather than a "conversion" because the result is still SGML, although restricted to the XML subset.</fn> The simple.sgm document of the last section can be adapted to XML as follows:

```
C>sx simple.sgm

<?xml version="1.0"?>
<SIMPLE
>Hello World</SIMPLE>
```

Note the end of line before the simple start-tag is closed. By default, SX will add such line breaks to reduce the likelihood of very long lines. Since XML ignores white space occurring in this part of a start-tag, the line break has no effect on the output produced by an XML parser, as shown here. First, I adapt the full SGML to XML using SX:

```
C>sx simple.sgm > simple.xml
```

Now I parse the XML document with EsisDemo:

```
C>jview EsisDemo simple.xml

(SIMPLE
-Hello World
)SIMPLE
```

SX provides a number of options to control how and what is generated in the resultant XML. Some of the most important ones are listed in Table 16.1. You can see some of them in action later on in this chapter.

Table 16.1   Some Command-Line Options to SX

Option	*Interpretation*
-x no-nl-in-tag	Disables the insertion of newlines in start-tags to break the XML output into lines.
-x cdata	Generates XML CDATA sections for both SGML CDATA sections and elements with CDATA declared content
-x comment	Outputs comments
-x empty	Generates the <foo/> syntax for empty elements.
-x attlist	Generates attribute list declarations in the internal DTD subset

16.5 | Some examples

In this section, my favorite SGML features are illustrated, along with examples of how they can be used in the process of creating XML documents.

16.5.1 *Omitted tag minimization*

In SGML, element types can be declared so that start-tags, end-tags, or both can be omitted. The tag omission required is declared immediately to the right of the element type name in the element type declaration. The "-" character means "no omission allowed." The "O" character means "omission allowed." The first character refers to the start-tag, and the second to the end-tag. Here is an example of an SGML document that allows end-tags to be omitted from **p** elements:

```
C>type note.sgm

<!DOCTYPE note [
<!ELEMENT note - O (p)+>
<!ELEMENT p - O (#PCDATA)>
]>
<note>
<p>first para
<p>second para
</note>
```

Parsing this with NSGMLS produces the following output:

```
C>nsgmls note.sgm

(NOTE
(P
-first para
)P
(P
-second para
)P
)NOTE
C
```

Note that it includes events for the end of P elements even though no end-tags are present in the SGML document. The parser has *inferred* their presence. I offer no prizes for guessing what happens when I convert this into XML.

```
C>sx note.sgm

C>sx -x no-nl-in-tag note.sgm

<?xml version="1.0"?>
<NOTE><P>first para</P><P>second para</P></NOTE>
```

As you can see, the p element end-tags have been slotted into the output, giving us a fully conformant XML document:

```
C>sx -x no-nl-in-tag note.sgm >note.xml

C>jview EsisDemo note.xml

(NOTE
(P
-first para
)P
(P
-second para
)P
)NOTE
```

Note the use of the no-nl-in-tag option to stop SX from inserting line breaks in start-tags. The output without this option looks like this:

```
C>sx note.sgm

<?xml version="1.0"?>
<NOTE
><P
>first para</P><P
>second para</P></NOTE>
```

Armed with this knowledge of how omitted tag minimization works in SGML, you can see how the designers of HTML have used SGML minimization techniques in the HTML DTD. Partial and simplified declarations from the HTML 3.2 DTD for the HTML, HEAD, and BODY elements look like this:

```
<!ELEMENT HTML O O (HEAD,BODY)>
<!ELEMENT HEAD O O (...)>
<!ELEMENT BODY O O (...)>
<!ELEMENT TITLE - - (#PCDATA)>
```

Note that both start- and end-tags for HEAD and BODY are declared omissible. In contrast, start- and end-tags for TITLE are mandatory. As a result of these declarations, the following HTML document is valid, per the HTML3.2 DTD:

```
C>type test.htm

<!DOCTYPE HTML SYSTEM "HTML32.DTD">
<HTML>
<TITLE>Hello World</TITLE>
<P>Hello World
```

The slightly abridged output from NSGMLS appears here:

```
C>nsgmls test.htm

(HTML
(HEAD
(TITLE
-Hello World
)TITLE
)HEAD
BODY
P
-Hello World
)P
)BODY
)HTML
C
```

Note how the parser has inferred start- and end-tags in all the right places. I now have a properly SGML-parsable HTML document. For fun, I can convert this into valid XML as follows:

```
C>sx test.htm

<?xml version="1.0"?>
<HTML
VERSION="-//W3C//DTD HTML 3.2 Final//EN"
><HEAD
><TITLE
```

```
>Hello World</TITLE></HEAD><BODY
><P
>Hello World</P></BODY></HTML>
```

HTML as XML! This switch is certainly fun, but a serious point to it exists as well. An HTML document that is also a fully compliant XML document is a doubly useful thing. It can be just as good for display in an HTML browser but is also fully programmable with XML tools and can be processed like any other XML document by XML-aware editors, databases, XSL style-sheet implementations, and so on.

16.5.2 *Conditional sections*

Sometimes, having a single document that holds multiple variations of its content is useful. Examples include documents where, say, 80% of the content is common to two uses of the document and 20% of the content differs. Another common example is maintaining multiple language versions of the same content in a single document.

Unlike XML, SGML allows conditional sections to occur within the document content. In this example, one paragraph is common to two uses, whilst the other two need to be included, depending on intended use:

```
C>type cond.sgm

<!DOCTYPE legalstuff [
<!ELEMENT legalstuff - O (p)+>
<!ELEMENT p - O (#PCDATA)>
]>
<legalstuff>
<p>This product is provided as is...
<!-- European version -->
<![INCLUDE[
<p>Contact Europe 1234 for help
]]>
<!-- American version -->
<![IGNORE[
<p>Contact America 1234 for help
]]>
```

As it stands, the paragraph aimed at American use is "commented out" by the IGNORE keyword to the conditional section. The European paragraph is included. Parsing with NSGMLS produces the following output:

```
C>nsgmls cond.sgm

(LEGALSTUFF
(P
-This product is provided as is...
)P
(P
-Contact Europe 1234 for help\n
)P
)LEGALSTUFF
C
```

In practice, using a parameter entity to control which sections are included and which ones are ignored is often more useful, as shown here:

```
C>type cond.sgm

<!DOCTYPE legalstuff [
<!ENTITY % EuropeanStuff "INCLUDE">
<!ENTITY % AmericanStuff "IGNORE">

<!ELEMENT legalstuff - O (p)+>
<!ELEMENT p - O (#PCDATA)>
]>
<legalstuff>
<p>This product is provided as is...
<!-- European version -->
<![%EuropeanStuff;[
<p>Contact Europe 1234 for help
]]>
<!-- American version -->
<![%AmericanStuff;[
<p>Contact America 1234 for help
]]>
```

This document parses to produce exactly the same output:

```
C>nsgmls cond.sgm
```

```
(LEGALSTUFF
(P
-This product is provided as is...
)P
(P
-Contact Europe 1234 for help\n
)P
)LEGALSTUFF
C
```

A two-line change to swap the INCLUDE/IGNORE parameter entities is all that is required to get the parser to generate the American version.

```
C>type cond.sgm

<!DOCTYPE legalstuff [
<!ENTITY % EuropeanStuff "IGNORE">
<!ENTITY % AmericanStuff "INCLUDE">

<!ELEMENT legalstuff - O (p)+>
<!ELEMENT p - O (#PCDATA)>
]>
<legalstuff>
<p>This product is provided as is...
<!-- European version -->
<![%EuropeanStuff;[
<p>Contact Europe 1234 for help
]]>
<!-- American version -->
<![%AmericanStuff;[
<p>Contact America 1234 for help
]]>

C>nsgmls cond.sgm

(LEGALSTUFF
(P
-This product is provided as is...
)P
(P
-Contact America 1234 for help\n
)P
)LEGALSTUFF
C
```

I am now within a stone's throw of XML versions of the two variations, thanks to the magic of SX.

```
C>sx cond.sgm

<?xml version="1.0"?>
<LEGALSTUFF
><P
>This product is provided as is...</P><P
>Contact America 1234 for help
</P></LEGALSTUFF>
```

The beauty of SGML conditional sections is that I have to do literally no programming work to generate multiple, stand-alone XML
variations of a single-source document. I can go further and arrange
for the selection between the two to be command-line driven. The "i
foo" command-line option to NSGMLS causes the parser to behave
as if

```
<!ENTITY % foo "INCLUDE">
```

occurs in the internal declaration subset. Such a declaration then takes
precedence over any others in the document. To use this feature, I
start by setting both the AmericanStuff and EuropeanStuff parameter
entities to IGNORE:

```
C>type cond.sgm

<!ENTITY % AmericanStuff "IGNORE">
<!ENTITY % EuropeanStuff "IGNORE">
<!ELEMENT legalstuff - O (p)+>
<!ELEMENT p - O (#PCDATA)>
]>
<legalstuff>
<p>This product is provided as is...
<!-- European version -->
<![%EuropeanStuff;[
<p>Contact Europe 1234 for help
]]>
<!-- American version -->
<![%AmericanStuff;[
<p>Contact America 1234 for help
]]>
```

As they stand, the parser ignores both conditional sections:

```
C>nsgmls cond.sgm

(LEGALSTUFF
(P
-This product is provided as is...\n
)P
)LEGALSTUFF
C
```

Using the -i switch, I can generate the American version like this:

```
C>nsgmls -i AmericanStuff cond.sgm

(LEGALSTUFF
(P
-This product is provided as is...
)P
(P
-Contact America 1234 for help\n
)P
)LEGALSTUFF
C
```

Switching the command line generates the European version:

```
C>nsgmls -i EuropeanStuff cond.sgm

(LEGALSTUFF
(P
-This product is provided as is...
)P
(P
-Contact Europe 1234 for help\n
)P
)LEGALSTUFF
C
```

The SX application also has this magical -i switch. So in order to generate an XML version of the European variation of this document, I simply do the following:

```
C>sx -i EuropeanStuff cond.sgm

<?xml version="1.0"?>
```

```
<LEGALSTUFF
><P
>This product is provided as is...</P><P
>Contact Europe 1234 for help
</P></LEGALSTUFF>
```

Producing the American version is equally difficult.

```
C>sx -i AmericanStuff cond.sgm

<?xml version="1.0"?>
<LEGALSTUFF
><P
>This product is provided as is...</P><P
>Contact America 1234 for help
</P></LEGALSTUFF>
```

16.5.3 *CDATA elements*

In XML, sections of text can be shielded from the attentions of the parser using a CDATA section. Such protection is particularly important for elements intended to contain programming language scripts that tend to make liberal use of characters such as "<", and "&," that have special meaning in XML. A CDATA section looks like this:

```
C>type script.xml

<!DOCTYPE script [
<!ELEMENT script (#PCDATA)>
]>
<script>
<![CDATA[
for (i = 0;i<foo;i++)
 a = a&b;
]]>
</script>
```

In SGML, you can use an element with CDATA declared content to achieve a similar effect.

```
C>type script.sgm
```

```
<!DOCTYPE script [
<!ELEMENT script - O CDATA>
]>
<script>
for (i = 0;i<foo;i++)
 a = a&b;
</script>
```

This approach removes the need for the marked section tagging but it is not a complete panacea. Just as the string "]]>" must be avoided within a CDATA section, a string that looks like an end-tag (i.e., starting with "</") must be avoided in a CDATA element. This proviso notwithstanding, CDATA elements, with their reduced tagging requirements, are particularly useful for creating program code. When you need XML versions of SGML documents using CDATA declared content, you can use the cdata switch to the SX application, which will insert the CDATA section tagging automatically.

```
C>sx -x cdata script.sgm

<?xml version="1.0"?>
<SCRIPT
><![CDATA[for (i = 0;i<foo;i++)
 a = a&b;]]></SCRIPT>
```

16.6 | SGML viewers

For many organizations, SGML is used as a data source from which multiple output formats are generated via conversion software. For some uses, a perfectly acceptable approach is to simply have viewing software that reads the SGML, applies style, and displays the result on the screen, perhaps in a Web browser via an SGML viewer plug-in. Even when down translation to say, HTML or RTF, is the ultimate destination format, having tools to allow you to quickly create and view styled versions of the SGML documents is useful.

A variety of these SGML viewers have been developed over the years. Perhaps the most well known is the Panorama SGML viewer from Softquad, which is available as a Web browser plug-in (see http://www.softquad.com).

In this section, I look at an SGML viewer/publishing package known as Multidoc Pro. A trial version is included on the accompanying CD. I create another little products database for acmepc.com and illustrate how you can use Multidoc Pro to very quickly set up an SGML viewer for the database.

These viewers are of interest from an XML perspective for a number of reasons:

- They provide organizations using SGML as their data source with a rapid SGML viewing/browsing capability. The SGML can be down translated to XML for delivery, via SX, for example.
- They provide "rapid application development" environments for designing and playing with style sheets.
- Native XML versions of these viewers will soon be available.

First, I need an SGML document for the products database. I use a very simple model in which the products database consists of a collection of **product** elements. Each product has a **description** and a **unit-price.** The description consists of a mixture of character data interspersed with **B** (bold) and **I** (italic) elements. Note that because this viewer is an SGML viewer, I can take advantage of omitted tag minimization, as you see here:

```
C>type products.sgm

<!DOCTYPE Products [
<!ELEMENT Products - O (Product+)>
<!ELEMENT Product - O (Description,UnitPrice)>
<!ATTLIST Product type (PC|Printer) #REQUIRED>
<!ELEMENT Description - O (Para+)>
<!ELEMENT UnitPrice - O (#PCDATA)>
```

```
<!ELEMENT Para - O (#PCDATA|B|I)+>
<!ELEMENT B - O (#PCDATA|I)+>
<!ELEMENT I - O (#PCDATA|B)+>
]>
<Products>
<Product type = "PC">
<Description>
<Para>Acme Blaster 555.
<Para>A <B>fantastic</B> PC.
</Description>
<UnitPrice>
1000
</UnitPrice>
</Product>
<Product type = "PRINTER">
<Description>
<Para>Sprinter Printer 123
<Para>Included patented <I>sixth sense</I> technol-
   ogy.
</Description>
<UnitPrice>
500
</UnitPrice>
</Product>
</Products>
```

Before proceeding, I use NSGMLS to ensure that I have valid SGML.

```
C>nsgmls -s products.sgm
```

The -s switch to NSGMLS suppresses normal output and just emits error messages. I get no output from the above command, so the coast is clear. Multidoc also does a parse of the SGML, but it is a nonvalidating parse somewhat akin to the well formedness check of nonvalidating XML parsers.

Loading this document into Multidoc Pro produces the result you see in Figure 16–1.

To the right, you see all the data content of the products.sgm document in an essentially unformatted form. On the left, you see two views of the document. The default view is a table of contents view (I have not set one up yet). The other is the SGML Tree view. Clicking

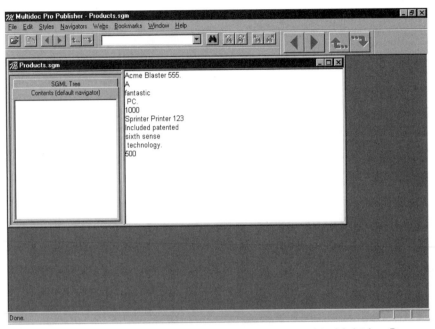

Figure 16–1 The products.sgm document viewed in Multidoc Pro

this SGML Tree tab (and expanding a few nodes by clicking them) produces the result in Figure 16–2.

Clicking any element node in this tree view highlights the entire contents of the element in the data view on the right. In Figure 16–3, the second **product** element is highlighted.

I can now proceed to create a style sheet to produce a pleasant view of the data content of products.sgm. In Multidoc Pro, a single document can have any number of style sheets providing different views of the same data. The various style sheets to choose from will be displayed under the Styles menu. To create a new style sheet, choose "new style sheet" under the styles menu. In Figure 16–4, a style called style1 is defined and given the filename style1.ssh.

A style sheet can be associated with an SGML document in a variety of ways. The most powerful way is to use a separate file called entityrc to associate style sheets with documents conforming to particular DTDs. For this simple demonstration of Multidoc Pro, I use an alter-

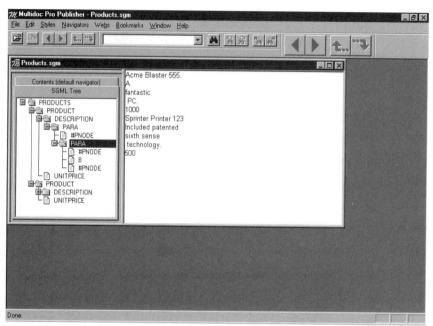

Figure 16–2   The SGML Tree view of products.sgm

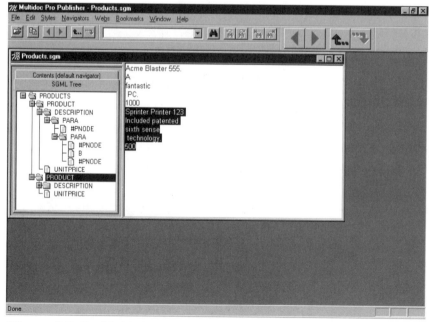

Figure 16–3   Highlighting an element using the SGML tree view

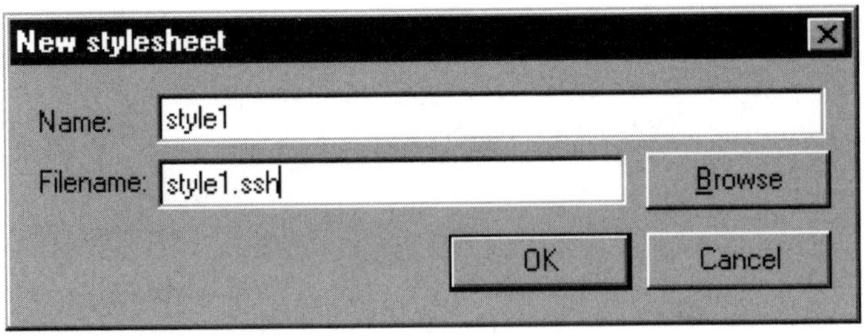

Figure 16–4   Creating a style sheet

native technique. I insert a style-sheet processing instruction into the products.sgm document. I insert it just after the doctype line, but it can go anywhere in the DTD.

```
<!DOCTYPE Products [
<?STYLESPEC "style 1" "style1.ssh">
```

To make this change take effect, I need Multidoc Pro to reparse the document. This action is most conveniently achieved by pressing the **F5** key. Once done, the style sheet appears for selection under the Styles menu, as Figure 16–5 shows.

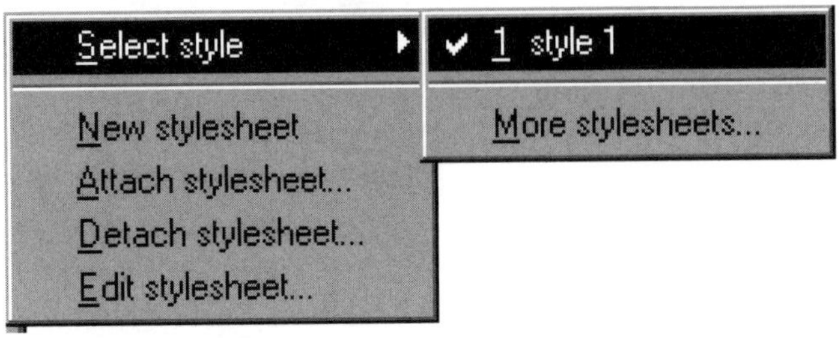

Figure 16–5   Selecting the style from the Style menu

I can now proceed to interactively create the style sheet and immediately view how the style changes affect the SGML document. Selecting the B element from the SGML Tree view and selecting "Edit stylesheet" from the right-click submenu produces the dialog box in Figure 16–6.

Notice that the effect of setting the font weight to bold is immediately previewed in the preview window. The document now looks like Figure 16–7.

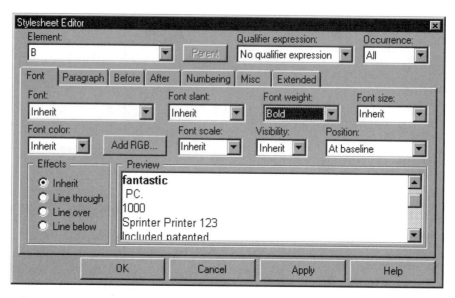

Figure 16–6   Modifying the element style with the style dialog box

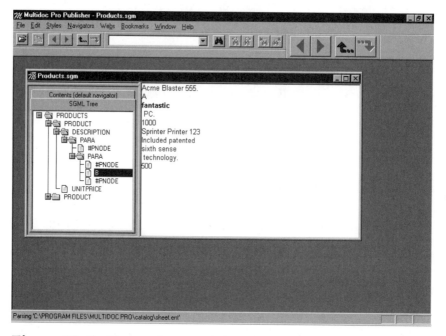

Figure 16–7   The products sgml document with a bold style attached to **B** elements

I am not finished with B elements yet, however. Notice how the word **fantastic** appears on a line on its own. The reason is that the default behavior of Multidoc is to break elements into separate lines. B is an example of an *in-line* element. You typically want it to flow in line with surrounding text. You can arrange this flow in the paragraph tab of the Stylesheet Editor dialog box, as you see in Figure 16–8.

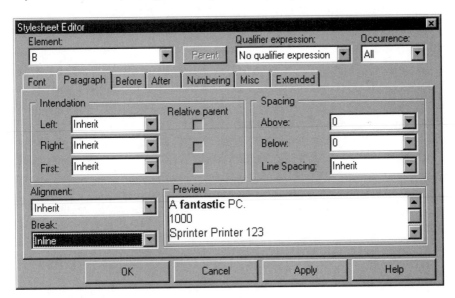

Figure 16–8   Making **B** elements in line

While I am at it, I can do a similar job for I (italic) elements. The resultant document view appears in Figure 16–9.

And so on it goes! You simply select the element type to which you wish to apply style, modify the style sheet dialog as desired, and voila! The result appears in the document window. Figure 16–10 shows the resultant document after more style has been applied to various element types.

Note that I have merely scratched the surface of the style-sheet capabilities of Multidoc Pro. For full information, consult the on-line documentation (which is an SGML document, of course!). The manual itself is a good demonstration of what Multidoc Pro can achieve. A sample screen shot appears in Figure 16–11.

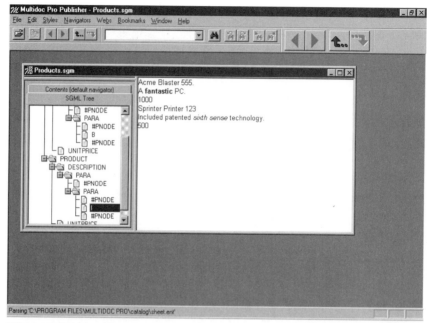

Figure 16–9   The document after applying style to **B** and **I** elements

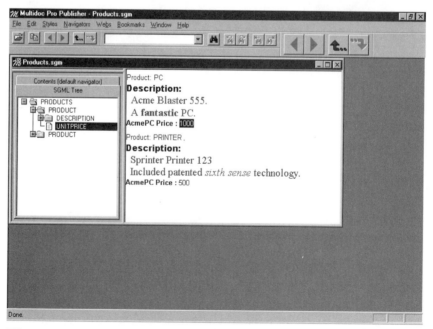

Figure 16–10   A reasonably readable version of the products SGML document

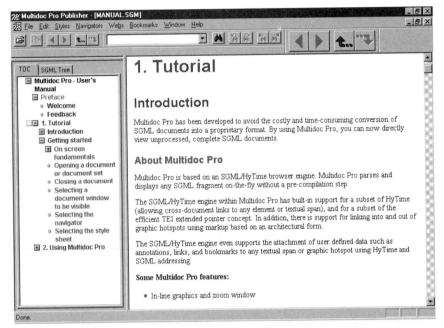

Figure 16–11   The Multidoc Pro manual displayed in Multidoc Pro

16.6.1 *The style-sheet language*

As befits an SGML viewer, the style sheets created in Multidoc Pro are
themselves SGML documents conforming to a style sheet DTD. Here
are some snippets of the one I created earlier in this chapter for prod-
ucts.sgm, with some comments added to explain what is going on.

```
<!-- Style for the UNITPRICE element -->
<STYLE TAG="UNITPRICE">
<A-TEXT V='AcmePC Price : '> <!-- Text to add before -->
<!-- Font weight is bold -->
<FONT-WEIGHT V=Bold>
</STYLE>

<!-- Style for the PRODUCT element -- >
<STYLE TAG="PRODUCT">
```

```
<SPC-ABOVE V="5"> <!-- 5 points vertical spacing above-->
<SPC-BELOW V="3"> <!-- 3 points vertical spacing below-->
<!-- prepend the text of the element with "Product: "
followed by the value of the type attribute -->
<A-TEXT V='Product: \att(type)'>
</STYLE>
```

16.6.2 *Viewing tags*

Selecting the "view tags" option from the right-click popup causes the tags to be displayed in the document window. Figure 16–12 shows an example from the Multidoc Pro manual SGML documents.

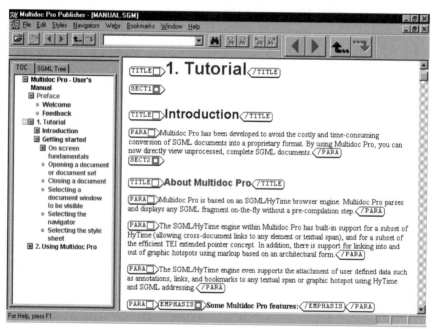

Figure 16–12   Viewing tags in the document window

16.6.3 *Structure-aware searching*

Multidoc knows all about the element structure of an SGML document and allows you to take advantage of it when performing searches. Using the search dialog box, you can restrict searches to particular elements. In Figure 16–13, the word "tutorial" is searched for but restricted to occurrences of the word within **title** elements.

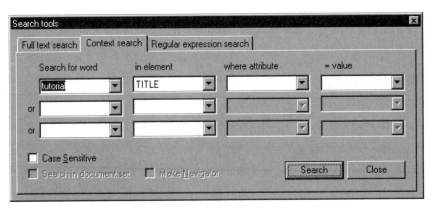

Figure 16–13   Structure-aware searching

16.6.4 *Creating hypertext*

Multidoc Pro supports a subset of the HyTime Hypertext standard for SGML. The features supported are very similar to the feature set planned for XLL. It also supports some TEI extended pointer features. If you wish to get a feel for what XLL allows you to achieve with XML documents, Multidoc Pro is a good place to start.

16.6.5 *Processing Multidoc Pro style sheets*

Multidoc Pro style sheets are themselves valid SGML documents that can easily be hand edited and even generated completely automatically.

This fact is particularly useful if you have, say, database data that you wish to export in an XML-ready format. You could generate an appropriate Multidoc Pro style sheet directly from the database schema.

Not only that, but you can also process these style sheets directly with tools such as NSGMLS. You can even store them in SGML databases, edit them in SGML editors, and, of course, adapt them into XML!

16.6.6 *From Multidoc Pro to XML*

SGML documents viewed under Multidoc Pro are a stone's throw away from conformant XML, thanks to tools like SX. This similarity applies equally well to the style sheets. One interesting possibility is that an off-the-shelf Multidoc Pro style-sheet-to-XSL converter could be developed to allow a "no-brainer" transformation of SGML + Multidoc Pro style-sheet-to-XML + XSL style sheet. This would allow organizations that wish to leverage SGML facilities such as minimization and so on to do so safe in the knowledge that a fully XML/XSL- and indeed XLL-compliant suite of documents can be automatically generated.

16.7 | The Jade DSSSL engine

No raid on the SGML larder would be complete without taking a peek at the DSSSL standard for SGML style sheets. DSSSL is a comprehensive environment based on the Scheme programming language for transforming and formatting SGML. DSSSL specifies a core set of flow objects for formatting SGML in such a way that a single DSSSL style sheet can be used to generate output for a variety of target type-setting formats such as RTF, TeX, and so on. The principle appears in Figure 16–14.

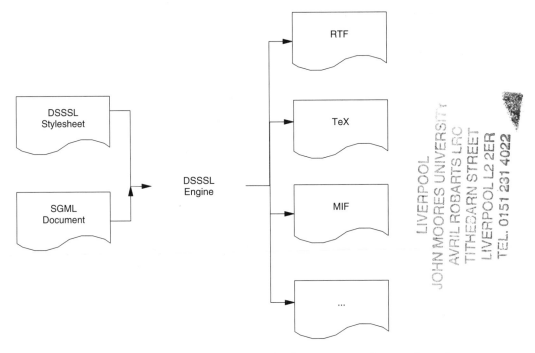

Figure 16–14 Using DSSSL to target multiple outputs with a single style sheet

Although the syntax of DSSSL style sheets may look foreign unless you have a background in Lisp-like languages, the fundamental philosophy is the same as that used in XSL. In this section, I use the Jade DSSSL engine by James Clark (available on the accompanying CD) to generate a number of output formats from the acmepc products SGML document of the last section. Here is the DSSSL style sheet, commented to show what is going on.

```
C>type products.dsl

<!-- DSSSL style sheets are SGML documents conforming
to a style sheet DTD defined in the standard -->

<!doctype style-sheet SYSTEM "style-sheet.dtd">

<!-- A style rule for the Description element
Make a sequence of two things, a piece of literal
```

```
text "Description" followed by the results of
processing the children of the Description element -->

(element Description (make paragraph
    space-before: 4pt
  (make sequence
    font-weight: 'bold
    font-size: 16pt
    (literal "Description:")
    )
  (process-children)
  ))

<!-- For Para elements, make a paragraph -->
(element Para (make paragraph))

<!-- For B elements, make the font weight bold -->
(element B (make sequence
  font-weight: 'bold))

<!-- For I elements, use italic -->
(element I (make sequence
  font-posture: 'italic))

<!-- A style rule for the UnitPrice element
Make a sequence of two things, a piece of literal
text "Unit Price:" followed by the results of
processing the children of the UnitPrice element -->
(element UnitPrice (make paragraph
    space-before: 8pt
  (make sequence
    font-weight: 'bold
    font-size: 12pt
    (literal "Unit Price:")
    )
  (process-children)
))
```

With this simple style sheet, I can proceed to generate RTF as follows:

```
C>jade -t rtf products.sgm
```

The Jade DSSSL engine by default searches for a style sheet with the same base name as the SGML document. It also defaults to producing its output in a document with the same base name and an extension that changes depending on the "back end" being used—in this case, RTF. The RTF that Jade generates from this example appears in all its gory detail here:

```
c>type products.rtf

{\rtf1\ansi\deff0
{\fonttbl{\f0\fnil\fcharset0 Times New Roman;}}
{\colortbl;}
{\stylesheet
{\s1 Heading 1;}{\s2 Heading 2;}
\s3 Heading 3;}{\s4 Heading 4;}
{\s5 Heading 5;}{\s6 Heading 6;}
{\s7 Heading 7;}{\s8 Heading 8;}
{\s9 Heading 9;}}
\deflang1024\notabind\facingp\hyphauto1\widowctrl
\pard\sb80\sl-240 \b\fs32 Description:
\hyphpar0\par\pard\sl-240 \b0\fs20 Acme Blaster 555.
\hyphpar0\par\pard\sl-240 A \b fantastic\b0  PC.
\hyphpar0\par\pard\sb160\sl-240 \b\fs24 Unit Price:\b0\fs20 1000
\hyphpar0\par\pard\sb80\sl-240 \b\fs32 Description:
\hyphpar0\par\pard\sl-240 \b0\fs20 Sprinter Printer 123
\hyphpar0\par\pard\sl-240 Included patented \i sixth sense\i0
   technology.
\hyphpar0\par\pard\sb160\sl-240 \b\fs24 Unit Price:\b0\fs20 500}
```

Figure 16–15 shows the document in Microsoft Word.

I would be doing DSSSL an injustice to even say that I have scratched its surface in this section! With its built-in, fully fledged programming language, little exists that DSSSL cannot do to SGML documents. Since XML documents are also SGML documents, it can work equally well with XML. Take comfort in the knowledge that if you need to achieve a formatting effect beyond what XSL or XSL back ends can achieve, DSSSL is available to crank up the power.

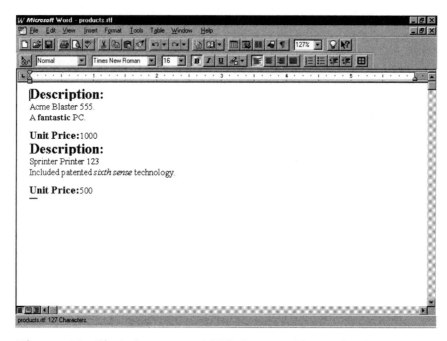

Figure 16–15   Jade-generated RTF shown in Microsoft Word

To find out more about DSSSL, visit http://www.jclark.com. For some powerful examples of DSSSL style sheets in action, see http://www.berkshire.net/~norm/dsssl/docbook/.

Part Four

E-Commerce Initiatives Based on XML

OFX—Open Financial Exchange

- Design principles
- Architecture overview
- Applications supporting OFX
- Sources of more information

T he OFX standard is an initiative from Checkfree Corp., Intuit Inc., and Microsoft Corp. aimed at standardizing the format of financial data that needs to be interchanged between communicating parties. Application areas covered by OFX include:

- Checking Account Transactions
- Credit Card Payments
- Brokerage
- Fund Transfer

Some examples of entities that can benefit from OFX appear in Table 17.1.

The OFX standard initiative predates the development of XML. It is still based, at the time of writing, on XML's parent, SGML. As multiple parties are involved in the development and promulgation of the standard, the decision to make OFX fully XML compliant is likely to take some time. Having said that, the impetus behind XML is such

Table 17.1   OFX Links Customers and Institutions

Customers	< -- >	Institutions
Private Individuals		Banks
Taxpayers		Financial Advisors
Small Businesses		Government Agencies
		Merchants
		Transaction Processors

that a move to full XML compliance seems very likely. that a move to XML compliance seems very likely. Moreover, the principle area in which OFX currently diverges from XML is in allowing various forms of markup minimization. As those features need not be used, XML documents can also be perfectly valid OFX documents. This is what I have done in the example documents in this chapter.

As well as using an open standard for describing financial transactions, OFX uses widely accepted standards for communicating those transactions (such as TCP/IP and HTTP), and for security (such as SSL).

17.1 | Some of the design principles of OFX

The main design principles of OFX are that it should be:

- Open
- Extensible
- Client Independent

- Robust
- Secure
- Support batch processing
- International

17.1.1   *Open*

OFX is an open standard; the specification is freely available to all. Being based on SGML/XML means that nothing is hidden about the specification and no reliance on any one vendor or institution is possible.

17.1.2   *Extensible*

OFX is designed so that transaction types not covered by the standard can be added without breaking existing applications. OFX processors, that encounter elements they are not aware of, will simply skip over them (as long as the full OFX document is well formed).

17.1.3   *Client independent*

OFX is a data format, not an application. Developers are free to use stand-alone PC applications, Web browsers, or cash dispensing machines to deploy OFX-compliant applications. Although it does not intrinsically rely on HTTP, the current version of the specification uses HTTP as its *transport layer*. Consequently, an institution wishing to use OFX can, in principle, use any off-the-shelf Web server platform to implement its support for OFX.

17.1.4   *Robust*

OFX transaction documents must conform to one of the OFX DTDs. As a consequence, much of the odious and error-prone task of developing transaction-validation software can be avoided with OFX. Developers can use off-the-shelf SGML/XML validation tools and libraries to verify the validity of transaction documents.

17.1.5   *Secure*

OFX provides a framework upon which layers of security can be added, using standards such as SSL (Secure Sockets Layer) and SET (Secure Electronic Transactions).

17.1.6   *Batch processing*

OFX is structured as a collection of request/response OFX documents that do not depend on user interaction. You can thus just as easily develop an OFX application that works in batch mode in the background as you can develop an interactive application.

17.1.7   *International*

OFX is intended to be a truly international standard for financial transactions. It supports multiple currencies, country-specific extensions, and the Unicode character set.

17.2 | OFX architecture

OFX is an inherently client/server architecture. A client (typically a Web browser) initiates a conversation by sending a request message to the server (typically a Web server). The server in return sends back a response. This is called the request/response architecture.

Clients send OFX data using the POST capability of HTTP to a particular URI, say, http://www.greatbank.com/accounts.gw.

This URL will typically act as a gateway to relay the OFX part of the message through to the OFX-aware application. An example of an OFX conversation is illustrated here:

```
<!-- Begin OFX Conversation -->
<OFX>
<SIGNONMSGSRQV1>
 <!-- Begin sign on process -->
 <SONRQ>
 <!-- Oct. 29, 1996, 10:10:00 am -->
 <DTCLIENT>19961029101000</DTCLIENT>
 <!-- User ID (i.e. Social Security Number) -->
 <USERID>123-45-6789</USERID>
 <!-- Password (encrypted using SSL) -->
 <USERPASS>Open Sesame</USERPASS>
 <!-- Language used for text -->
 <LANGUAGE>ENG</LANGUAGE>
 <!-- ID of receiving institution -->
 <GREATBANK>
  <!-- Name of ID owner -->
  <ORG>NCH</ORG>
  <!-- Actual ID -->
  <FID>1001</FID>
 </GREATBANK>
 <!-- Application details -->
 <APPID>TransactMaster</APPID>
 <APPVER>0500</APPVER>
 </SONRQ> <!-- End of sign on -->
</SIGNONMSGSRQV1>

<!-- First request in file -->
<BANKMSGSRQV1>
 <!-- Request a statement -->
```

```
<STMTTRNRQ>
 <TRNUID>1001</TRNUID>
 <STMTRQ>
  <!-- Identify the account -->
 <BANKACCTFROM>
  <!-- GreatBank ID -->
  <BANKID>121099999</BANKID>
  <!-- Account number -->
  <ACCTID>999988</ACCTID>
   <!-- Account type -->
  <ACCTTYPE>CHECKING</ACCTTYPE>
  </BANKACCTFROM>
 <!-- Begin include transaction -->
 <INCTRAN>
  <!-- Include transactions == yes -->
  <INCLUDE>Y</INCLUDE>
 </INCTRAN>
 </STMTRQ>        <!-- End of statement request -->
 </STMTTRNRQ>     <!-- End of first request -->
 </BANKMSGSRQV1>
 </OFX>
```

A typical OFX-based architecture appears in Figure 17–1.

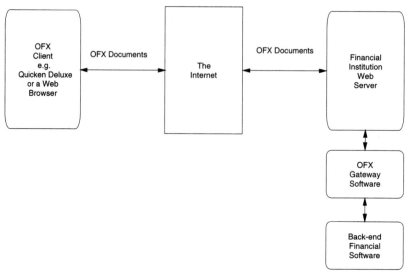

Figure 17–1   A typical OFX-based architecture

17.3 | For more information

More information about OFX is available at the following Web sites.

- **http://www.ofx.net** A site set up to promote the use of OFX

- **http//www.onestandard.com** A site set up to promote the use of OFX

- **http://www.innovision.com** A supplier of OFX-enabled client and server solutions

- **http://www.etrade.com** E*TRADE is a supplier of on-line investment services—allows customers to integrate their account information into Money or Quicken with OFX

- **http://www.livebiz.com** Xenosys have developed an OFX toolkit for Java (JOFX). It is aimed at developers building financial client applications such as accounting packages, internet banking, bill presentation, on-line invoicing, bill payment, and PC based ATMs.

- **http://www.microsoft.com/finserv/ofxdnld.htm** Microsoft hosted site containing all the OFX specification documents

17.4 | PC Application software supporting OFX

- Microsoft Money 98
- Quicken Deluxe 98

XML/EDI— XML and Electronic Data Interchange

- Relating XML and EDI
- Advantages of XML and EDI
- XML/EDI application areas
- Sources of more information

T he way in which the hype around the Internet has grown over the last few years would lead one to believe that concepts such as electronic commerce did not exist prior to the Internet becoming a household word. In fact, Electronic Commerce has been bubbling away for at least 25 years. Specifically, various efforts have led to the creation of a variety of Electronic Data Interchange standards. The best known of these are EDIFACT[1] and ANSI X12. With the amount of business forecast to be conducted via the Web and related technologies, no wonder people have asked where traditional EDI fits into the Internet scheme of things. Specifically, where does EDI sit with respect to XML? In this chapter, I explore these questions.

The EDIFACT standard is a *message format* for business-oriented transactions such as purchase orders, invoices, and so on. The EDIFACT message format is very definitely not directly related to HTML or XML, as the following snippet aptly illustrates.

---

1. **E**lectronic **D**ata **I**nterchange **F**or **A**dministration, **C**ommerce, and **T**ransport

```
UNB+UNOA:2+ESTEC(JBUTU)+ESA(CMO)+920316:0000+1'
UNH+1+PCINFR:1:2:ES'
RFF+AEP:COLUMBUS PHASE 1:048'
DTM+317:920301:101'
UNS+D'
RFF+WBS:048'MOA+209:110700:AU'DTM+295:920301:101'
RFF+WBS:048'MOA+211:55400:AU'DTM+295::101'
RFF+WBS:048'MOA+209:241800:AU'DTM+295:920401:101'
RFF+WBS:048'MOA+211:83800:AU'DTM+295::101'
```

An EDIFACT message consists of compressed *data segments* that are interpreted via a separate field definition table. Fields are themselves interpreted with reference to a data element dictionary. The mechanism by which the order of data segments is prescribed for transmission is reminiscent of the functionality provided by XML DTDs. Segments can be mandatory, optional or conditional. They can be repeated a predefined number of times. For each data segment, the field definition table and element dictionary allow control over the number of characters in each segment and their types (numeric, alphabetic and so on).

Parties wishing to exchange EDIFACT messages would contract between themselves to establish a private, often proprietary communications link (known as a VAN—**V**alue **A**dded **N**etwork). They would then develop a conversion program to convert between their own data formats and the EDIFACT format agreed upon for transmission. As a consequence of this design, each new party to join in the EDIFACT conversation had to develop new software. The closed/per-user-customized nature of EDI has contributed to the significant cost of using EDI and has restricted its uptake to large enterprises.

The original intent of EDIFACT was to provide a digital version of a paper *form*. The idea was to reduce the inherent waste in the paper loops so common in business. An example loop appears in Figure 18–1.

According to the XML/EDI Group (http://www.xmledi.net), a Washington D.C. based organization promoting the benefits of XML for EDI, less than 2% of the 2.6 million businesses in the United

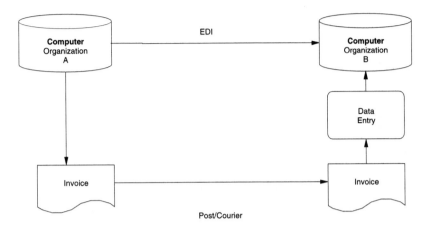

Figure 18–1   Removing the need for paper and data-entry via EDI

States currently use EDI. This low figure is attributed to the technical and financial obstacles presented by traditional EDI. Obstacles that XML can help to overcome.

18.1 | XML/EDI

EDIFACT messages can be converted to XML and vice-versa. More-over, once represented in XML, the Internet can be used in place of a VAN for communicating EDIFACT messages. These simple-to-state facts hold out the possibility of spreading the potential user base of traditional EDI beyond the proprietary networks from which it came into the global Internet. Perhaps most importantly, the metalanguage nature of XML allows XML DTDs to be used to customize messages rather than hand-craft conversion programs as is the case with traditional EDI.

The EDI community stands to benefit from this in many ways. The Internet is clearly where a lot of electronic commerce is headed!

XML, as I hope this book helps to illustrate, is where the Internet is headed! A marriage between EDI and XML would seem to be pre-ordained.

The world of business has changed significantly since EDIFACT was first designed. Perhaps the biggest change has been the Internet itself. Electronic business transactions no longer consist primarily of the batch transfer of paper form-oriented data fields from one computer to another. Modern business transactions are more immediate, more interactive.

The XML/EDI initiative aims to join XML and EDI together whilst retaining the best features of each from an electronic commerce perspective.

- XML will be used as the data interchange format.
- XSL will be used as the presentation format.
- XML/EDI will convert to/from traditional EDI formats such as EDIFACT.
- XML/EDI will run on the Web, i.e., it will be able to use standard TCP/IP and HTTP protocols.

The Web will bring other possibilities into play such as the use of web automation, search engines, and web agents to perform electronic commerce tasks.

18.2 | XML as an EDI format

XML has many advantages as an EDI data format. A lot of time and money is being spent on XML and XML expertise. The primary goal of EDI—reducing the cost of commerce—is well served by piggy-backing on this phenomenon! Apart from its market success, the XML open systems format, human readability, and the concept of a DTD all have much to offer EDI.

18.3 | Data manipulation agents (databots)

Developers of XML/EDI envision the emergence of specialized data manipulation applets that are XML/EDI aware. XML/EDI transactions routed through Web-based databots could be used to automate processes such as forms processing, business-document routing, regulation compliance, and so on.

18.4 | XML/EDItors

XML/EDItors are envisioned as interactive tools for the creation of business forms. The idea is to download XML/XSL descriptions of the business document to a Web browser, where the user is guided through the process of filling in the form in order to meet the requirements of the business transaction.

18.5 | Electronic Catalogs

The creation of Electronic Catalog formats based on XML/EDI standards will open up a whole new world for buyers and sellers alike. No longer will a visitor to a virtual store need to be a human being! Purchasing Web Agents will roam XML/EDI sites, gathering pricing information. They may report back their findings to a human user. They may even be embued with discretionary e-cash buying power by their creators.

18.6 | For more information

More information about the various initiatives to combine traditional EDI technologies and XML can be found at the following sites:

- http://www.geocities.com/WallStreet/Floor/5815
- http://www.commerce.net
- http://www.xmledi.net
- http://www.premenos.com/Resources/

Open Trading Protocol

- Design principles
- Benefits of OTP
- OTP trading roles
- Structure fo an OTP message
- Sources of more information

19

The burgeoning interest in Electronic Commerce has brought with it a flurry of technologies developments. Some examples are:

- SET (Secure Electronic Transactions). Developed by Mastercard, Visa, American Express
- JEPI (Joint Electronic Payment Initiative) from CommerceNet and the World Wide Web Consortium
- Cyber cash
- Micropayment technologies such as Millicent
- OFX —Open Financial Exchange (discussed in Chapter 17)
- XML/EDI (discussed in Chapter 18)

The subject of this chapter, Open Trading Protocol (OTP) is an over-arching, XML-based initiative to allow electronic commerce technologies such as these to interoperate and peacefully coexist. OTP is aimed at smoothing the path towards the development of a pervasive retail trade infrastructure on the Internet. The idea is that OTP-compliant applications will present the user with an easy-to-use, consistent, and familiar interface to the electronic purchasing experience irrespective of the actual payment method or software application being used. The principle developers of the standard are:

- AT&T
- Hewlett-Packard/Verifone
- Mastercard International
- Sun Microsystems
- Wells Fargo Bank

19.1 | Design of OTP

OTP seeks to facilitate electronic commerce by providing digital equivalents of the familiar, paper-based trading methods. It uses XML to describe the structure and content of the various types of messages that are required to achieve an electronic transaction, and in so doing, provides an open standard that will ensure that shoppers, traders, and purchasers alike can all speak the same language in the emerging electronic marketplace. The overall model of OTP is that of invoice-payment-receipt, as you see in Figure 19–1.

OTP supports formats and specifies rules concerning the following activities:

- Offers of sale
- Agreements to purchase
- Payment
- Transfer of goods and services
- Delivery
- Receipts
- Problem resolution

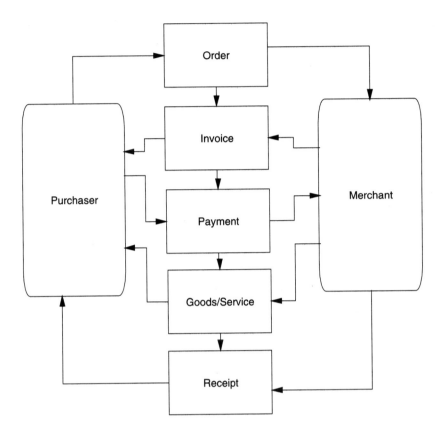

Figure 19–1   The overall trading model of OTP

An important part of OTP is the creation and storage of records of transactions for tax purposes, expense claims, financial management, refunds, and so on.

19.2 | Benefits of OTP

OTP promises to bring benefits to a wide range of users including shoppers, financial institutions, merchants and software developers:

- **Customers** benefit from having a wide selection of merchants from whom they can make purchases—all of which will support the same familiar "look and feel" to the electronic shipping experience. Also, the transaction records OTP produces can be used for tax/accounts purposes.
- **Financial Institutions** benefit by being able to offer OTP-based financial services to merchants. Their potential merchant customer base is extended to any merchant using OTP anywhere on the Internet.
- **Merchants** benefit by being able to offer purchasers a wide variety of payment options. Their potential customer base is extended to any user of an OTP-compliant application on the Internet. The use of authentication and the creation of records in OTP allow merchants to trade with confidence.
- **Software Developers** benefit by knowing that any OTP-compliant applications they develop will readily interoperate with applications developed by others.

In a sense, everyone stands to benefit from the OTP standard. A standard way of trading over the Internet encourages competition and can thus lower the cost of trading for all concerned.

19.3 | Trading types in OTP

The OTP model offers two main ways of performing a trade. Cash trading allows a consumer to deal directly with the merchant selling the goods or service, as illustrated in Figure 19–2.

Debit/Credit trading involves a third party—typically a financial institution to authorize purchases. The financial institution then set-

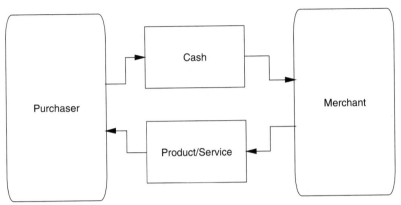

Figure 19–2   Cash trading on the Internet with OTP

tles with the merchant and takes on the payment seeking itself (see Figure 19–3).

The standard is intended to cover the gamut of transactions/communications occurring between five trading roles, as you see in Figure 19–4.

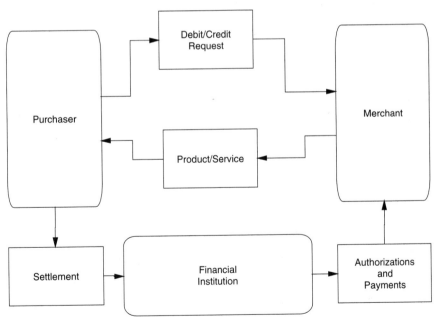

Figure 19–3   Debit/Credit trading on the Internet with OTP

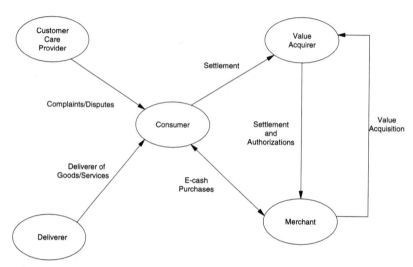

Figure 19–4   Trading roles addressed by OTP

Five entities are identified that can partake in OTP trading:

- **The consumer:** The entity wishing to pay for and subsequently receive goods or services
- **Customer Care Provider:** The entity responsible for dealing with trading disputes
- **Value Acquirer:** The organization that settles Debit/ Credit transactions with the merchant and receives payment from the consumer
- **Merchant:** The entity selling goods or services
- **Deliverer:** The entity responsible for delivering the goods traded from the merchant to the consumer

19.4 | Structure of an OTP message

An OTP message consists essentially of a collection of trading blocks that themselves consist of a collection of individual OTP transaction components, as illustrated in Figure 19–5.

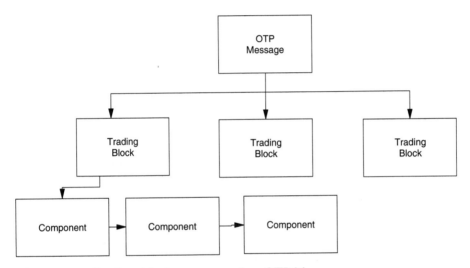

Figure 19–5   Simplified structure of an OTP Message

Some examples of OTP components are discussed in the following sections.

19.4.1 *Order component*

A slightly simplified element type declaration for an OTP order is shown here. Table 19.1 lists the attributes you can use with order components.

```
<!ELEMENT Order ANY>
<!ATTLIST Order
  OrderRef          CDATA    #REQUIRED
  ShortDesc         CDATA    #REQUIRED
  ContentFormat     NMTOKEN  #IMPLIED
  XML:Lang          NMTOKEN  #REQUIRED
>
```

Table 19.1   Attributes of the Order element type

Attribute	Usage
OrderRef	A code or reference number that can be used by whatever created the order to uniquely identify it
ShortDesc	A description of the order in the language specified by the XML:lang attribute
Content-Format	Specifies how the contents of the order (if any) are structured; some permissible values are XML : an XML-based order PCDATA : text that can be correctly parsed as XML but without any structure HTML : HTML text Base64 : binary data encoded using the Base64 encoding standard.
XML:lang	Specifies the language used within the element and ShortDesc attribute

19.4.2 *Brandlist component*

This component is used to list payment brands and payment protocols from which the user may select one. Table 19.2 lists the component's attributes.

```
<!ELEMENT BrandList (Brand+,PayProtocol+)>
<!ATTLIST BrandList
  XML:lang            NMTOKEN #REQUIRED
  ShortDesc           CDATA #REQUIRED
  PayDirection (Debit|Credit) #REQUIRED>
```

Table 19.2 Attributes of the Brandlist element type

Attribute	*Usage*
PayDirection	The direction in which payment is being made: debit indicates that the consumer will make the payment to the value acquirer (i.e., a bank); credit indicates that the consumer will receive a payment from the value acquirer
ShortDesc	A description of the brand list that may be displayed by an OTP-compliant application to help the user select a brand; the text is in the language specified by the XML:lang attribute.
XML:lang	Specifies the language used within the element and Short-Desc attribute

A *brand* element describes a brand of payment to be used to make the payment. Table 19.3 lists the brand element attributes.

```
<!ELEMENT Brand ANY>
<!ATTLIST Brand
  XML:Lang NMTOKEN #REQUIRED
  Name CDATA #REQUIRED
  ShortDesc CDATA #REQUIRED
  ProtocolChoices IDREFS #REQUIRED>
```

Table 19.3   Attributes of the Brand element type

Attribute	Usage
Name	A payment brand name such as Visa, MasterCard, and so on
Protocol-Choices	Identifies the protocols available for use with this brand; this is one or more IDs corresponding to individual elements of type Protocol. The sequence in which they occur indicates the preference of the sender; software processing the ProtocolChoices list should use the first one it can support.
ShortDesc	A description of the protocol that may be displayed by an OTP-compliant application to help the user select a protocol. The text is in the language specified by the XML:lang attribute.
XML:lang	Specifies the language used within the element and ShortDesc attribute

A *PayProtocol* element specifies how a protocol can be used to make a payment. Table 19-4 lists the element's attributes.

```
<!ELEMENT PayProtocol ANY>
<!ATTLIST PayProtocol
  Name             CDATA    #REQUIRED
  Version          NMTOKEN  #REQUIRED
  PayReqNetLocn    CDATA    #IMPLIED
  SecPayReqNetLocn CDATA    #IMPLIED
  ContentFormat    NMTOKEN  #IMPLIED>
```

Table 19.4   Attributes of the PayProtocol element type

Attribute	*Usage*
Name	A payment protocol name such as SET
Version	The version of the protocol
SecPayReqNetLocn	Indicates where a payment request message should be sent if a secured transmission is requested
PayReqNetLocn	Indicates where a payment request message should be sent if an unsecured transmission is requested
XML:lang	Specifies the language used within the element and ShortDesc attribute
ContentFormat	Specifies how the contents of the order (if any) are structured; some permissible values are XML : an XML-based order PCDATA : text that can be correctly parsed as XML but without any structure HTML : HTML text Base64 : binary data encoded using the Base64 encoding standard

An example of a BrandList is shown here:

```
<BrandList XML:Lang = "en-us"
ShortDesc = "Please select a payment method."
PayDirection = "Debit">

<Brand Name = "MC"
ShortDesc = "MasterCard Credit"
ProtocolChoices = "SET"
ContentFormat = "Base64">
</Brand>
<Brand Name = "Visa"
ShortDesc = "Visa Credit"
ProtocolChoices = "SCCD"
```

```
ContentFormat = "Base64">
</Brand>
<PayProtocol id = "SET"
Name = "SET"
Version = "1.0"
PayReqNetLocn = "http://www.merchant.com/set">
<!-- Payment Protocol Specific info here  -- >
</PayProtocol>
<PayProtocol id = "SCCD"
Name = "Secure Channel Credit Debit"
Version = "1.0"
PayReqNetLocn = "http://www.merchant.com/sccd">
<!-- Payment Protocol Specific info here  -- >
</PayProtocol>
```

19.5 | Miscellaneous points

The standard recognizes that too high a level of homogeneity between, say, merchants, makes it difficult for individual entities to differentiate themselves from the competition. As a result, an overly restrictive standard would inhibit its acceptance in the marketplace. To combat this problem, OTP has optional features such as various grades of security, various forms of receipts, payment-method choices, and so on. Also, the OTP protocol is deliberately extensible. Innovators can invent new trading blocks, trading components, and even new elements within trading components.

The initial specification for OTP is termed a *baseline* specification. It is intended to be used to develop working systems and then naturally evolve with market demand. One area where extension is currently envisioned is in payment methods where support for payment based on connection time, loyalty cards, and so on, is being considered.

19.6 | For more information

For more information on OTP visit http://www.otp.org/

Appendix A
Some Details

This appendix contains some further detailed information about aspects of XML and related standards.

A.1 White space handling

In Chapter 11, I discuss how XML handles white space, which depends on whether the element type the white space occurs in was declared to have <i>mixed content</i> or <i>element content</i>. In both cases, white space that occurs outside markup is considered significant; that is, it is passed on to the application by the XML processor. However, in a valid document, white space occurring in element content is identified as such by a validating parser, which enables an application to discard it.

An element with mixed content is one that has #PCDATA somewhere in its content model. For example, in the following document, the para element has mixed content. White space occurring within the element is passed on to the application.

```
C>type para.xml

<!DOCTYPE para [
<!ELEMENT para (#PCDATA|list)*>
]>
<para>
This is a
paragraph of
text
</para>


C>jview esisdemo para.xml

(para
-\nThis is a\nparagraph of\ntext\n
)para
```

Note the "\n" strings in the output indicating the presence of significant newline characters. In the following document, the list element has element content and the #PCDATA keyword does not occur.

```
C>type list.xml

<!DOCTYPE list [
<!ELEMENT list (item)*>
<!ELEMENT item (#PCDATA)>
]>
<list>
<item>I am an item</item>
<item>So am I</item>
</list>


C>jview esisdemo list.xml

(list
(item
-I am an item
)item
(item
-So am I
)item
)list
```

Note the absence of newline characters in the output. The parser has detected that the list item has element content, and as such no white space can occur that is significant. All the white space has in fact been detected and passed through by the core parser (in this case, Ælfred), but some of it has been flagged as insignificant. The Esis-Demo application has been written in such a way as to output only the white space it receives from the parser that is significant.

The EsisDemo application can make the distinction between significant and insignificant white space because Ælfred is *DTD aware*. It processes all of the Document Type Declaration and notes elements that have element content. In this respect, Ælfred is providing more functionality than is strictly required in a nonvalidating XML parser. Parsers that validate are *required* to make the distinction between significant and insignificant white space and communicate both to the application. Nonvalidating parsers are not so required.

If the application that is processing the output of a validating XML parser is discarding white space in element content and you would prefer that it did not, you can use the reserved attribute xml:space to force the application to leave the white space alone, like the following:

```
C>type list.xml

<!DOCTYPE list [
<!ELEMENT list (item)*>
<!ELEMENT item (para)+>
<!ELEMENT para (#PCDATA)>
]>
<list xml:space = "preserve">
<item>
<para>I am an item<para>
</item>
<item xml:space = "default">
<para>
So am I
</para>
</item>
</list>
```

The xml:space attribute can take two values. The value "preserve" informs the XML processor that all white space should be preserved in the element. The value "default" informs the processor that its default behavior is acceptable. The "default" value can be used to arrange for subelements of an element to have different white space treatment from other elements, as shown here:

```
C>type list.xml

<!DOCTYPE list [
<!ELEMENT list (item)*>
<!ELEMENT item (para)+>
<!ELEMENT para (#PCDATA)>
]>
<list xml:space = "preserve">
<item>
<para>I am an item<para>
</item>
<item xml:space = "default">
<para>
So am I
</para>
</item>
</list>
```

A.2 | System and public identifiers

In SGML, external entities can have two types of identifier associated with them. *System Identifiers* are provided to allow references to local resources such as physical files and so on. So-called *Public Identifiers* are also allowed. These identifiers are intended to allow formal names to be established in some central registry of names in order to make completely unambiguous what the identified entity is.

Perhaps the most famous PUBLIC identifier is the one commonly seen at the start of HTML documents:

```
<!DOCTYPE HTML PUBLIC "-//W3C//DTD HTML 3.2 Final//EN">
```

Public identifiers are retained in XML but only as an ancillary device. That is to say, an external entity declaration must have a system identifier and can optionally have a public identifier. The system identifier is always interpreted as a URI.

A.3 | Attribute value normalization

Attribute values, prior to being passed on to the application, are processed by the parser in a number of ways to *normalize* their contents. For CDATA attributes, the following normalization takes place:

- any entity references are expanded
- newlines and tabs are replaced by spaces

In the following document, an entity reference, a newline, and a tab occur in the attribute value:

```
C>type doc.xml

<!DOCTYPE text [
<!ELEMENT text EMPTY>
<!ATTLIST text attr CDATA #REQUIRED>
]>
<text attr = "P&amp;L

        account"/>

C>jview esisdemo doc.xml

A attr  P&L account
(text
)text
```

Attributes other than CDATA attributes undergo further normalization:

- leading and trailing spaces are removed
- sequences of spaces are replaced by a single space

In the following document, leading spaces, trailing spaces, and newlines occur in the attribute value specification:

```
C>type text.xml

<!DOCTYPE text [
<!ELEMENT text EMPTY>
<!ATTLIST text attr NMTOKENS #REQUIRED>
]>
<text attr = "  apple

orange      banana  "/>

C>jview esisdemo text.xml

A attr  apple orange banana
(text
)text
```

A.4 | Language identification

The reserved attribute "xml:lang" can be used to specify the language used in the contents and attribute values of any element in an XML document. The attribute consists of a language code optionally followed by a subcode to provide an extra level of classification. First, we will look at some examples and then at the details:

```
<!-- English -->
<p xml:lang="en">My name is Sean</p>

<!-- English - Great Britain -->
<p xml:lang="en-GB">My name is Sean</p>

<!-- English - United States of America -->
<p xml:lang="en-US">My name is Sean</p>

<!-- Irish (Gaelic)-->
<p xml:lang="GA">Seán is anim dom.</p>
```

Three techniques are supported for specifying language information:

1. Use a two-letter language code from the ISO639 standard. This is what I used in these examples.
2. Use a language code registered with the Internet Assigned Numbers Authority (IANA).
3. Use a custom identifier. The standard suggests that this should start with "x" or "X-" in order to avoid potential conflicts with the IANA codes, which all begin with "i-" or "I-."

Note that these codes are case sensitive.

A.5 | Deterministic content models

In SGML, constraints exist on the way content models are constructed, in order to allow the parser to do its job more easily in matching elements against content models. Specifically, in SGML, element content models must be *deterministic* (the term *unambiguous* is used in the SGML standard). A deterministic content model is one in which the parser need look only one element ahead during a parse to be able to uniquely identify to which part of the model the element conforms. An example illustrates the idea; consider the following document:

```
<!-- well-formed, but not valid XML document -->
<!DOCTYPE person [
<!ELEMENT person
   ((name,address,telephone)|(name,address))>
<!ELEMENT name (#PCDATA)>
<!ELEMENT address (#PCDATA)>
<!ELEMENT telephone (#PCDATA)>
]>
<person>
<name>Joe Bloggs</name>
<address>Tumbolia</address>
```

```
<telephone>555 - 1234</telephone>
</person>
```

When an SGML parser is processing the person element, it first encounters the name element. At that point, it cannot determine to which of the two possible person models the element is intended to conform. It could be name, address, and telephone, or it could be just name and address. To disambiguate between the two, the parser needs to look ahead at the elements that follow, before making its final decision. SGML disallows this sort of look ahead, and so does XML. In the majority of cases, this problem is not great because the content model can be rearranged. In my example, I can recast the content model as shown here, to remove the ambiguity.

```
<!-- well-formed, and valid XML document -->
<!DOCTYPE person [
<!ELEMENT person (name,address,telephone?)>
<!ELEMENT name (#PCDATA)>
<!ELEMENT address (#PCDATA)>
<!ELEMENT telephone (#PCDATA)>
]>
<person>
<name>Joe Bloggs</name>
<address>Tumbolia</address>
<telephone>555 - 1234</telephone>
</person>
```

A.6 | Pernicious mixed content

Experience over the years with SGML has shown that elements with mixed content lead to surprising parsing results unless you follow certain recommended practices. The problems mostly relate to white space handling. In SGML, you can (but probably should not) create an element content model like this:

```
<!ELEMENT foo (#PCDATA,bar)+>
```

This sort of content model causes all sorts of trouble for the parser in working out where the PCDATA starts and ends in the presence of new lines. The details of the problems are rather complex. For details, see my book, *ParseMe.1st: SGML for Software Developers,* ISBN 0-13-488967-3.

To avoid the problems that such so-called *pernicious* content models can cause, the XML standard requires that #PCDATA can only appear:

- on its own, i.e..

    ```
    <!ELEMENT foo (#PCDATA)>
    ```

- at the start of a repeatable "or" model group, i.e.,

    ```
    <!ELEMENT foo (#PCDATA|bar)*>
    ```

A.7 | Character encoding in external entities

In XML, each entity is free to use a different character encoding. An external entity that uses an encoding other that UTF-8 (the default) can signal its encoding using a character encoding declaration. The character encoding declaration is very similar to the XML declaration. It can specify XML version information but cannot specify the "stand-alone" information allowed in the XML declaration. Here is an example of character encoding declaration specifying that the entity uses UTF-16.

```
<?xml  version = "1.0" encoding = "UTF-16"?>
```

A.8 | Recognizing character encodings in XML

The XML declaration allows the character encoding of a document to be specified.

```
<?xml version = "1.0" encoding = "8859-1"?>
```

At first sight, this might look like a straightforward way of dealing with character set issues, but it presents a chicken-and-egg situation for the parser. In order to get at the string "encoding = '8859-1'" it has to have decided upon a character encoding to read this very text. The encoding declaration is necessary but it is not sufficient. You need to allow a document to specify what variation of character encoding it is using, i.e., the various subparts of 8859 or EBCDIC.

The XML declaration is optional in general, but it is mandatory if a document is encoded in anything other than UTF-8 or UTF-16. As a result, an XML parser can look at the first few bytes and detect the encoding because it will know that it is a representation of the text "<?xml".

Here are some examples of the first few bytes of an XML entity and the conclusions an XML processor can draw from them regarding character set encoding:

```
FE FF       Must be UTF-16 on a big-endian machine
FF FE       Must be UTF-16 on a little-endian machine
3C 3F 78 6D UTF-8, ASCII, ISO-646, and others
4C 6F A7 9A EBCDIC
```

A.9 | Rule arbitration in XSL

In XSL, only one construction rule triggers for any particular source element. This fact raises the question as to what happens when more than one rule matches a particular pattern. Consider the following example:

```
C>type chapter.xml

<chapter>
<title>Chapter Title</title>
<sect>
<title>Section Title</title>
</sect>
</chapter>

C>type chapter.xsl

<xsl>
<rule>
<element type = "sect">
<target-element type = "title"/>
</element>
<DIV>
Title under sect rule fired.
</DIV>
<children/>
</rule>

<rule>
<target-element type = "title"/>
<DIV>
Title rule fired.
</DIV>
<children/>
</rule>
</xsl>
```

Both rules apply to **title** elements, so which one will fire for each of the title elements? Take a look at the output.

```
C>msxsl -i chapter.xml -s chapter.xsl -o chapter.htm
C>type chapter.htm
```

```
<DIV>
 <DIV> Title rule fired. </DIV>
 Chapter Title

 <DIV> Title under sect rule fired. </DIV>
 Section Title
</DIV>
```

The XSL proposal includes the specification for an algorithm that implementations will use to decide what rules to fire. It also allows a stylesheet to override the default behavior.

If an element in the source document matches more than one pattern, the most specific pattern will be chosen.

The most specific pattern is determined by the following criteria (applied in this order):

- The highest value of the **importance** attribute
- The pattern with the largest number of **id** attributes
- The pattern with the largest number of **class** attributes
- The pattern with the largest number of **type** attributes
- The pattern with the largest number of **element** or **target-element** elements that have a type attribute
- The pattern with the least wildcards
- The pattern with the highest value of the **priority** attribute
- The pattern with the highest number of **only** qualifiers
- The pattern with the highest number of **position** qualifiers
- The pattern with the highest number of attribute specifications

Appendix B
About the CD-ROM

The CD-ROM attached to this book has three subdirectories:

- Software—software packages (free and trial versions of various applications)
- Gallery—Sample XML documents and DTDs
- Docs—assorted standards documents

B.1 | The software subdirectory

The contents of the software subdirectory appear in Table B.1.

Table B.1   Contents of the Software Subdirectory

Subdirectory	Contents
msxml	Microsoft's validating XML parser (Java)
xp	James Clark's nonvalidating XML parser (Java)
Ælfred	Microstar's nonvalidating XML parser (Java)
xmltok	James Clark's nonvalidating XML parser (C)
xparse	Jeremie Miller's non-validating XML parser (JavaScript)
sx	James Clark's SGML-to-XML adapter
jade	James Clark's DSSSL engine + SGML parser (nsgmls)
amaya	The World Wide Web Consortium's testbed Web browser
multidoc	CITEC's SGML viewer
widl	Web Methods Toolkit Evaluation Edition
cdfgen	Microsoft's CDF editor
cfusion	Cold Fusion Evaluation Edition

B.2 | The gallery subdirectory

The gallery subdirectory contains two subdirectories called docs and dtds. You can see the contents of these directories in Table B.2.

Table B.2   Contents of the Gallery Subdirectory

File	Contents
docs\shake.zip	The plays of William Shakespeare marked up in XML
docs\religion.zip	Various religious texts marked up in XML
docs\xmltest.zip	James Clark's parser test suite
dtds\ofx*.dtd	DTDs for Open Financial eXchange
dtds\nff.dtd	Notes Flat File DTD
dtds\acmepc.dtd	DTD for the AcmePC catalog
dtds\tstmt.dtd	DTD for the religious texts in the docs subdirectory
dtds\play.dtd	DTD for the plays of William Shakespeare in the docs subdirectory
dtds\xmldata.dtd	XML-Data DTD
dtd\smil.dtd	Synchronized Multimedia Integration Language DTD
dtds\widl.dtd	WebMethods Web Automation DTD
dtds\bsml.dtd	Bioinformation Sequence Markup Language DTD

B.3 | The docs subdirectory

The contents of the docs subdirectory appear in Table B.3.

Table B.3   Contents of the Docs Subdirectory

File	Contents	Format
xmlspec.htm	XML standard	HTML
xslspec.htm	XSL proposal	HTML
xllspec.htm	XLL proposal	HTML
dom.zip	Document Object Model proposal	Zipped HTML
ECMA-262.DOC	The ECMAScript (JavaScript) standard	Microsoft Word 6.0
smil.htm	The Synchronized Multimedia Integration Language proposal	HTML

Appendix C
OTP Specification Preface

This appendix contains the preface of the OTP specifications. We have included in here because it provides a good overview of this key E-commerce tool. The full specification can be found at http://www.otp.org

Preface

The interest in electronic commerce is everywhere. As merchants, financial institutions, technology providers and newcomers scramble to understand the market and establish their presence it is clear that there is little overall cohesion to the myriad efforts.

There have been some co-ordinated activities that while not guaranteeing success have demonstrated the benefits of a co-operative multi-enterprise effort to produce something for the advancement of this phenomenon known as electronic commerce.

Examples are the development of:

- SET—Secure Electronic Transaction from MasterCard, Visa, American Express etc.
- JEPI—Joint Electronic Payment Initiative from CommerceNet and W3C (the World Wide Web Consortium)
- EMV—Debit/credit cards using chip technology from Europay, MasterCard and Visa
- E-Check—Electronic Checkbook on a smart card from the US based Financial Services Technology Consortium and FSTC members; Federal Reserve Bank, NationsBank, Bank of Boston, Huntington Bancshares, IBM and Sun Microsystems and others.

OTP shares many of the high level objectives of these efforts and in part builds on some of them. The OTP specification provides a unifying framework within which these and others not named or even contemplated can co-exist and successfully interoperate.

OTP seeks to enable electronic commerce by supplying analogues of traditional, mostly paper based, methods of trading. The negotiation of who will be the parties to the trade, how it will be conducted, the presentment of an offer, the method of payment, the provision of a payment receipt, the delivery of goods and the receipt of goods. These are events that are taken for granted in the course of our real world and OTP has been produced to provide the same for the virtual world, and to prepare and provide for the introduction of new models of trading made possible by the expanding presence of the virtual world.

The other fundamental ideal of this effort is to produce a definition of these trading events in such a way that no matter where produced, two unfamiliar parties using electronic commerce capabilities to buy and sell that conform to the OTP specifications will be able to complete the business safely and successfully.

In summary, OTP supports:

- Familiar trading models
- New trading models
- Global interoperability

6.2 | Commerce on the Internet— A Different Model

The growth of the Internet and the advent of electronic commerce are bringing about enormous changes around the world in society, politics and government, and in business. The ways in which trading partners communicate, conduct commerce, are governed have been enriched and changed forever.

One of the very fundamental changes about which OTP is concerned is taking place in the way consumers and merchants trade. Characteristics of trading that have changed markedly include:

- **Presence**: Face-to-face transactions become the exception, not the rule. Already with the rise of mail order and telephone order placement this change has been felt in western commerce. Electronic commerce over the Internet will further expand the scope and volume of transactions conducted without ever seeing the people who are a part of the enterprise with whom one does business.
- **Authentication**: An important part of personal presence is the ability of the parties to use familiar objects and dialogue to confirm they are who they claim to be. The seller displays one or several well known financial logos that declaim his ability to accept widely used credit and debit instruments in the payment part of a purchase. The

buyer brings government or financial institution identification that assures the seller she will be paid. People use intangibles such as personal appearance and conduct, location of the store, apparent quality and familiarity with brands of merchandise, and a good clear look in the eye to reinforce formal means of authentication.

- **Payment instruments**: Despite the enormous size of bank card financial payments associations and their members, most of the world's trade still takes place using the coin of the realm or barter. The present infrastructure of the payments business cannot economically support low value transactions and could not survive under the consequent volumes of transactions if it did accept low value transactions.

- **Transaction values**: New meaning for low value transactions arises in the Internet where sellers may wish to offer for example, pages of information for fractions of currency that do not exist in the real world.

- **Delivery**: New modes of delivery must be accommodated such as direct electronic delivery. The means by which receipt is confirmed and the execution of payment change dramatically where the goods or services have extremely low delivery cost but may in fact have very high value. Or, maybe the value is not high, but once delivery occurs the value is irretrievably delivered so payment must be final and non-refundable but delivery nonetheless must still be confirmed before payment. Incremental delivery such as listening or viewing time or playing time are other models that operate somewhat differently in the virtual world.

C.3 | Benefits of OTP

C.3.1 *Electronic Commerce Software Vendors*

Electronic Commerce Software Vendors will be able to develop e-commerce products which are more attractive as they will inter-operate with any other vendors' software. However since OTP focuses on how these solutions communicate, there is still plenty of opportunity for product differentiation.

C.3.2 *Payment Brands*

OTP provides a standard framework for encapsulating payment protocols. This means that it is easier for payment products to be incorporated into OTP solutions. As a result the payment brands will be more widely distributed and available on a wider variety of platforms.

C.3.3 *Merchants*

There are several benefits for Merchants:

- they will be able to offer a wider variety of payment brands,
- they can be more certain that the customer will have the software needed to complete the purchase
- through receiving payment and delivery receipts from their customers, they will be able to provide customer care knowing that they are dealing with the individual or organization with which they originally traded
- new merchants will be able to enter this new (Internet) market-place with new products and services, using the new trading opportunities which OTP presents

C.3.4 *Banks and Financial Institutions*

There are also several benefits for Banks and Financial Institutions:

- they will be able to provide OTP support for merchants
- they will find new opportunities for OTP related services:
  —providing customer care for merchants
  —fees from processing new payments and deposits
- they have an opportunity to build relationships with new types of merchants

C.3.5 *Customers*

For Customers there are several benefits:

- they will have a larger selection of merchants with whom they can trade
- there is a more consistent interface when making the purchase
- there are ways in which they can get their problems fixed through the merchant (rather than the bank!)
- there is a record of their transaction which can be used, for example, to feed into accounting systems or, potentially, to present to the tax authorities

C.4 | Baseline OTP

The team working on the OTP see an extended version of this specification being developed but at this stage feel a need to develop a limited function specification in order that technology providers can soon develop pathway-pilot[1] products that will be placed in the market in order to understand the real "market place" demands and requirements for electronic trading or electronic commerce. To proceed otherwise would be presumptuous, time consuming, expensive and foolish.

Accordingly the OTP Baseline specification has been produced for pathway-pilot product development, expecting to transact live trades over the open networks by mid '98.

At the same time that the pathway-pilot products are being developed and brought to market the developers of the OTP specification will be studying and working on the protocol to both preserve the original work (and the initial investment made by early technology suppliers) and to enhance the specification.

An area that is most likely to be extended is the "Trading Exchanges" as it is here that many new possibilities and options are expected; the ability to make multiple payments in one purchase, the ability to pay for units of time connected to a service, the ability to earn and or use loyalty points all are recognized and need to be brought into a fuller and extended OTP while at the same time preserving the initial specification.

6.5 | Objectives of the Document

This document provides an overview of the Baseline version (0.9) of the Open Trading Protocol. The Open Trading Protocol is designed to support electronic commerce on the Internet independent of payment instrument. For completeness, some functions described below are not part of the Baseline version. It is acknowledged that these are

---

1. "Pathway-Pilot" is used to draw a distinction between pilot products that within our industry are often considered to be temporary with set end dates and our intent to build off these early products as the specification is extended.

necessary and ordinary functions and they are noted here to indicate that they will be included as part of the trading functions added in the first of the succeeding versions.

To provide for:

- optional authentication by the consumer that merchants are "bona-fide",
- optional authentication by the merchant, that consumers are who they appear to be,
- submission by the merchant of an offer for goods or services which the consumer can then accept or reject,
- payment for the goods or services by the consumer using potentially any electronic payment method,
- optional issuing of receipt for a purchase or other type of trade by the merchant,
- optional provision to the consumer by the merchant of proof of shipment of the goods (not Baseline OTP)
- optional provision, by the consumer or the delivery system, of proof of delivery of the goods and services (not Baseline OTP),
- enablement and facilitation in the resolution of purchase related problems between a consumer and the merchant, (not Baseline OTP) and
- provision of a refund from a merchant to a consumer.
- For electronic cash, as a payment mechanism, the Open Trading Protocol provides support for:
- the transfer of electronic cash between consumers and banks,
- the withdrawal or deposit of electronic cash between a provider of the electronic cash (e.g. a Bank) and a consumer or merchant,
- optional authentication by the bank of the account holder as part of account access and withdrawal transactions

- value exchange transactions which result in the exchange of value from one combination of currency and payment method to another, for example foreign exchange

- enablement and facilitation in resolution of customer care related problems between the bank (value acquirer) or merchant and their customers (not Baseline OTP).

6.6 | Purpose

The purpose of the document is:

- to allow potential developers of products based on the protocol to:

  —comment on the applicability of the protocol to their environment,

  —start development of software/hardware solutions which use the protocol[2].

- to allow the financial services industry to understand a developing electronic commerce trading protocol that encapsulates (without modification) any of the current or developing payment schemes now being used or considered by their merchant customer base.

- to describe the intent of the protocol developers to submit the OTP for consideration as the basis for a governed industry standard for conducting electronic commerce which is independent of the payment method.

---

2. Please see disclaimer at the start of this document.

C.7 | Scope of Document

The protocol describes the content, format and sequences of messages that pass among the participants in an electronic trade - consumers, merchants and banks or other financial institutions. These are required to support the electronic commerce transactions outlined in the objectives above.

The protocol is designed to be applicable to any electronic payment scheme[3] since it targets the complete purchase process where the movement of electronic value from the payer to the payee is only one, but important, step of many that may be involved to complete the trade.

Each payment scheme contains some message flows which are specific to that scheme. These scheme-specific parts of the protocol are contained in a set of payment scheme supplements of this standard.

The document does not prescribe the software and processes that will need to be implemented by each participant. It does describe the framework necessary for trading to take place.

This document also does not address any legal or regulatory issues surrounding the implementation of the protocol or the information systems which use them.

---

3. A Payment Scheme is a method of making a payment such as MasterCard Credit, Visa Credit, Mondex Cash, Visa Cash, GeldKarte, ecash, Cybercoin, Millicent, Proton etc. where rules apply which define the methods, policies and processes used to make payments.

C.7.1 *Relationship to other payment methods or initiatives*

The table below shows for a number of payment methods or initiatives:

- whether it is a published and open standard
- whether it is an open standard or a proprietary standard
- the extent to which it can be integrated into OTP

The table is not exhaustive and has not been verified with all the organization's concerned. However the author's of this specification believe the information to be correct.

Table C.1   Payment methods

Payment Method or Initiative	*Comment*
Bankcard (Mag Stripe) CR/DR	Protocol for carrying out magnetic stripe credit card and debit card transactions over proprietary networks. Open proprietary standard. No OTP integration as currently provided on proprietary and private networks.
CyberCash	A software based electronic cash product.
CyberCoin	See http://www.cybercash.com/cybercash/merchants/paytypes.html Unpublished proprietary standard. Can integrate with OTP.
DigiCash ecash	A software based electronic cash product. See http://www.digicash.com/ Unpublished proprietary standard. Can integrate with OTP.

Table C.1   Payment methods *(continued)*

Payment Method or Initiative	Comment
E-check	Developed by the FSTC – Financial Services Technology Consortium and being piloted by the US Treasury. A secure electronic check payment product for use on the open networks between unfamiliar parties, clears through ACH or ECP. See http://www.fstc.org/ Unpublished proprietary standard. In pilot with the US Treasury. Can integrate with OTP
EDI	Electronic Data Interchange. A method of exchanging information such as order information between organizations. Some proprietary and some open EDI standards exist. Can integrate with OTP.
EMV	The standard for carrying out smart card based credit and debit payments developed by Europay, MasterCard and Visa. See http://www.mastercard.com/emv/index.html Published open standard. Can integrate with OTP.
GeldKarte	The smart card based electronic cash product developed by the Association of German Savings Banks. Unpublished proprietary standard. Can integrate with OTP.
JEPI	JEPI provides the means to negotiate payment methods. JEPI describes launching a payment protocol, which would be the point at which the purchase protocol described in this document would be initiated. See http://www.w3.org/ECommerce/specs/ Open draft standard. Working paper published. Not applicable to OTP.

Table C.1 Payment methods *(continued)*

Payment Method or Initiative	*Comment*
Mondex	A smart card based electronic cash product. See http://www.mondex.com/ Unpublished proprietary standard. Can integrate with OTP
OBI	OBI - Open Buying on the Internet. For companies wanting to conduct business-to-business commerce over the Internet a set of electronic purchasing specifications being tested by American Express Co. which assume a pre-existing relationship. See http://www.supplyworks.com/obi/ Published open standard. Cannot integrate with OTP.
Other Micro-payment schemes	Examples are IBM's mini-pay (see http://www.ibm.net.il/ibm_il/int-lab/mpay/), or Digital's Millicent (see http://www.millicent.digital.com/). Generally unpublished proprietary standards. Can integrate with OTP.
Proton	A smart card based electronic cash product developed by Banksys. See http://www.proton.be or http://www.proton-world.com. Unpublished proprietary standard. Can integrate with OTP.
SET	Secure Electronic Transactions. A software based electronic payment product for credit/debit transactions. See http://www.mastercard.com/set/technologies.html Published open standard. Can integrate with OTP.
Visa Cash	A smart card based electronic cash product. See http://www.visa.com/cgi-bin/vee/nt/cash/main.html?2+0 Unpublished proprietary standard. Can integrate with OTP

C.8 | Intended Readership

Software and hardware developers; development analysts; business and technical planners; industry analysts; merchants; bank and other value providers; owners, custodians, and users of payment protocol.

C.9 | Document Structure

Part 1 provides the business description. The focus is on explaining OTP more from a business than a technical point of view.

Part 2 provides the detailed protocol specification which describes the content and structure of the messages within the protocol

Both of the above are independent of the payment scheme, and the transport mechanism used to transmit the messages within the protocol.

Therefore there are (or will be) supplements to the protocol which describe:

- how OTP works with specific payment methods, for example SET,
- how the messages within the protocol map to specific transport mechanisms, for example HTTP
- At the time of writing this specification (late 1997):
- a mapping OTP to HTTP has been developed
- approaches to how OTP works with, for example, SET have been identified.

The OTP web site http://www.otp.org contains information on both of the above.

C.10 | Related Documents

This section contains the descriptions of related documents identified in this specification.

Table C.2   Related Documents

[Base64]	Base64 Content-Transfer-Encoding. A method of transporting binary data defined by MIME. See: RFC 2045: Multipurpose Internet Mail Extensions (MIME) Part One: Format of Internet Message Bodies. N. Freed & N. Borenstein. November 1996.
[DNS]	The Internet Domain Name System which allocates Internet names to organizations for example "otp.org," the Domain Name for OTP. See RFC 1034: Domain names - concepts and facilities. P.V. Mockapetris. Nov-01-1987, and RFC 1035: Domain names - implementation and specification. P.V. Mockapetris. Nov-01-1987.
[DSA]	The Digital Signature Algorithm (DSA) published by the National Institute of Standards and Technology (NIST) in the Digital Signature Standard (DSS), which is a part of the U.S. government's Capstone project.
[ECCDSA]	Elliptic Curve Cryptosystems Digital Signature Algorithm (ECCDSA). Elliptic curve cryptosystems are analogs of public-key cryptosystems such as RSA in which modular multiplication is replaced by the elliptic curve addition operation. See: V.S. Miller. Use of elliptic curves in cryptography. In Advances in Cryptology - Crypto '85, pages 417-426, Springer-Verlag, 1986.
[HTML]	Hyper Text Mark Up Language. The Hypertext Markup Language (HTML) is a simple markup language used to create hypertext documents that are platform independent. See RFC 1866 and the World Wide Web (W3C) consortium web site at: http://www.w3.org/MarkUp/

Table C.2   Related Documents *(continued)*

[HTTP]	Hyper Text Transfer Protocol versions 1.0 and 1.1. See RFC 1945: Hypertext Transfer Protocol — HTTP/1.0. T. Berners-Lee, R. Fielding & H. Frystyk. May 1996. and RFC 2068: Hypertext Transfer Protocol — HTTP/1.1. R. Fielding, J. Gettys, J. Mogul, H. Frystyk, T. Berners-Lee. January 1997.
[ISO4217]	ISO 4217: Codes for the Representation of Currencies. Available from ANSI or ISO.
[MIME]	Multipurpose Internet Mail Extensions. See RFC822, RFC2045, RFC2046, RFC2047, RFC2048 and RFC2049.
[OPS]	Open Profiling Standard. A proposed standard which provides a framework with built-in privacy safeguards for the trusted exchange of profile information between individuals and websites. Being developed by Netscape and Microsoft amongst others.
[RFC822]	The Standard for the Format of ARPA Internet Messages. 13 August 1982
[RSA]	RSA is a public-key cryptosystem for both encryption and authentication supported by RSA Data Security Inc. See:R.L. Rivest, A. Shamir, and L.M. Adleman. A method for obtaining digital signatures and public-key cryptosystems. Communications of the ACM, 21(2): 120-126, February 1978.
[SET]	Secure Electronic Transaction Specification, Version 1.0, May 31, 1997. Supports credit and debit card payments using certificates at the Consumer and Merchant to help ensure authenticity. Download from: <http://www.mastercard.com/set/specs.html>.

Table C.2   Related Documents *(continued)*

[SHA1]	[FIPS-180-1] "Secure Hash Standard," National Institute of Standards and Technology, U.S. Department Of Commerce, April 1995. Also known as: 59 Fed Reg 35317 (1994).
[UTC]	Universal Time Coordinated. A method of defining time absolutely relative to Greenwich Mean Time (GMT). Typically of the form: "CCYY-MM-DDTHH:MM:SS.sssZ+n" where the "+n" defines the number of hours from GMT. See ISO DIS8601.
[UTF16]	The Unicode Standard, Version 2.0. The Unicode Consortium, Reading, Massachusetts. See ISO/IEC 10646 1 Proposed Draft Amendment 1
[X.509]	ITU Recommendation X.509 1993 I ISO/IEC 9594-8: 1995, Including Draft Amendment 1: Certificate Extensions (Version 3 Certificate)
[XML Namespace]	See Design decisions reached at the XML WG meeting in Montreal, Canada, August 22, 1987
[XML]	Extensible Mark Up Language. See http://www.w3.org/ TR/PR-xml-971208 for the 8 December 1997 version.

Index

■ *E*

N

name property, Element Definition object, 358
Nested HTML tables, displaying hierarchical XML as, 162–64
NMTOKEN/NMTOKENS attributes, 281
NodeEnumerator object, 349, 353
NodeList object, 349, 353
Nonvalidating XML processor, 119
NOTATION attribute, 281–82
Notation declarations, 288–89
    external notation entities, 288
notations, Document Type object, 358
Notes Flat File (NFF) (Digitome Electronic Publishing), 67–68
Notes Import Filter, 68, 116
nsgmls, 115
NSGMLS parser, 364–65

O

OFX (Open Financial Exchange), 105–6, 396–403, 413
    application areas, 397
    architecture, 401–2
    and batch-processing, 400
    as client-independent standard, 399
    definition of, 397
    design principles, 398–400
    as extensible standard, 399
    home page, 43fn
    as international standard, 400
    as open standard, 399
    PC application software supporting, 403
    robustness of, 400
    security of, 400
    Web sites for, 403
OpenTag format, 64
OSD (Open Software Distribution), 47–48
OTP (Open Trading Protocol), 10, 105–6, 412–25
    Dan financial institutions, 416
    benefits of, 415–16

brandlist component, 421–22
    attributes of, 421
    example of, 423–24
consumer, and OTP trading, 418
Customer Care Providers, and OTP trading, 418
and customers, 416
deliverer, and OTP trading, 418
design of, 414–15
merchant, 416
    and OTP trading, 418
message, structure of, 419–24
order component, 419–20
    attributes of, 420
PayProtocol element, 422–23
    attributes of, 422
and software developers, 416
trading types in, 416–18
value acquirers, and OTP trading, 418
Web site for, 425
Out-of-line link, definition of, 295

P

Parameter entities, 284–85
parameterEntities, Document Type object, 358
Parsing, 256
Partial attribute list declarations, 144
path function, 331–32
Perl, 49, 234–38, 241
Physical structure, XML documents, 117, 255
PI object, 354
Plain text, 26–27
Position qualifier, 319–20
PRECEDING keyword, XPointer, 302
Predefined entities, 130
println function, 232
Processing instructions, 135–36, 261–62
Programming languages, and Unicode, 343–44
prolog, 251, 255
Proprietary language, XML vs., 26–27
Protocol transparency, and WIDL, 199
PSIBLING keyword, XPointer, 302
Pull publishing, 32–33

Company does not warrant that the SOFTWARE will meet your requirements or that the operation of the SOFTWARE will be uninterrupted or error-free. The Company warrants that the media on which the SOFTWARE is delivered shall be free from defects in materials and workmanship under normal use for a period of thirty (30) days from the date of your purchase. Your only remedy and the Company's only obligation under these limited warranties is, at the Company's option, return of the warranted item for a refund of any amounts paid by you or replacement of the item. Any replacement of SOFTWARE or media under the warranties shall not extend the original warranty period. The limited warranty set forth above shall not apply to any SOFTWARE which the Company determines in good faith has been subject to misuse, neglect, improper installation, repair, alteration, or damage by you. EXCEPT FOR THE EXPRESSED WARRANTIES SET FORTH ABOVE, THE COMPANY DISCLAIMS ALL WARRANTIES, EXPRESS OR IMPLIED, INCLUDING WITHOUT LIMITATION, THE IMPLIED WARRANTIES OF MERCHANTABILITY AND FITNESS FOR A PARTICULAR PURPOSE. EXCEPT FOR THE EXPRESS WARRANTY SET FORTH ABOVE, THE COMPANY DOES NOT WARRANT, GUARANTEE, OR MAKE ANY REPRESENTATION REGARDING THE USE OR THE RESULTS OF THE USE OF THE SOFTWARE IN TERMS OF ITS CORRECTNESS, ACCURACY, RELIABILITY, CURRENTNESS, OR OTHERWISE.

IN NO EVENT, SHALL THE COMPANY OR ITS EMPLOYEES, AGENTS, SUPPLIERS, OR CONTRACTORS BE LIABLE FOR ANY INCIDENTAL, INDIRECT, SPECIAL, OR CONSEQUENTIAL DAMAGES ARISING OUT OF OR IN CONNECTION WITH THE LICENSE GRANTED UNDER THIS AGREEMENT, OR FOR LOSS OF USE, LOSS OF DATA, LOSS OF INCOME OR PROFIT, OR OTHER LOSSES, SUSTAINED AS A RESULT OF INJURY TO ANY PERSON, OR LOSS OF OR DAMAGE TO PROPERTY, OR CLAIMS OF THIRD PARTIES, EVEN IF THE COMPANY OR AN AUTHORIZED REPRESENTATIVE OF THE COMPANY HAS BEEN ADVISED OF THE POSSIBILITY OF SUCH DAMAGES. IN NO EVENT SHALL LIABILITY OF THE COMPANY FOR DAMAGES WITH RESPECT TO THE SOFTWARE EXCEED THE AMOUNTS ACTUALLY PAID BY YOU, IF ANY, FOR THE SOFTWARE.

SOME JURISDICTIONS DO NOT ALLOW THE LIMITATION OF IMPLIED WARRANTIES OR LIABILITY FOR INCIDENTAL, INDIRECT, SPECIAL, OR CONSEQUENTIAL DAMAGES, SO THE ABOVE LIMITATIONS MAY NOT ALWAYS APPLY. THE WARRANTIES IN THIS AGREEMENT GIVE YOU SPECIFIC LEGAL RIGHTS AND YOU MAY ALSO HAVE OTHER RIGHTS WHICH VARY IN ACCORDANCE WITH LOCAL LAW.

ACKNOWLEDGMENT

YOU ACKNOWLEDGE THAT YOU HAVE READ THIS AGREEMENT, UNDERSTAND IT, AND AGREE TO BE BOUND BY ITS TERMS AND CONDITIONS. YOU ALSO AGREE THAT THIS AGREEMENT IS THE COMPLETE AND EXCLUSIVE STATEMENT OF THE AGREEMENT BETWEEN YOU AND THE COMPANY AND SUPERSEDES ALL PROPOSALS OR PRIOR AGREEMENTS, ORAL, OR WRITTEN, AND ANY OTHER COMMUNICATIONS BETWEEN YOU AND THE COMPANY OR ANY REPRESENTATIVE OF THE COMPANY RELATING TO THE SUBJECT MATTER OF THIS AGREEMENT.

Should you have any questions concerning this Agreement or if you wish to contact the Company for any reason, please contact in writing at the address below.

Robin Short

Prentice Hall PTR

One Lake Street

Upper Saddle River, New Jersey 07458

About the CD-ROM

The CD-ROM contains the following tools for Windows 95 and Windows NT platforms.

- MSXML XML Parser
- Ælfred XML Parser
- XP XML Parser
- XmlTok XML Parser
- Xparse XML Parser
- NSGMLS SGML/XML Parser
- Jade DSSSL Engine
- SX SGML to XML Adaptor
- The WebMethods Web Automation Toolkit
- The ColdFusion Database Publishing Toolkit
- The Amaya Web Browser
- The Multidoc SGML/XML Viewer

System Requirements

Windows 95/NT
HTML 3.2 compatible Web browswer
The Java based tools will require a Java Virtual Machine (JVM)

Technical Support

Prentice Hall does not offer technical support for this software. However, if there is a problem with the media, you may obtain a replacement copy by emailing us with your problem at:

discexchange@phptr.com